NASDAQ-100® INVESTOR'S GUIDE 2001—2002

FEATURING COMMENTARY AND ANALYSIS BY
MICHAEL P. BYRUM
AND
THE EDITORS OF THE
NEW YORK INSTITUTE OF FINANCE

NEW YORK INSTITUTE OF FINANCE
NEW YORK • TORONTO • SYDNEY • TOKYO • SINGAPORE

Library of Congress Cataloging-in-Publication Data

Byrum, Michael P.
NASDAQ-100 : investor's guide 2001-2002 / Michael P. Byrum and the editors of the New York Institute of Finance.
p. cm.
Includes index.
ISBN 0-7352-0249-4
1. Nasdaq Stock Market. 2. Stocks—Prices. 3. Stock price indexes. I. Title:

HG4574.2 .B97 2001
332.63´22—dc21 00-068451

Associate Publisher: Ellen Schneid Coleman
Production Editor: Mariann Hutlak
Interior Design: Nicola Evans
Executive Editor for Literary Productions: Kirk Kazanjian

Printed in the United States of America
10 9 8 7 6 5 4 3 2 1

ISBN 0-7352-0249-4

ATTENTION: CORPORATIONS AND SCHOOLS

Prentice Hall books are available at quantity discounts with bulk purchase for educational, business, or sales promotional use. For information, please write to: Prentice Hall Special Sales, 240 Frisch Court, Paramus, New Jersey 07652. Please supply: title of book, ISBN, quantity, how the book will be used, date needed.

NEW YORK INSTITUTE OF FINANCE
An Imprint of Prentice Hall Press
Paramus, NJ 07652

http://www.phdirect.com

CONTENTS

FOREWORD

John L. Jacobs

Much has been said in the press and throughout the securities industry about the tremendous success of The Nasdaq-100®. This index was established in 1985 and has seen its value grow by more than 4,000 percent since inception. The Nasdaq-100 reflects the performance of the 100 largest nonfinancial Nasdaq-traded companies across several major industry groups, including computer hardware and software, telecommunications, retail/wholesale trade, and biotechnology.

The Nasdaq-100 adjusts its component companies based purely on market capitalization values at the end of each year. It has therefore been said that the index self-selects winning stocks on an ongoing basis. In turn, the tremendous growth of The Nasdaq-100 can be attributed to the fact that it benefits from the performance of whatever sector is strongest in any given year.

Like most overnight success stories, the rise of the Nasdaq-100 has been an evolving process, rooted in years of hard work and creative effort undertaken by the dedicated staff members at The Nasdaq Stock Market®.

There are many ways to invest in the Nasdaq-100 companies found throughout this book. You can buy all 100 stocks in the index individually, which is impractical for most small investors. You can select a handful of your favorite names and create your own representative sampling, which this book can help you with. Or, you can buy the entire index through a single mutual fund or exchanged-traded vehicle, such as The Nasdaq-100 Tracking Stock®, which trades on the American Stock Exchange under the symbol QQQ.

The explosive acceptance of QQQ, as well as the entire exchange traded fund (ETF) sector, can be traced back to the stock market crash of 1987. This watershed event had a tremendous affect on both the market and the economy as a whole. The aftershocks are still being felt today. Studies show that had the crash not occurred, exchange traded funds might not be in existence today.

The market's gyrations in October 1987 demonstrated the power of computerized—or program—trading. Program trading was developed by investors looking for a fast and efficient way to move in and out of baskets of stocks as an automated means of exploiting volatility in a rapidly moving market. The Securities and Exchange Commission finally opened the doors to allowing ETFs in the early 1990s. In 1993, after years of diligent work in the face of a somewhat slow-moving securities industry, the American Stock Exchange created and launched the first ETF known as SPDRS (Standard & Poor's Depositary Receipts).

Nasdaq used what it learned from the crash of 1987 and embarked on a mission to evolve its market structure into a more inclusive model, enhancing transparency and including such features as automated execution, negotiation facilities, and orders in the quote system. At the same time, it became clear that Nasdaq's brand value would play an integral role in the continued improvement of our underlying market model. Earlier efforts to extend and define the Nasdaq brand were reestablished and, for the first time, we began to seriously develop, project, and protect what "Nasdaq" stood for in the minds of investors.

Today, the Nasdaq brand is synonymous with growth and performance. It is inextricably linked to the new economy and the rise of technology in our business and personal lives.

Creating the Nasdaq-100 index was one of the earliest means we used to establish the Nasdaq brand. But it wasn't until March 10, 1999 that the first shares of QQQ began to trade. The Nasdaq-100 Index Tracking Stock is one of the few instruments investors can use as a pure proxy for the Nasdaq benchmark.

Given the extraordinary growth of the companies it contains, it should come as no surprise that The Nasdaq-100 Index has been the most successful ETF launched to date. In just six months, assets in

QQQ grew from almost $15 million to $2 billion. By the one-year anniversary, assets had reached a staggering $12 billion. In the past year, the average trading volume of this security has jumped from 2.6 million to almost 17 million shares a day. That makes QQQ the most heavily traded ETF on the market.

What's the secret to the success of The Nasdaq-100? In short, and to paraphrase a line from the popular movie *Field of Dreams*, give investors what they want and they will come. Investors were clearly looking for a way to easily invest in some of the nation's most innovative and fastest-growing companies. The Nasdaq-100, and QQQ in particular, gave them that opportunity.

I congratulate you for taking the next step to learning about the exciting companies contained in The Nasdaq-100 Index. The *Nasdaq-100 Investor's Guide 2001–2002* is the first book devoted exclusively to showing readers how to tap into the potential of this index and the stocks it contains. I wish you a prosperous and successful journey as you learn more about the opportunities available through the Nasdaq-100.

John L. Jacobs
Senior Vice President, Nasdaq

1

INTRODUCTION TO THE NASDAQ–100

Where can you find many of the world's fastest-growing, most innovative, and cutting-edge companies? The answer is on the best-performing U.S. stock market index that, until recently, rarely got the respect it deserved.

The Nasdaq-100 was first launched in January 1985. Since then, it has grown at the incredible rate of 29.85 percent annually, compared with 14.55 percent for the better-known Standard & Poor's 500 index, with only one losing year. Cumulatively, the index has returned close to 2,000 percent during this 16-year stretch, versus 1,200 for the broad Nasdaq Stock Market, and roughly 400 percent for both the S&P 500 and Dow Jones Industrial Average.

Nasdaq–100 vs. S&P 500 and DJ Industrial

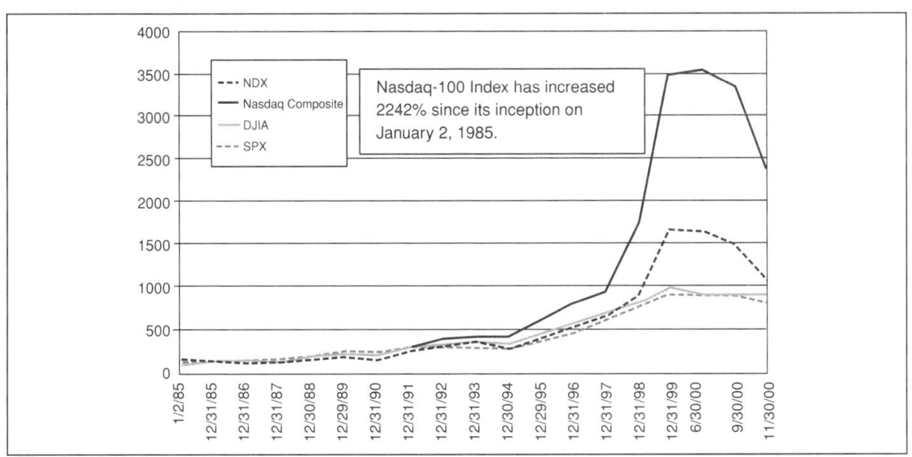

The Nasdaq-100 contains the largest and most active nonfinancial stocks listed on The Nasdaq Stock Market based on market capitalization. Market capitalization is determined by taking a stock's share price and multiplying it by the number of outstanding shares. For instance, if a stock trades for $100 per share, and there are 1 million shares outstanding, the company's market capitalization would be $100 million.

The index includes both domestic and international issues, including such recognizable names as Microsoft, Intel, Amgen, WorldCom, Oracle, Starbucks, Costco Wholesale, and Amazon.com. It also contains many lesser-known companies that are charging ahead with innovative products and services, such as Siebel Systems, Comcast Corporation, Abgenix, Adelphia Communications, Biomet, and Atmel.

How can you put some of your investment dollars to work in the Nasdaq-100 companies? And which of the 100 stocks in the index look most promising for the year ahead? You're about to find out in the pages that follow. In fact, this is the first guide to the Nasdaq-100 companies that has ever been written. It is by far the most comprehensive resource to these investment powerhouses around.

In addition to giving you an overview of the index, and the various ways to tap into its potential, *Nasdaq-100 Investor's Guide 2001–2002* provides complete profiles of each stock, complete with charts and graphs from well-known data provider Baseline. What's more, you'll discover which 25 companies are best positioned for the immediate future, according to one of America's top analysts of Nasdaq-100 companies—Michael P. Byrum. Byrum manages the largest mutual fund designed to track this venerable index. He not only reveals his favorite picks, but also gives you a list of things to look out for as you venture further into the stocks in this index.

Before we continue, let's look at how the Nasdaq-100 got to where it is today.

A Brief History of Popular Indexes

The oldest and most often quoted American stock market index is the Dow Jones Industrial Average (DJIA). This benchmark was created by journalist Charles Dow in 1884. Dow compiled a list of 11 companies—mostly railroad operators—and began tracking their performance. Two years later, he added another stock to the index, and began tracking its performance in the pages of his publication, *The Wall Street Journal.*

Dow wanted the index to give readers a better feel for how the overall stock market was doing.

By 1916, the number of stocks in the DJIA grew to 20. It blossomed to 30, where it stands today, in 1928. The list of included companies changes and evolves over the years, either to account for mergers and acquisitions, or to keep it better aligned with the economy.

At the end of World War II, manufacturing-based businesses were key drivers of the transforming U.S. economy, and well-represented in the DJIA. The aerospace, automobile, chemical, and oil industries were among the leaders of this era. Today, however, the DJIA includes several technology companies, including Intel and Microsoft, as well as drug companies and retailer Wal-Mart.

Another widely regarded market index is the Standard & Poor's 500. This benchmark, founded in 1926, holds a basket of 500 large-capitalization stocks from both the New York Stock Exchange and Nasdaq. It represents about 70 percent of the collective stock market's value. An eight-member panel selected by Standard & Poor's handpicks which companies get listed in the index. Included companies change on a regular basis, based on market value, financial conditions, and trading liquidity. The S&P 500 is a market-weighted index, meaning the higher a company's market valuation, the more emphasis it has on the index. Therefore, the biggest companies drive a large portion of the index's performance. In fact, the largest 60 stocks in the S&P 500 make up about half of its value.

Other widely accepted indexes include the Wilshire 5000—which tracks more than 6,000 publicly traded securities and is arguably the most accurate measure of the overall market's health—and the Russell 2000, which is comprised of smaller stocks trading on the Nasdaq.

The Nasdaq-100 is clearly the new kid on the block. Until recently, many professional investors regarded it as one of Wall Street's best-kept secrets. As previously discussed, the Nasdaq-100 includes the 100 largest companies, based on market capitalization, that trade on the Nasdaq Stock Market, excluding those in the financial services and utility sectors.

ABOUT THE NASDAQ STOCK MARKET

Nasdaq, which originally was an acronym for National Association of Securities Dealers Automated Quotation system, was created in 1971. It is the world's first electronic stock market. Unlike its rival, the New

York Stock Exchange (NYSE), Nasdaq trades take place among many different brokerages that are linked by a national computer network. By contrast, issues on the NYSE are physically bought and sold on a common floor in the heart of Wall Street.

The Nasdaq Stock Market is the gateway for newer companies to come to market. One reason is that listing requirements on the Nasdaq are more lenient than on the NYSE. The Nasdaq exchange currently contains the stocks of some 5,000 companies, compared with about 3,000 on the NYSE. However, the market value of all NYSE companies is more than double the approximate $5.2 trillion value of all Nasdaq companies, because a majority of the largest and most seasoned companies are found on the NYSE.

While the Nasdaq's listings cover the whole spectrum of the global economy—including retail, banking, transportation, construction, and agriculture—it is dominated by technology names. The Nasdaq contains:

- More companies than any other stock market in the world.
- More initial public offerings than any other U.S. stock market.
- More non-U.S. companies than any other market.
- The largest concentration of firms in technology, telecommunications, pharmaceuticals, and biotechnology.

CHARACTERISTICS OF COMPANIES IN THE NASDAQ—100 INDEX

It stands to reason that technology is the dominant sector represented in the Nasdaq-100. After all, that's the growth area for most new companies coming to market in the twenty-first century. Nasdaq-100 companies fall primarily into nine basic industry groups, all of which have enormous future potential: Computers & Office Equipment (39.7 percent), Computer Software/Services (27.3 percent), Telecommunications (18.2 percent), Biotechnology (6.5 percent), Services (2.9 percent), Retail/Wholesale Trade (3 percent), Manufacturing (0.8 percent), Healthcare (0.8 percent), and Transportation (0.1 percent).

Nasdaq–100 Industry Weightings by Market Value

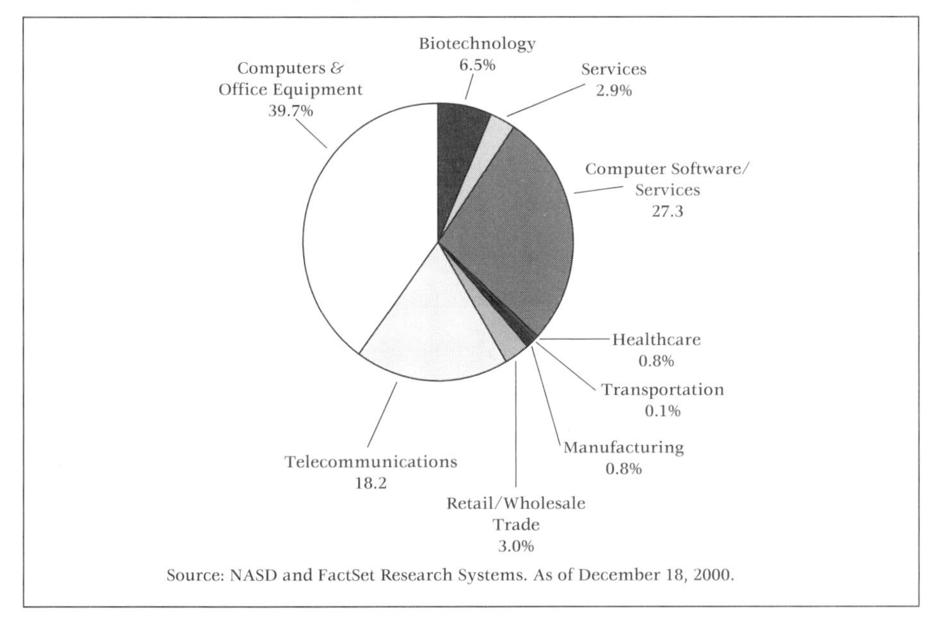

Source: NASD and FactSet Research Systems. As of December 18, 2000.

Within the index are many of today's leading-edge technology companies, several of which dwarf some of the big-name industrial companies that have been around for decades longer. For instance, at its peak, Microsoft's market capitalization was 22 percent greater than General Electric's. Intel's market capitalization is more than double that of Coca-Cola, and 12 percent larger than ExxonMobil's. Sun Microsystems's market capitalization is almost 150 percent bigger than the entire S&P 500 aluminum sector.

Because of its natural selection process, and continuous rebalancing, the Nasdaq-100 index will always contain the world's fastest-growing, most progressive companies. Stocks that underperform are continuously eliminated and replaced with more impressive names.

To make it into the index, a company's stock must have a minimum average daily trading volume of 100,000 shares. Companies generally must be seasoned, which means being listed for a minimum of two years. The exception is if a company's market capitalization falls in the top 25 percent of all issuers included in the index, then a one-year listing period applies. If the stock is a foreign security, the company must have a worldwide market value of at least $10 billion, a U.S. market value of at least $4 billion, and average trading volume of at least 200,000 shares per day. In addition, foreign securities must be eligible for listed options trading.

Leading Companies in the Nasdaq-100

TECHNOLOGY
- Microsoft
- Intel
- Cisco Systems
- Dell Computer
- Oracle

TELECOMMUNICATIONS
- WorldCom
- Nextel
- Qualcomm

RETAIL
- Starbucks
- Costco Wholesale
- Amazon.com

BIOTECHNOLOGY
- Amgen
- Immunex
- Biogen

QQQ—THE NASDAQ-100 TRACKING STOCK

In this book, you will not only discover which 25 stocks from the Nasdaq-100 index one leading analyst finds most attractive for the coming year, you'll also find complete profiles on each of the remaining 75 companies. This should give you the information you need to decide which stocks from the index you'd like to add to your portfolio. Keep in mind that this book will be updated on an annual basis, so you'll always have the freshest information and analysis at your disposal to make an informed decision.

How many stocks do you need to construct a diversified portfolio? The experts vary on the exact number, but given the volatility of the sectors represented in the index, you'll probably want at least 10–15. (We'll talk more about this subject shortly in the interview with Michael Byrum.)

But let's say you decide that all 100 companies look attractive, and you'd like to own the whole basket. How should you go about buying them? You could, of course, purchase shares in all 100 companies. Given that some online discount brokers execute trades for as little as $5, that's not an impossible or terribly expensive task. But you still need quite a bit of investment capital to make this approach practical.

There is, however, a much easier way to buy all 100 stocks in a single security. It's known as the Nasdaq-100 Index Tracking Stock, and trades on the American Stock Exchange under the symbol QQQ. (Incidentally, the American Stock Exchange merged with the Nasdaq Stock Market a couple of years ago, and both operate in a similar manner.)

For more on how this tracking stock was launched in March 1999, be sure to read this book's foreword by John L. Jacobs. Suffice it to say, QQQ tracks the price and yield performance of the entire Nasdaq-100 index. It is priced at approximately one-fortieth of the value of the Nasdaq-100 index itself. You can buy as many shares as you want, and the security is highly liquid, with average daily trading volume of 17–19 million shares. In fact, it's the most actively traded stock on the American Stock Exchange. That means you can liquidate your position almost instantly, although it normally makes sense to hold such securities for the long haul.

Rather than buying and keeping track of all 100 stocks individually, you can simply own QQQ, or "Qubes" for short. The security pays out only a tiny annual dividend, so it's highly tax-efficient. Plus, when the index is rebalanced each year, you don't have to do a thing, because any changes are automatically priced into the security.

Of course, many investors are more interested in finding the gems from the index that might potentially provide greater rewards than the basket as a whole. Our goal with this book is to help you uncover those special stocks. But for those looking for an easy solution for gaining exposure to the entire index, QQQ is worth a look.

What's more, it could make a lot of sense to keep part of your portfolio earmarked for the Nasdaq-100 in QQQ, and the rest in carefully selected individual names that you select with the help of this book. That way you spread some of your risk among the entire universe, and won't be affected so much if an individual name comes upon hard times.

For more information on the Nasdaq-100 and QQQ shares, visit:

www.nasdaq100.com

INVESTING IN THE NASDAQ–100 THROUGH MUTUAL FUNDS

There are also a growing number of mutual funds designed to replicate the performance of the Nasdaq-100 index. The largest is the Rydex OTC fund, which is run by manager Michael P. Byrum. You'll learn more about this fund in our exclusive interview with Byrum in Chapter 3. You'll also discover his top 25 favorite holdings for the coming year.

Funds designed to track the Nasdaq-100 on a one-to-one basis are also offered by both American Express and Ranson and Associates, which runs the aptly named Nasdaq 100 Fund. Note that while the Rydex fund is offered on a no-load basis (meaning there are no charges to buy or sell shares), the American Express and Nasdaq 100 funds come in several share classes with varying loads and expenses.

If you're a true believer in the index, Rydex, Potomac Funds, and ProFunds have super-charged funds designed to provide a return that's even greater than the index itself. The funds do this by leveraging the portfolio, often through the use of futures or options. For instance, the Potomac OTC Plus fund is designed to provide 125 percent of the Nasdaq-100's return. Even more aggressive are the Rydex Velocity 100 and ProFunds Ultra OTC funds, which are leveraged to generate 200 percent of the Nasdaq-100's performance. Keep in mind that these funds fall much harder when the index falls, so they certainly entail incredible risk.

Nasdaq–100 Mutual Funds

NASDAQ-100 INDEX FUNDS (EQUAL TRACKING FUNDS)	
Rydex OTC	(800) 820-0888
American Express Nasdaq 100	(800) 328-8300
Nasdaq 100 Index Fund	(877) 627-3272
Rydex Arktos (shorts index)	(800) 820-0888
LEVERAGED NASDAQ-100 INDEX FUNDS	
Rydex Velocity 100	(800) 820-0888
Potomac OTC Plus	(800) 851-0511
ProFunds UltraOTC	(888) 776-3637
Rydex Venture 100 (shorts index)	(800) 820-0888
Potomac OTC Short (shorts index)	(800) 851-0511
ProFunds Ultra Short (shorts index)	(888) 851-0511

If you're bearish on the Nasdaq-100, Potomac, ProFunds, and Rydex all have funds for you as well. The Potomac OTC Short fund shorts the Nasdaq-100 on a one-to-one basis. Meantime, the ProFunds Ultra Short OTC and Rydex Venture 100 funds short the Nasdaq-100 using leverage. Both funds are built to rise 200 percent more than the Nasdaq-100 when that index falls. By the same token, they will fall twice as hard when the market goes up. The catch phrase to remember when buying any type of leveraged fund is "investor beware."

Why buy a Nasdaq-100 mutual fund instead of QQQ shares? If you're a long-term investor, there isn't much difference, because the returns should be about the same. But QQQ shares are priced constantly with the market, and can be bought or sold throughout the trading day. By contrast, mutual funds are only priced once daily, at the market close. So if you're looking to do short-term trading, QQQ is probably a better way to go.

In addition, many of the mutual funds have higher expense ratios and larger minimum investment requirements. For instance, the Potomac and Rydex funds require $10,000 or more, while ProFunds' minimum is $15,000. Therefore, if you have less money to work with, QQQ shares may be your only option, although you can get into many of these funds for a lower initial minimum by going through one of the discount brokerage fund supermarkets.

2

HOW TO USE THIS BOOK

Chapters 4 and 5 of this book both contain profiles on all of the companies currently in the Nasdaq-100 index. Here's the difference: Chapter 4 features the 25 companies from the index that fund manager Michael P. Byrum views as being most attractive for the year ahead. Byrum manages the Rydex OTC fund, a mutual fund that invests exclusively in Nasdaq-100 companies, with the goal of replicating the performance of the index. Chapter 5 has profiles of the remaining 75 Nasdaq-100 stocks. In both chapters, companies are presented alphabetically, not necessarily in order of attractiveness.

About the Profiles

The profiles all follow a similar format. You will find the company's name, ticker symbol, and industry sector at the top of each page. (Of course, all stocks trade on the Nasdaq Stock Market.) Next comes a brief profile, discussing the company's primary business, key products, and recent acquisitions. Then you will find a discussion of the company's earnings and revenues over the past 12 months, along with an analysis of how those numbers compare with the period one year earlier.

Below that, you will find a plethora of information on such key ratios as price-to-earnings (P/E), price-to-book, price-to-cash flow, and price-to-sales, along with each company's return on equity percentage and beta factor. The figures include both the five-year range for each data point, along with the current reading. The five-year range is important because it shows you where a company has been, compared to where it is now. For instance, if a company's P/E has ranged from 10–50 over the past five years, and now stands at 11, you'll know it currently trades at the low end of its long-term range. These are the same numbers Wall Street pros use in determining whether a stock is attractive for purchase.

Following these important numbers in Chapter 5, you will find "Byrum's Commentary," written analysis from fund manager Michael P. Byrum on why he has selected the stock among his 25 favorites, along with his personal insights on what he expects from the company in the months ahead. Following this commentary is a discussion on some of the risk factors associated with each stock.

READING THE CHARTS

You will also find three very useful charts in each of the 100 profiles supplied by Baseline, one of the leading names in investment data.

First is the "Price Action" chart. This gives a graphic illustration of the company's share price over the past year, along with lines showing both its 50- and 200-day moving averages. Moving averages are a gauge often looked at by technical analysts. They show the average stock price over a given period of time, and are used to spot trends and possible future direction. Typically when a stock price moves below its 50- or 200-day moving average, it signals bad things to come. The opposite is also true. At the bottom of the "Price Action" chart is a graphical illustration of each stock's trading volume, plotted over a 12-month period. Technical analysts look for rising volume in periods when a stock goes up, and lower volume when it falls. If the opposite is happening, it's generally viewed negatively.

The "Earnings" and "Revenues" charts give you a quick graphical look at the trend for these two important variables over the last four quarters. Keep in mind that it's not unusual for earnings and revenues to fluctuate wildly from quarter to quarter due to seasonal factors. But, overall, you want to see the line trending up. (Note that all companies have earnings and/or revenues.)

At the bottom of each profile is the contact information for every company, including the address for corporate headquarters, main phone number, and Internet address.

Definitions of Key Terms

beta Means of measuring the volatility of a security or portfolio of securities in comparison with the market as a whole. Beta is calculated using regression analysis. A beta of 1 suggests that a security's price will move with the market. A beta greater than 1 suggests that a security's price will be more volatile than the market. A beta less than 1 suggests that it will be less volatile than the market.

price-earnings ratio (P/E) Price of a stock divided by its earnings per share. Sometimes referred to as the "multiple." Generally speaking, a high P/E indicates investors have large projected future earnings expectations for the company. It's helpful to compare a stock's P/E ratio with similar companies in the same industry, to the overall market, and to a company's own historical range. This will give you a feel for relative valuation.

price-to-book ratio alculated by dividing the current market price of a stock by the underlying company's book value. A low price-to-book ratio could mean a stock is undervalued. On the other hand, it could indicate that something is fundamentally wrong with the company.

price-to-cash flow ratio Price per share divided by cash flow per share. This is a measure of the market's expectations for a firm's future financial health. It provides an indication of relative value, similar to the price-earnings ratio.

price-to-sales ratio Calculated by dividing a stock's current price by its revenues per share. This is another way to look at a stock's valuation relative to its own past performance, other companies in the same industry, or the overall market.

return on equity Measure of a company's profitability, calculated by dividing net income by shareholders equity. This number is useful in comparing the return on equity on one company with other firms in the same industry.

In some cases, these figures are unavailable for various reasons. For instance, if a company does not have earnings, I cannot have a meaningful price-earnings ratio. Therefore, you will occasionally find either NM (not meaningful) or NA (not applicable) indicated in this section.

DIGGING DEEPER

While the information in this book is designed to help you select investments for your own personal portfolio, you should not buy any stock or other highlighted security without doing additional research, to make sure it's right for you. Call or write each company you're interested in and ask for an investor kit, including the latest quarterly and annual report, form 10-K (a required disclosure that must be filed annually with the Securities and Exchange Commission), form 10-Q (a quarterly abbreviated version of the 10-K), analyst reports, and any other information it can provide. Also visit the company's Web site. In fact, you can download all of this information from the investor relations section of most corporate Web sites.

3

Q&A: MICHAEL P. BYRUM, MANAGER, RYDEX OTC FUND

Mike Byrum has always been fascinated with the investments markets. He graduated with a finance degree from Miami University of Oxford, Ohio, and has spent much of his career working in and around the mutual fund industry. After a brief stint at the Rushmore Funds, Byrum joined Rockville, Maryland-based Rydex Global Advisors in 1993.

Rydex was just a start-up at the time. Byrum found himself doing everything from product development to marketing. His role eventually developed into overseeing the firm's investment department.

The company's first fund, Rydex Nova, was a leveraged portfolio tied to the S&P 500. It, like all other early Rydex funds, was especially designed for traders. Today Rydex boasts 33 funds with $9 billion in assets. All are run using quantitative models, and many track the performance of either recognized indexes or designated sectors. "We don't describe ourselves as pure indexers. Our investment philosophy drives us to seek to improve returns beyond that of a plain vanilla index fund. This is achieved through our portfolio construction process, our trading strategies, and through the use of consistently applied leverage."

The firm's largest fund, Rydex OTC, is designed to track the performance of the Nasdaq-100. Byrum is the $3-billion fund's chief portfolio manager. Rydex OTC was launched in February 1994. He also runs a leveraged fund tracking the Nasdaq-100, and several portfolios designed to short the index.

Byrum arguably knows more about the Nasdaq-100 and the companies inside the index than just about anyone else. In the following interview, Byrum discusses the various ways to invest in the index. He also talks about how he chose his favorite 25 stocks from the Nasdaq-100 for the year ahead, which are profiled in Chapter 5.

NASDAQ-100 OVERVIEW

What, in your opinion, makes the Nasdaq-100 index unique among all of the stock market indexes out there?

It's an extraordinary index. It has become what many view as the leading technology benchmark. Technology stocks represent a majority of the stocks in the index, accounting for roughly 80–90 percent of the index's total capitalization. In a lot of ways, it represents the companies that are driving the economy. That's why so many investors have been attracted to it.

One characteristic that has tended to help the Nasdaq-100's performance over time is that it has a higher turnover than most other indexes. In 1999, for example, the index turned over 29 percent of its component stocks, compared with only 10 percent for the S&P 500. This means that each year a significant number of new growth-oriented companies come into the index, while some of the nonperforming companies tend to be paired back or removed. You have almost a Darwinistic selection process, which has led to an index of growth-oriented companies that have performed well in the market environment we've enjoyed over the last several years.

You mentioned the Nasdaq-100 was mostly a technology index, but there are companies from other sectors in there.

That's true. Healthcare does have some representation. But, depending on how you classify it, some of the biotech companies are a hybrid between the healthcare and technology fields. Still, these companies have different characteristics from others in technology-related industries. Other areas represented include media and retail. Certainly as far as driving the performance of the index, they're a smaller consideration than technology. But they are not to be entirely ignored

Is the Nasdaq-100 representative of the performance of the Nasdaq composite overall?

To a large degree. It comprises about 60 percent of the Nasdaq's total capitalization. That's impressive because the Nasdaq-100 contains just 100 of the 4,500-plus stocks in the Nasdaq composite. These companies are real powerhouses.

We discussed it a bit earlier, but explain once again how companies are selected for inclusion in the Nasdaq-100.

It's more of a mechanical approach than what the S&P 500 selection committee uses. Nasdaq keeps a market-cap-weighted list of the 200 or so largest stocks from the composite. Each year, on the third Friday in December, they take a look at this list and check whether any companies included in the Nasdaq-100 have fallen below the top 150 in rank. If so, they generally get dropped from the index, and are replaced by companies that have moved up into the top 100. The Nasdaq committee does have other criteria, such as making sure each company has a reasonable trading volume of at least 100,000 shares per day. The included companies must also be seasoned, which generally means two years of listing on the Nasdaq Stock Market. Foreign issuers have some additional liquidity and capitalization requirements. But it's definitely a mechanical approach.

Financial services stocks are excluded from the Nasdaq-100. Why is that?

Nasdaq has another financial services index. My sense is they wanted to promote that as a separate animal. However, that index hasn't drawn the type of attention the Nasdaq-100 has.

Are there any common themes among the Nasdaq-100 companies?

Yes. The most notable among them is that they are growth-oriented. This is clearly a large-cap growth index. These are the cream-of-the-crop stocks from the Nasdaq, which has a greater number of listed companies than any other stock market. The Nasdaq-100 companies are usually leaders in their respective industries. The ones that find their way into the Nasdaq-100 normally have significant market share.

Some people say that the Nasdaq-100 really represents the companies of the twenty-first century, while the Dow and S&P 500 are made up mostly of "old economy" stocks. Is this a fair statement?

There's a lot of truth to that. The addition of Intel and Microsoft to the Dow was a big step in aligning that index with the drivers of the current and future economy. But I still think that the Nasdaq-100 has a considerable advantage, especially when you consider that technology continues to expand its role in our economy. Given that several of these companies are in hyper-growth segments, such as wireless data and semiconductors, there's going to be some volatility along the way. But those are the industries driving future growth, and the Nasdaq-100 captures it better than any other index.

PORTFOLIO ALLOCATION

How do you think the Nasdaq-100 companies should fit into an investor's overall portfolio?

It boils down to the investor's time horizon and risk tolerance. The Nasdaq-100 has considerably greater volatility than the S&P 500. It's about one and a half times more volatile. So it should appeal to investors with a high risk tolerance and long-term investment horizon. Assuming that someone has five years or more to invest and is reasonably aggressive, these companies should be a cornerstone of their investment portfolio, making up probably 15–25 percent of the total allocation. If you're talking about someone with a moderate or low risk tolerance, the percentages should be adjusted down accordingly. In any case, I don't feel it's prudent to put all of your investments into any one segment, even an index like this. It does make sense to diversify into other asset classes. Even though the Nasdaq-100 contains 100 stocks, and offers some diversification, it's still concentrated in technology, which, in my opinion, precludes it from being someone's entire investment.

A lot of investment experts tell people that you should also have small company stocks in your portfolio. Do you believe that's important and, if so, are you getting that exposure through the Nasdaq-100?

You should consider the different stock market capitalization dimensions (i.e., small-caps, mid-caps, etc.), along with growth versus value. The Nasdaq-100 is a large-cap growth index. It's important to have mid- and small-cap exposure, too, along with international exposure, and possibly alternative asset classes, such as real estate. This is a generalization, and every investor's situation is certainly unique.

You just mentioned international stocks. Are you getting much international exposure through these Nasdaq-100 companies?

As global as the economy is, there is significant exposure to the international arena through the Nasdaq-100. Several companies, such as Cisco, Dell, and Intel, get a significant portion of their revenues from overseas. There is one pure foreign issuer in the index, which is LM Ericsson Telephone. This is an American Depositary Receipt that makes up about 1 percent of the index. But to truly diversify, you'll probably want to own an international mutual fund, composed of foreign-issued securities, especially if you believe in overseas diversification.

THE CHANGING INDEX

Before we talk about the different ways to invest in the Nasdaq-100 companies, how does Nasdaq determine what percentage each company is going to represent in the index?

They use what is called a modified capitalization weighted scheme. It's similar to the market capitalization approach, like the S&P 500, which ranks companies by size. However, Nasdaq pares back some of the exposure from the larger companies and adds exposure to the smaller ones. They did that to make it easier to conform to some regulatory requirements for mutual funds, unit investment trusts, and exchange traded funds, such as QQQ.

Still, only a handful of companies make up a large part of the index.

That's right. If you look at the current weightings, Cisco Systems is the largest at about 7 percent. Microsoft is right behind at about 5.2 percent. At one point Microsoft made up almost a quarter of the index. We call that top heavy. The index is better diversified now, but still emphasizes larger companies over smaller ones.

Is it a function of the changing market values of these companies?

That's a big part of it. It reflects the relative size of the companies. For instance, Cisco is a bigger company now than Microsoft. The two flip-flopped.

WAYS TO INVEST

Let's talk about the various ways to invest in these stocks. There are 100 stocks in the index. Obviously one option is to go out and buy all 100 of these companies. Is that a feasible way for an individual investor to go?

That would be difficult, especially if the investor was trying to precisely duplicate the index. Replicating an index is a bit more complicated than it appears on the surface. Among other things, you must deal with corporate actions such as stock splits, mergers, and dividends, and stay on top of all the changes in the index in order to correctly weight the portfolio. Some may invest in the top 20 companies in the index, trying to match the performance of the index with fewer names. That will give you something that correlates reasonably well to the index, but your performance will still look different from an index-based fund. So, in sum, you can buy all 100 companies, but it will likely be more costly and certainly more difficult than using a mutual fund or exchange traded fund.

One alternative to this is QQQ, the Nasdaq-100 Tracking Stock. How would you describe QQQ?

QQQ, which is the ticker symbol for the Nasdaq-100 Tracking Stock, is what is known as an exchange traded fund. In essence, it's an open-ended mutual fund traded on the American Stock Exchange. You have specialists who are willing to make a market and buy and sell these shares on the exchange, just like a regular stock. The security gives you exposure to the entire Nasdaq-100. The nice thing about QQQ is that it trades continuously throughout the day. If you want to trade frequently, or pick spots to buy and sell within the day, you can. Exchange traded funds tend to be cost-effective and relatively tax-efficient, meaning they are unlikely to pay out significant distributions as long as they are growing in assets. However, one thing to note is that if they stay even or start to lose assets, they will be required to pay out distributions.

But there is an actual portfolio of securities underlying the index? It's not just a derivative, if you will?

Although the QQQ's represent a portfolio of stocks in a unit investment trust, the market price derives its value from the value of the portfolio. In that sense, it is considered a derivative.

Is it always going to follow the Nasdaq-100 index precisely during the day?

That's one disadvantage of exchange traded funds. Even though there is a portfolio of stocks behind them, they are traded like derivatives. There's a specialist who attempts to maintain an orderly market, but the QQQ will often trade at a premium or discount to the value of the underlying index. The deviations between what QQQ is doing and what the index is doing can be quite high. In fast-trading markets, the deviation can easily exceed 2 percent or more. Even on a typical day it's not uncommon to see a 1-percent deviation throughout the day, as well as at the close. This is one thing investors should consider. There are some nice advantages to QQQ, including the ability to sell it short, but it's not without its shortcomings. The derivative aspect can certainly work against investors.

So you can either buy the individual stocks in the index, invest in QQQ, or purchase an open-ended mutual fund, such as Rydex OTC, which you run. Do you buy all of the stocks in the index for your portfolio?

Let me give you a little bit of background on the Rydex OTC Fund. We started back in 1994 before all other Nasdaq-100 mutual funds and QQQ even existed. Our objective is to replicate the performance of the Nasdaq-100, and we can invest in anything that will help us achieve this objective. In truth, we're looking to marginally outperform the index over time, so we can make up for any possible transaction costs or expenses that shareholders may incur. We'll typically own a subset of the index—somewhere between 75 and 90 stocks—that we think will best replicate its performance.

Do you buy QQQ as well, or do you just own individual stocks?

Our preference is to purchase individual stocks. If we were to trade the QQQ, we would have to contend with its premium/discount issue, its bid/ask spread, and pay its management fee.

How have you performed compared to your goal?

Over time, we've been able to slightly outpace the index. In certain years, we've been ahead of the index by about 1.7 percent. Other years we've trailed it by 1.3 percent. On average, we're about four basis points (0.04 percent) per year ahead, which might not sound like a lot, but we're covering considerable transaction costs and the usual expenses of managing a mutual fund.

How has your tax efficiency been?

We've had great tax efficiency compared with our mutual fund peers. Our payouts have been well under 1 percent per year.

Tell me why someone would buy your fund versus QQQ, assuming they don't want to own individual stocks and prefer an all-in-one investment instead. What is the advantage or disadvantage of one versus the other?

The advantage of a fund like ours is that each day you are able to buy or sell at the value of the underlying securities. You avoid the possibility of buying at a premium or selling at a discount, a hazard that is always present with QQQ. If we do our job well, it puts you in a position to keep pace with or hopefully slightly outperform the index over time, which we think serves a great purpose. To the degree we succeed in enhancing the performance of the index to cover our expenses, we're providing costless exposure to the index. That's our goal. For those who want to buy and sell on a minute-by-minute basis, QQQ makes sense. For most people, a fund like ours probably has an edge.

Speaking of traders, you originally designed your fund specifically for them. How do traders impact your ability to efficiently manage the portfolio if money is constantly coming in and out?

The proportion of traders in our fund has diminished over time. The nice thing is we've built the fund to withstand considerable turnover, both from a tax standpoint and from a liquidity standpoint. We try to keep distributions down and emphasize the more liquid and tradable companies. During the early days of the fund, when turnover was high, we learned to efficiently move shares at the end of the day and were able to generally trade better than the closing price. It's something you learn to do through experience.

Not only do you have a fund that tracks the Nasdaq-100 one-to-one, but you also have some leveraged portfolios both on the long and short side. Let's first talk about Rydex Velocity, which tries to outdo the performance of this index.

That fund is designed to give investors 200-percent exposure on a daily basis to the Nasdaq-100. We created our leveraged portfolio because of shareholder demand. Investors wanted a way to garner additional exposure to a particular index when they were bullish and they were seeking a lower cost alternative than buying stocks on margin. If you consider that the index is already more volatile than the

S&P 500, and then multiply it by two, it's clear that Velocity is going to be a highly volatile fund. It's certainly not for the faint of heart. But for those who can handle the added risk, it offers a much higher potential reward over time, assuming this index does well.

How do you achieve that 200-percent performance?

We use a mixture of Nasdaq-100 futures, Nasdaq-100 options, options on futures, and stocks. It tends to be a complicated mix. We're always trying to optimize the fund to achieve this leverage at the lowest possible cost. Much of the exposure comes directly from the stocks, but we overlay some derivatives to gain additional exposure. In that regard, we are not borrowing money to get leverage and our investors are not in a position to lose more money than they put in the fund.

A lot of leveraged funds really haven't achieved their goal, if you look closely at the numbers.

We've been quite successful at matching our goal of 200-percent exposure to the index each and every day. What you must pay attention to is the daily returns. One misconception is that if you take the index and multiply it by two at the end of a time period, you can determine what a leveraged fund should do. That calculation ignores the compounding effect of each day's return. For example, in markets with consistent trends, our leveraged funds have exceeded their benchmark, while in choppy markets, leveraged funds often underperform their benchmarks. We've had a number of exciting academic studies that argue in favor of consistently applying leverage over time to beat a particular index. It certainly gives the investor a much better chance to beat the index than if they were to use an active fund manager who is not using leverage.

If you buy the notion that over time the stock market will do well, might it make sense to leverage some part of your long-term portfolio?

Absolutely. We're true believers. If you feel that over time the economy will continue to grow, translating into greater earnings and profits for companies, then it does make sense to invest in leveraged funds.

What percentage of a portfolio would it be prudent to leverage?

It boils down to your risk tolerance and time horizon. For aggressive investors, 10–20 percent isn't out of the ordinary.

The flip side is if you are negative on the market, you might want to short the Nasdaq-100. You also manage a fund for that, right?

We have two. Rydex Arktos shorts the index on a one-for-one basis. Arktos is a unique name. It's Greek for "bear." Our leveraged version of this is called the Venture Fund.

How do you manage those to short the market?

Arktos is really the inverse of the Rydex OTC Fund. It shorts the stocks in the index and also sells Nasdaq-100 futures. The Venture Fund takes a similar approach, primarily by buying puts on Nasdaq-100 futures.

Isn't there a possibility that you could really get under water if the market takes off to the upside?

When you have a short position, you do theoretically have unlimited exposure. We are required to cover some of that exposure by buying call options. We'll purchase out-of-the-money call options that really don't affect the performance on a daily basis. If things became extreme and the market started running away from you, these call options would protect some of the downside exposure.

So you keep a little insurance for that.

It's required because, as a mutual fund, you're not allowed to have unlimited exposure of your shareholder's money. You won't lose more money than you put into the fund, even in a theoretical market that doubles in a day.

Do you think all investors should have some short exposure in their portfolio?

We position our short funds as specialized products. They certainly would not be considered buy and hold investments.

And that's because you theorize that the market always goes up over time?

Right. We are believers that the economy is generally going to be expanding and that the market rises a majority of the time. It doesn't make sense to park your money in a short fund. You'll end up losing. We look at the short funds as hedging vehicles. By that I mean if a person has investments in the market and feels that we're potentially due for a correction, he or she can hedge some of that potential downside by putting money into a short fund. That can be especially attractive if an investor doesn't want to sell out of a position and incur a tax consequence. The other use for a fund like this is outright speculation. It's not a good idea for most investors, but for those willing to speculate on the downside and comfortable shorting either stocks or the market, a fund like this could be appropriate.

VALUATION

Despite the huge correction in 2000, the overall valuation of the Nasdaq-100 companies is still pretty high by many numerical standards, especially when compared with the Dow Jones Industrial Average and S&P 500. We know this has been the best-performing index over the past number of years. But is there reason to be concerned it has come too far too fast?

Investors should always concern themselves with valuation. It's important to consider how expensive these companies are and how much you're paying for the potential future earnings. The reason the Nasdaq-100 has a considerably higher price-to-earnings (PE) ratio than the S&P 500 is because you're dealing with a lot of growth-oriented companies. Interestingly, one of the reasons the PE ratio is so high is because of the modified capitalization scheme that Nasdaq has put into place. In essence, it gives more weighting to some of the smaller companies with high PE ratios. Investors must put the valuation question into perspective. One of the most effective ways to do that is to consider what's called the PEG ratio, which is price-to-earning-to-growth. It's a way of normalizing the PE figure by factoring in the expected future growth of a particular company or index. So even if a stock has a very high PE, but a relatively higher growth rate than a stock with a lower PE, it can be a more attractive investment from a valuation standpoint. It's important not to get fixated on one particular ratio because it won't necessarily give you the complete picture.

From what you said earlier, it sounds like this is really a momentum index.

It is. The index has a higher expected growth rate than the market in general. You're buying the growth and that's what's driving the performance of these companies.

And when a company's growth stops, it may get kicked out of the index because its capitalization is going to drop.

Precisely.

What do you expect from the Nasdaq-100 index and the companies it contains going forward?

My guess is that the nature of the index will remain relatively consistent with the trend we've seen. Companies in fast-growing industries will continue to dominate and drive not only the index, but also the economy. Specifically, the semiconductor segment, the Internet, software, hardware, networking, and even telecommunications are the industries that will be favored. Since those are the fastest growing industries, this argues for the Nasdaq-100 to have a higher PE multiple than most other indexes. It's going to continue to be a growth-oriented, large-cap-oriented, and even a technology-oriented index.

BUYING THE PICKS

You've selected 25 companies to highlight in this book that are especially attractive to you looking out over the next year or so. What criteria did you use in selecting these companies?

My goal was to identify companies in the index that have exhibited strong growth and determine which ones had the best prospects going forward. Consideration is given to relative valuation. However, in this volatile market, it's difficult to speculate on the valuation of these companies over the next few months. That being said, the most important factor is earnings growth. I also considered business momentum, strategic vision and strength of the management team, and competitive risks.

I tried to capture important themes that are driving economic growth going forward. Two of these themes are the emergence of biotechnology and the rapid growth of wireless data communications. In the coming months, companics developing wireless technologies offer some very exciting possibilities to efficiently move this data and may be well positioned for rapid growth. Also, certain companies involved in the semiconductor industry have great potential considering the continued strong demand for chips to power these new technologies. Many of the companies profiled are positioned as an important piece of the Internet infrastructure build-out. With Internet traffic doubling every 100 days, these companies have a lot of room to grow.

It's not surprising, then, that almost all of your names are technology related.

There are a couple of reasons they tend to be technology oriented. First, the pool of potential picks from the index is clearly dominated by technology. It's also the theme I tried to pick up on. I'm a big believer that the influence of technology will continue to grow over time. I feel the better growth prospects are in the technology sector.

How did USA Networks make your list?

USA Networks is a well-diversified media company. If you look at what the company has been able to accomplish, and the revenues it generates, you see that several of its diversified units have really started to contribute to performance. This seems like a business with a very bright future.

Let's talk briefly about a couple of companies that didn't make your list. One is a somewhat controversial name—Amazon.com. Why didn't that make the cut, and what do you think of this Internet retailer's prospects going forward?

The main reason I avoided the Internet retailers is because I feel companies in that segment will be challenged to sustain, or even produce, attractive operating margins over time. Retailers, online or otherwise, have traditionally encountered intense competition, and few have been able to carve out and defend a competitive niche. Amazon has yet to prove its ability to execute its business plan. My opinion is that it's best to take a wait-and-see attitude. To me, the build-out of the Internet infrastructure is the more attractive segment. Several companies, profiled later in this book, have tremendous potential going forward.

On the biotechnology side, you chose Amgen but not some other notable names, such as Biogen and Chyron. What made Amgen stand out?

Biotechnology is unique, in terms of the matrix investors want to look at when considering biotech shares. Certainly Amgen is the most profitable and largest biotechnology company in the index. It really benefits from powerful sales and revenues from its two blockbuster drugs. Amgen quickly moved from losses to profitability and positive cash flows. That's important because the ability to commit money and resources to drug development is the lifeblood of these companies. If they don't have an exciting drug pipeline and the ability to commit dollars to the research and development effort, you get a little nervous about their potential to stay in a leadership position. When you talk about biotechnology companies, it's all about the drug pipeline and what they can do for their next act. They must be in a position to bring out new drugs for the treatment of different diseases.

Two very different companies in a somewhat related industry didn't make your list, those being Apple Computer and Dell. Do you worry about box makers in general, or is there another particular reason those weren't included?

I worry about the growth of the PC market and future demand. Some of the estimates for 2001 put PC industry growth at somewhere around 10 percent. That's certainly come way off from where it's been. The box makers are potentially going to have a tough time over the next couple of years meeting revenue and sales expectations. They're trying to fight it out in a slower growing segment.

None of the specialty retailers, such as Bed, Bath & Beyond and Costco Wholesale, made your list. Any reason for that?

As far as specialty retailers go, it boils down to the company's ability to defend against competitive pressures and sustain its margins. These are well-run companies with strong brands. However, I feel their growth potential is overshadowed by companies in more attractive industries, such as communications, Internet infrastrucutre, and semiconductors.

LOOKING AHEAD

We've included your comments on the highlighted 25 stocks in each profile, along with the potential risks. What additional research should readers do before buying any of these stocks?

The most important thing is to get a good sense of the valuation of the stock at the point you plan to buy it. Having said that, I did choose these companies based on what I felt was their staying power. Most are well-established leaders. I believe they'll continue to be relatively strong in that sense. But understand that these companies are rather volatile and can move quickly. Investors should be careful to consider just where a company is at the point in time they are ready to buy it. They can also look at some of the other numerical indicators, such as the PE ratio, along with how those measures look now in relation to a few quarters back. Does it seem to be higher than it's been in the past, or is it a bit cheaper? Valuation is important. The nice thing is that these days this information is readily available, both in this book and on the Internet. You can also read recent news articles and other research reports to get a sense of just where these companies stand right now. Don't forget to visit their Web sites, too. The addresses are included in the profiles.

These companies tend to grow rapidly. How can you tell if that growth is going to continue?

There's no magic formula. One thing is to ask yourself whether the company makes sense in the overall scheme of things. Everyone is familiar with what's going on in the economy. Do the economic trends bode well for the company's position, or have things changed? I know that's not always easy to analyze, especially if you're dealing with complicated emerging technologies. But many stocks tend to get over-hyped without consideration for just what those companies do. I feel it's important to conduct a reality check.

Obviously one reason to sell one of these stocks, especially for you, is if it gets deleted from the index. But investors in general struggle with when to sell a stock. What are some other reasons you would eliminate a position?

The notion of when to sell is probably the most difficult consideration. Absent any fundamental changes to either the company or the industry, I would try to avoid selling. For instance, if a company misses its earnings and sells off, I would tend to be careful not to sell in that environment. Most investors have learned that panic selling just because earnings come out lower than expected is certainly not the way to go. It has to be more of a broader fundamental reason; for instance, if the company looks like it's headed toward bankruptcy or there are some important revisions to prior earnings or earnings restatements. Those events deserve more investigation and may sometimes warrant selling a particular company. More often than not it's going to make sense to hold on to these companies over the long term.

Over the past few years, the stocks within the index have been so volatile. We've seen even some large blue chips—including Intel, Nokia, and Apple—blow up, and it's not unusual for the index to go up or down 5 percent on any given day. Is that going to continue, and how should investors react to this incredible volatility?

It will continue. That's the nature of this current environment. If companies aren't perfectly in sync and matching their expectations, there's certainly the potential to have significant revisions in valuation. As long as the economy is favorable, once a company comes out with bad news or misses earnings expectations, you'll have these big drops in valuation. But that's not necessarily reason to get rid of a particular company. In fact, it may be an opportunity to add to your position. A short-term or myopic focus can cause you to sell at precisely the wrong time. Quick revaluations of companies that once had everything going in their favor will continue. The nice thing is that, especially if you're investing in a broad index, including the Nasdaq-100, you won't get hurt that badly. The diversification helps out.

Which presumably also means you shouldn't just buy one or two stocks. Do you have any idea of how many stocks investors need in their portfolio at a minimum?

The general rule of thumb is that a portfolio of more than 20 stocks will give you decent diversification, but if you're buying all 20 from the same industry, the benefit is reduced. If you're looking within the Nasdaq-100, buying 25–30 names will give you a pretty good mix and spread your bets out well.

Since we know you have a crystal ball on your desk, what is the market going to look like in 2001–2002? Give us your overall feel for what's ahead.

I see continued growth, but more within the normal parameters. A healthy 10 to 15 percent, annual return, and possibly more for the Nasdaq-100, is expected. We'll see a moderately healthy investment environment.

You said a 10 to 15 percent return is expected. Is that realistic?

I think so.

Many pundits say the U.S. stock market indexes have come so far in recent years that you must have a long stretch of lower returns to make up for this abnormally high performance.

I don't buy that. To a large extent the growth is justified, mainly due to the increase in productivity and the companies' ability to sustain strong earnings growth. I don't agree that we need to pay back for the good times, or that we've been living on borrowed time. I think we're just about right.

4

BYRUM'S TOP 25 FOR 2001–2002

1. ADC Telecommunications
2. Altera
3. Amgen
4. Applied Materials
5. Cisco Systems
6. Comverse Technology
7. Intel
8. JDS Uniphase
9. Level 3 Communications
10. Linear Technology
11. McLeodUSA
12. MedImmune
13. Metromedia Fiber Network
14. Microsoft
15. Network Appliance
16. Nextel Communications
17. Oracle
18. Paychex
19. PMC-Sierra
20. Sanmina
21. Sun Microsystems
22. USA Networks
23. Xilinx
24. XO Communications
25. Yahoo!

1. ADC TELECOMMUNICATIONS

Symbol: ADCT
Sector: Technology (Communications Equipment)

COMPANY PROFILE

ADC Telecommunications provides systems that enable communications service providers to offer integrated solutions in the local loop, which runs from local service provider offices through interfaces to end-user homes or businesses. ADC's broadband connectivity products link different components from the communications systems and provide access to system-related circuits. The technology also enables telephone companies to deliver voice, video, Internet, and data services to business customers, while allowing cable TV operators to transmit high-speed digital signals for two-way in-home voice, data, Internet, and video service. Additionally, ADC offers consulting, software, and systems integration services. The company acquired PairGain Technologies and Centigram Communications in 2000.

EARNINGS

During the past 12 months, ADC Telecommunications earned $0.52 per share, up 63 percent from the previous year.

REVENUES

Revenues during the past 12 months totaled $2.7 billion, up 686 percent from a year earlier.

KEY RATIOS & MEASURES	5-YEAR RANGE	CURRENT
P/E	14–97	76.9
Price-to-Book	2.3–19.8	16.1
Price-to-Cash Flow	10–73	59.6
Price-to-Sales	1.4–12.2	9.9
Return on Equity	8.1–25.5%	25.5%
Beta		1.28

Byrum's Comments

As a result of the world's seemingly insatiable urge to push information through wires, ADC Telecommunications, dubbed "The Broadband Company," finds itself in the right business at the right time. ADC provides network equipment, software, and integration services to companies that deliver telephone, cable, Internet broadcast, and wireless communications to homes and businesses. Its network solutions enable service providers to deliver high-speed transmission over fiber optic, copper, coaxial, and wireless media.

ADC is organized into three main product groups. The Broadband Access and Transport Group has the simple purpose of helping its customers increase capacity. This group supports fiber, copper, cable/coax, and wireless networks, and works with a host of leading technologies, including xDSL and ATM. The Integrated Solutions Group focuses on developing and integrating operations support software and network applications. The Systems Integration Group supplies teams of experts in network design and product integration. Services from this division include technical consulting, installation, and operations support system software.

More than most Nasdaq-100 companies, ADC appeals to investors primarily on the basis of its numbers. Revenue growth has been consistently stellar, and management has tended carefully to its enviable profit margins.

Risk Factors

ADC is enjoying its decade in the sun as a key player in the construction of a new global infrastructure. Sooner or later, however, the world will be adequately wired for voice and data transmission, and ADC shows a bit less innovation and a little more opportunism than many Nasdaq companies. In 1983, it was one of the few equipment suppliers available to the new Baby Bells. Later in the decade, it capitalized on the shift from analog to digital. It remains to be seen what businesses ADC will attempt to grab when the broadband boom comes to an end.

CONTACT INFORMATION

ADC Telecommunications, Inc., 12501 Whitewater Drive, Minnetonka, MN 55343
(952) 938-8080
www.adc.com

ADC Telecom (ADCT)

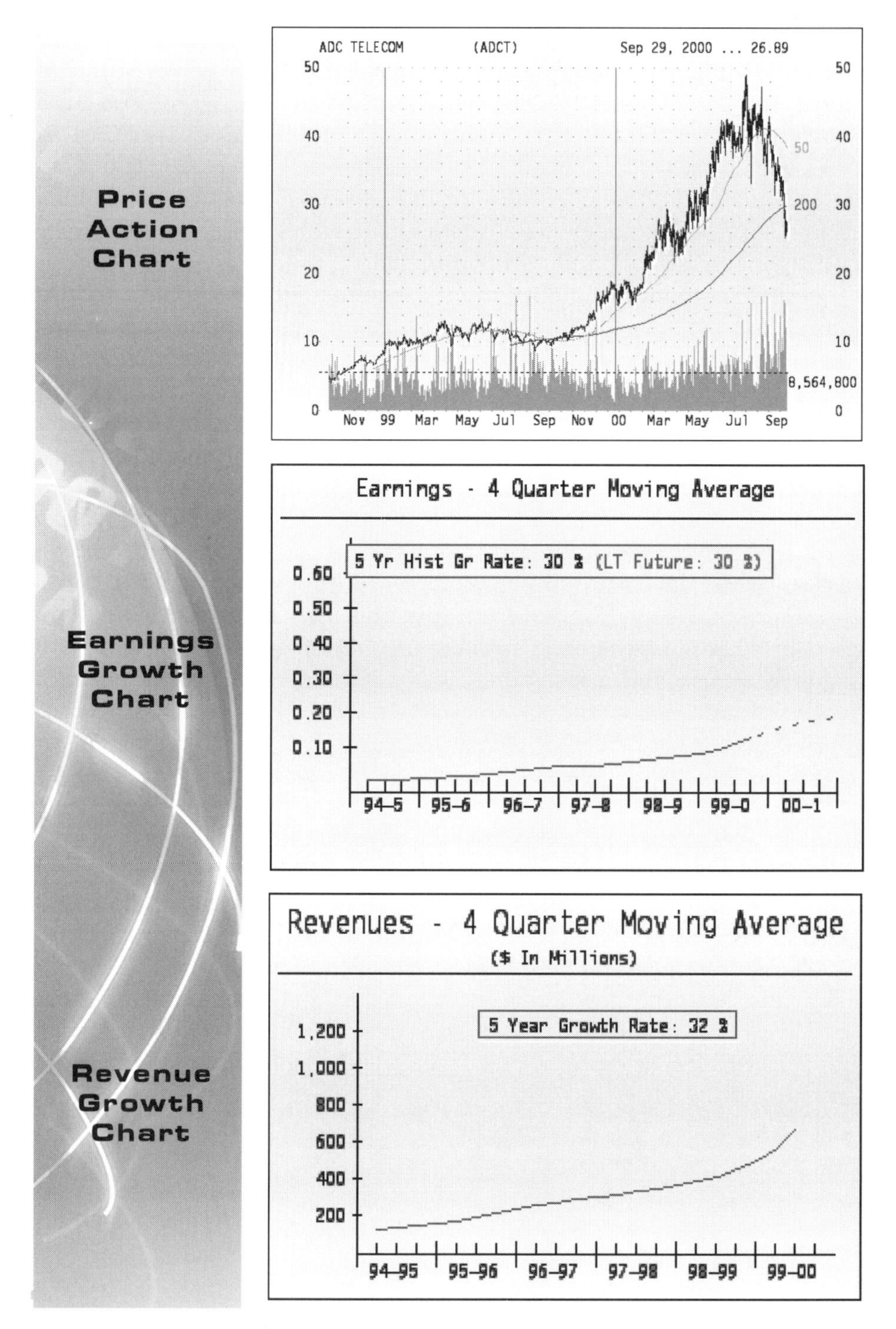

Charts provided by Baseline Financial Services.

2. ALTERA

Symbol: ALTR
Sector: Technology (Semiconductors)

COMPANY PROFILE

Altera manufactures and designs programmable logic devices (PLD) and associated development tools. PLDs are semiconductor integrated circuits that offer on-site programmability to customers using the company's proprietary software. The software operates on both PCs and engineering workstations. Altera's products are used for a wide range of functions, including electronic data processing, telecommunications, data communications, and industrial applications. The company offers more than 1,000 product options among its PLD line, along with an array of hardware used in programming PLDs. Altera markets its products in the United States, Canada, Europe, and Asia, primarily through direct sales personnel and a network of distributors. International sales make up nearly half of the overall total. In 2000, Altera also acquired DesignPRO, Inc.

EARNINGS

During the past 12 months, Altera earned $0.72 per share, up 54 percent from the previous year.

REVENUES

Revenues during the past 12 months totaled $1.1 billion, up 48 percent from a year earlier.

KEY RATIOS & MEASURES	5-YEAR RANGE	CURRENT
P/E	11–98	86.5
Price-to-Book	3.1–20.8	19.1
Price-to-Cash Flow	9.3–85.1	78.4
Price-to-Sales	2.3–25.1	23.1
Return on Equity	21.8–34.9%	25.5%
Beta		1.69

BYRUM'S COMMENTS

Altera Corporation designs, manufactures, and markets a broad range of high-performance, high-density logic devices (PLDs). PLDs are standardized, digital integrated circuits that can be customized by computer system designers. Working on Altera's proprietary software at PCs or workstations, designers using PLDs can avoid the hundreds of hours otherwise needed to program and test the logical sequences to be executed by semiconductors. Founded in 1983, Altera was the first supplier of reprogrammable logic devices and remains a global leader in this market.

PLDs are found in thousands of products, from traffic lights to medical imaging devices. Major customers, such as Cisco Systems and 3Com, use Altera devices for the routers and switches that keep the Internet and other worldwide networks running. By creating a product that reduces the time needed to bring new technology to market, Altera keeps itself on the front edge of technological change.

The programming flexibility of PLDs has made them especially popular for designers of communications equipment, who must be able to adapt to rapidly changing standards. Altera's growth has been fueled largely by the expansion of the communications industry, for which it has developed a number of new products. It is especially impressive that Altera's revenue from this area has continued to grow, even while the communications companies themselves have been cutting back on spending for new product development.

RISK FACTORS

Although the PLD companies have generally been stronger than semiconductor producers, Altera is by no means immune from the volatility of that industry. Despite analysts' preference that companies keep minimal inventories, Altera has been open about its intention to keep inventory levels high. This strategy is designed to ensure customer satisfaction, especially during periods of new product rollouts, but could be costly in the event of a sudden glut in semiconductor supply or a downturn in demand.

CONTACT INFORMATION

Altera Corporation, 101 Innovation Drive, San Jose, CA 95134-2020
(408) 544-7000
www.altera.com

Altera (ALTR)

Price Action Chart

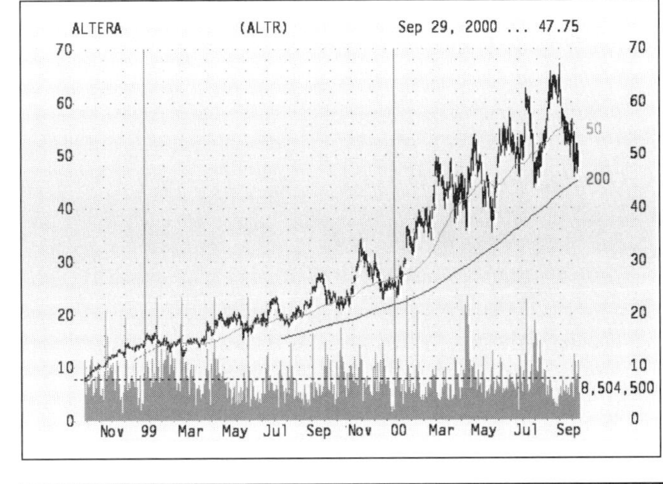

Earnings Growth Chart

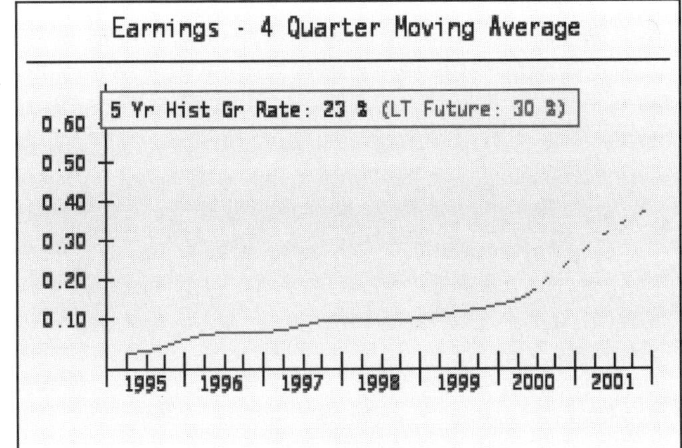

Revenue Growth Chart

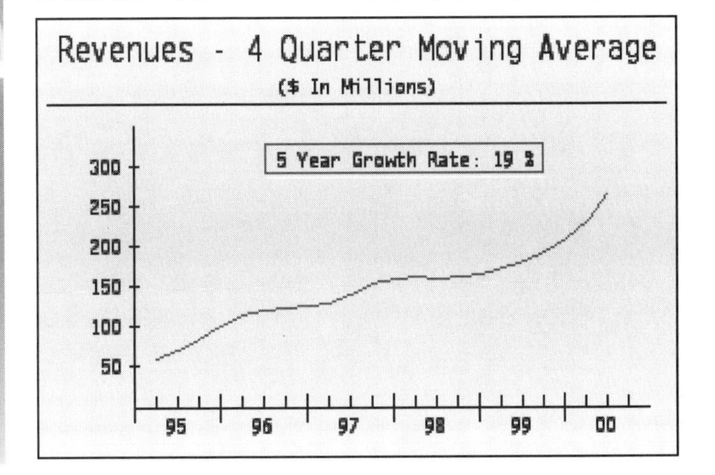

Charts provided by Baseline Financial Services.

3. AMGEN

Symbol: AMGN
Sector: Healthcare (Major Drugs)

COMPANY PROFILE

Amgen discovers, develops, manufactures, and markets drugs based on advances in cellular and molecular biology. Amgen's four principal products include Epogen, used for the treatment of anemia associated with chronic renal failure; Neupogen, which stimulates the production of certain white blood cells; Infergen, which helps the immune system fight certain viral infections; and Stemgen, used to support stem-cell transplants. Amgen focuses its research efforts on secreted-protein and small-molecule human therapeutics, with particular emphasis on neurobiology, inflammation, and cancer. Amgen places heavy emphasis on developing human therapeutics in hematology, cancer, infectious disease, endocrinology, neurobiology, and inflammation. It is one of the world's premier biotechnology companies.

EARNINGS

During the past 12 months, Amgen earned $1.04 per share, up 14 percent from the previous year.

REVENUES

Revenues during the past 12 months totaled $3.5 billion, up 16 percent from a year earlier.

KEY RATIOS & MEASURES	5-YEAR RANGE	CURRENT
P/E	16–78	73.5
Price-to-Book	4.6–23	21.8
Price-to-Cash Flow	12.1–66.4	63.1
Price-to-Sales	4.3–23.6	22.41
Return on Equity	31.9–39.3%	34.1%
Beta		0.87

Byrum's Comments

By most accounts, Amgen is the leading company in the biotechnology industry. It also has the most sales, earnings, and largest market capitalization within the sector. Amgen develops therapies for diseases of the hematopoietic, nervous, inflammatory, endocrine, and soft tissue systems. It currently markets the two largest drugs developed by a biotech firm, Epogen, for the treatment of anemia, and Neupogen, which stimulates white blood cell growth in patients undergoing cancer chemotherapy or bone marrow transplants. Each of these two blockbuster products commands more than $1 billion in annual sales and drives Amgen's earnings. A third product, Infergen, contributes approximately 10 percent of the company's annual sales. This drug is an effective treatment for hepatitis C.

Positioned as the leading biotech concern, and leveraging off the immense success of its two blockbuster drugs, Amgen is in a favorable position to continue its success for years to come. Sales of its two leading drugs, Epogen and Neupogen, are likely to enjoy double-digit growth going forward. In addition, after years of weakness, Amgen's pipeline now has several exciting new opportunities. The pipeline includes Abarelix, a treatment for prostate cancer, which has completed phase III trials, and SD-01, a long-acting version of its blockbuster, Neupogen, currently in phase III. It also is developing early-stage products for osteoporosis, rheumatoid arthritis, oral mucositis, and neurodegenerative diseases. Other products in the final stages of development include NESP and Kineret. It is likely that Amgen's new products (NESP, Kineret, Abarelix, and Neupogen SD-01) will be brought to market in 2001 and 2002, which may lead to earnings growth acceleration.

Risk Factors

Amgen is in a considerably more favorable position than many of its biotech peers, given the steady revenue stream it enjoys from its blockbuster drugs. However, pricing pressure on Epogen, as a result of a proposal to cut Medicare reimbursements for the drug to dialysis centers, may lower the profitability of this product. Additionally, an ongoing patent dispute could pose a serious threat to potential revenues from incremental sales of existing drugs.

CONTACT INFORMATION

Amgen, Inc., 1 Amgen Center Drive, Thousand Oaks, CA 91320-1799
(805) 447-1000
www.amgen.com

Amgen (AMGN)

Price Action Chart

Earnings Growth Chart

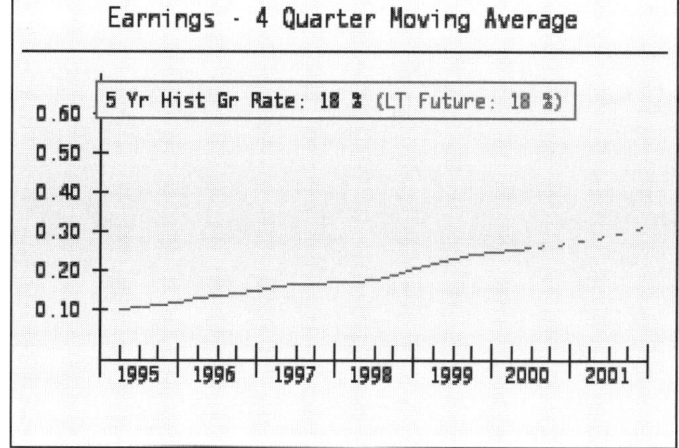

Revenue Growth Chart

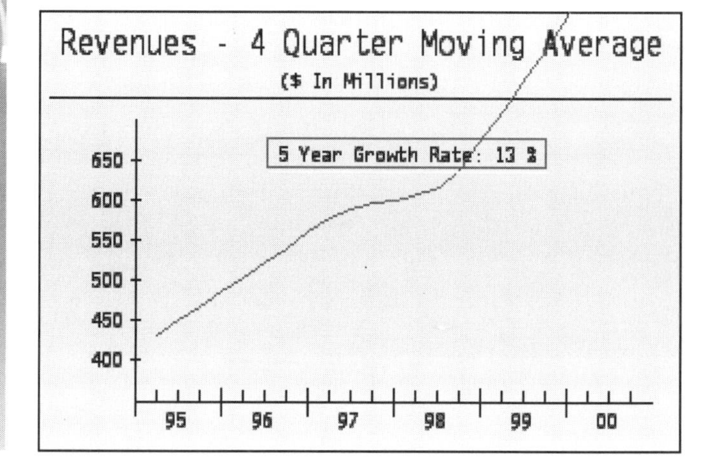

Charts provided by Baseline Financial Services.

4. APPLIED MATERIALS

Symbol: AMAT
Sector: Technology (Semiconductors)

COMPANY PROFILE

Applied Materials develops, manufactures, markets, and services semiconductor wafer-fabrication equipment and related spare parts for the worldwide semiconductor industry. Customers for these products include semiconductor wafer and semiconductor integrated circuit (IC or chip) manufacturers. These customers either use the ICs Applied Materials manufactures in their own products or sell them to other companies. These ICs are the key components in most advanced electronic products, such as telecommunications devices, computers, electronic games, and automotive engine management systems. Applied Materials also has a flat panel display division, called AKT, and provides manufacturing execution system software for the semiconductor industry through its Consilium subsidiary. Most recently, the company announced its acquisition of Etec Systems.

EARNINGS

During the past 12 months, Applied Materials earned $1.99 per share, up 246 percent from the previous year.

REVENUES

Revenues during the past 12 months totaled $8.2 billion, up 106 percent from a year earlier.

KEY RATIOS & MEASURES	5-YEAR RANGE	CURRENT
P/E	5–103	42.6
Price-to-Book	1.6–15.8	11.6
Price-to-Cash Flow	5.2–51.1	36.4
Price-to-Sales	0.9–11.4	8.4
Return on Equity	8.3–36.2%	36.2%
Beta		1.82

BYRUM'S COMMENTS

Applied Materials is a leading developer and manufacturer of semiconductor wafer-producing equipment and parts. The company provides equipment and services to producers of semiconductors and integrated circuits (chips). These integrated circuits play a vital role in a wide range of advanced electronic products, most notably computers and telecommunications products. Since acquiring Consilium in 1998, Applied Materials has been a leading provider of manufacturing execution system software for the semiconductor industry.

Product diversity and innovation have largely contributed to Applied Materials's ability to build a dominant position in the semiconductor equipment market. The three key sources of revenue for the company are integrated circuit deposition, chip polishing, and products that test integrated circuits. Applied Materials is a technological leader in providing equipment used in the preparation of chips. The company is currently in the process of developing technology to work with copper in integrated circuits. It's crucial for manufacturers to have effective testing mechanisms due to the great expense in fabricating integrated circuits. This gives Applied Materials an opportunity to further enhance its product line.

At present, the company's primary markets are North America, Japan, Taiwan, Europe, Southeast Asia, and Korea. As you can tell, Applied Materials's distribution channels and customer base is diverse and well balanced.

RISK FACTORS

Sustained sales growth for the company's products rests largely on the global demand for semiconductors. Demand has been high of late, and the company's inability to keep up has hindered revenue growth. To this end, Applied Materials has focused spending on expanding capacity and widening its product line. Sustaining this pattern is essential to fully capture profits on what is a relatively high-margin product. Balance is another key to Applied Materials's success. The company must continue to find ways of increasing market share while becoming the leading supplier in each subcategory of the semiconductor fabrication equipment industry.

CONTACT INFORMATION

Applied Materials, Inc., 3050 Bowers Avenue, Santa Clara, CA 95054-3299
(408) 727-5555
www.appliedmaterials.com

Applied Materials (AMAT)

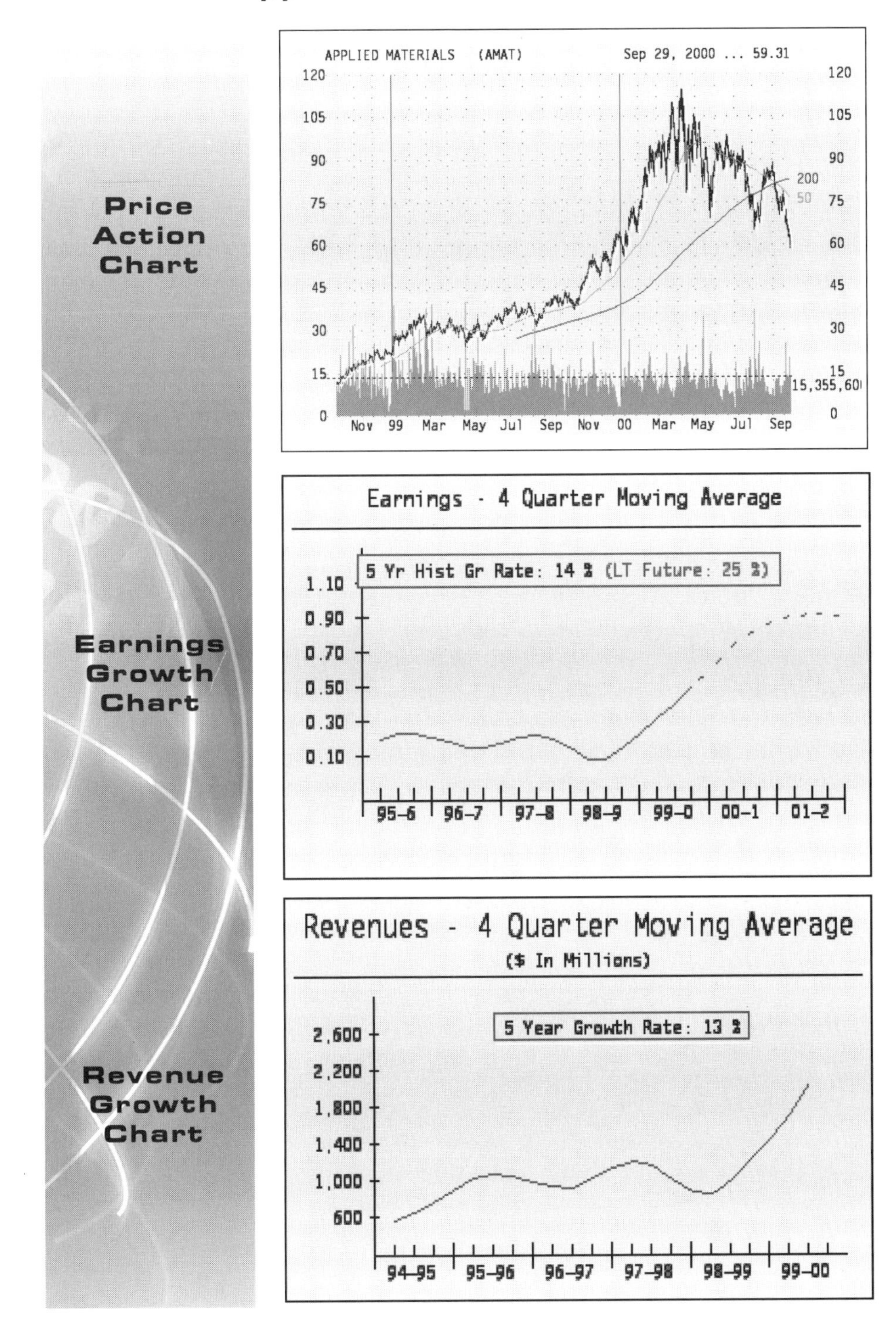

Charts provided by Baseline Financial Services.

5. CISCO SYSTEMS

Symbol: CSCO
Sector: Technology (Computer Networks)

COMPANY PROFILE

Cisco Systems produces hardware and software products that link computer networks worldwide. It makes an array of routers, which move information from one network to another, and switches, which are used in local area networks (LAN) and wide area networks (WAN) to control routing. Cisco also manufactures a range of remote-access devices, including ISDN remote-access routers, dial-up-access servers, DSL access multiplexers, and cable universal broadband routers. Its products include network security software (PIX Firewall, NetSonar, and others), intelligent network services software (Cisco IOS), and a network of various management products. The company is constantly growing through acquisition. Its most recent purchases include Aironet Wireless, Compatible Systems, JetCell, Atlantech, Arrowpoint Communications, SightPath, Pentacom, IPmobile, and PixStream.

EARNINGS

During the past 12 months, Cisco Systems earned $0.55 per share, up 45 percent from the previous year.

REVENUES

Revenues during the past 12 months totaled $18.9 billion, up 55 percent from a year earlier.

KEY RATIOS & MEASURES	5-YEAR RANGE	CURRENT
P/E	22–185	125.8
Price-to-Book	7–35.5	29.6
Price-to-Cash Flow	19.1–133.4	111.5
Price-to-Sales	3.8–30.3	25.28
Return on Equity	22.3–43.5%	25%
Beta		1.69

BYRUM'S COMMENTS

A perennial favorite among technology investors, Cisco Systems has grown to become one of the most successful technology companies in the world. Central to Cisco's remarkable performance over the past decade has been the explosive growth of the Internet. The associated build-out of the networking infrastructure that supports data traffic along the information superhighway has been the key long-term growth driver for sales of Cisco's data-networking products. Over the years, Cisco has matured to become a key strategic vendor for global corporations that rely on data-networking solutions for mission-critical applications. It has also become the world's largest supplier of data-networking products.

To date, the rewards for investors who recognized Cisco's importance relative to the Internet have been nothing short of phenomenal. Over the past decade, Cisco's stock price has achieved an average annual return of approximately 90 percent, greatly exceeding that of the general stock market.

Considering its stellar performance and relatively high valuation, investors often pause to consider whether Cisco's exceptional growth will continue in the future. Although it may become increasingly difficult for Cisco to sustain its past growth rate, several key positive fundamental factors suggest that Cisco is favorably positioned to continue to outperform the market, although perhaps at a less brisk pace. Simply put, Cisco is the dominant player in a rapidly growing segment of the market. Cisco has a powerful brand name and highly effective marketing and distribution, earning the company a highly loyal customer base. The company also benefits from a proven management team that has consistently implemented a strategic business plan to dominate Internet infrastructure and data-transport solutions. Its leadership position has created significant barriers to entry, making it difficult for competitors to gain market share.

RISK FACTORS

With solid core competencies and proven ability to execute, Cisco is perhaps less risky than most technology companies. Being the dominant player within a segment of the market, however, is pause for concern. Over the next several years, the market in which Cisco competes will continue to change rapidly. Cisco will have to identify changes early enough to position itself, through acquisition or internal development, to capitalize on these changes. Although Cisco dominates the corporate market for networking-equipment products, it faces stiffer competition from Lucent and Nortel Networks in other key growth areas, such as regional telephone companies and Internet service providers.

CONTACT INFORMATION

Cisco Systems, Inc., 170 West Tasman Drive, San Jose, CA 95134-1706
(408) 526-4000
www.cisco.com

Cisco Systems (CSCO)

Price Action Chart

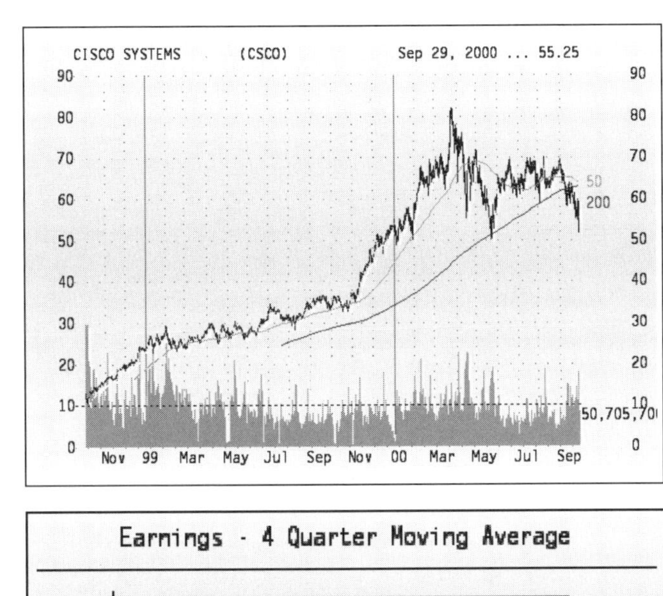

Earnings Growth Chart

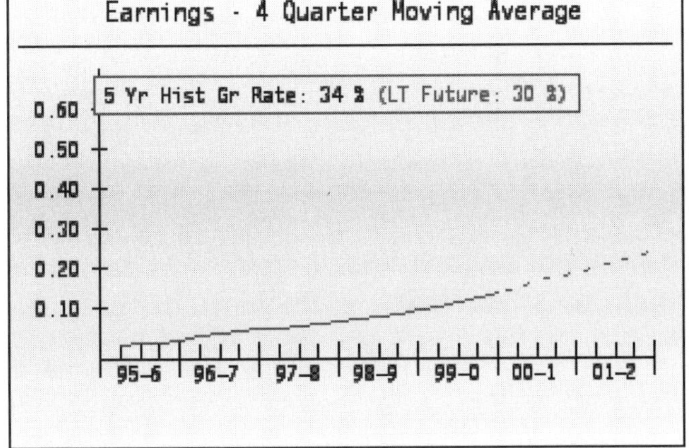

Revenue Growth Chart

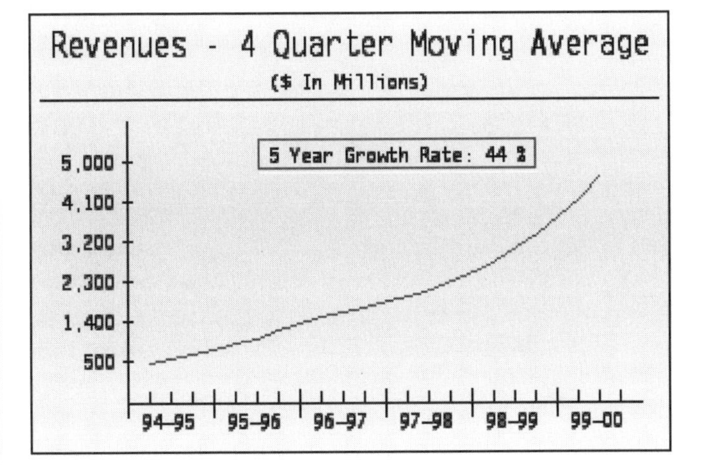

Charts provided by Baseline Financial Services.

6. COMVERSE TECHNOLOGY

Symbol: CMVT
Sector: Technology (Communications Equipment)

COMPANY PROFILE

Comverse Technology designs and manufactures computer and telecommunications systems and software for multimedia communications. It makes enhanced services platform products that enable telecommunications network operators to offer various revenue-generating services, such as call answering, voice and fax mail, prepaid services, audiotext, short-text messaging, and unified messaging. Comverse also provides multiple-channel multimedia digital-monitoring systems to support the surveillance activities of law enforcement and intelligence agencies. More than 320 wireless and fixed telephone network operators in some 90 countries have chosen Comverse's platforms to enhance their services. The company's clients include AT&T, Cable & Wireless, Deutsche Telecom, and Hong Kong Telecom.

EARNINGS

During the past 12 months, Comverse Technology earned $1.27 per share, up 37 percent from the previous year.

REVENUES

Revenues during the past 12 months totaled $1 billion, up 31 percent from a year earlier.

KEY RATIOS & MEASURES	5-YEAR RANGE	CURRENT
P/E	14–115	74.1
Price-to-Book	1.5–23.4	17.7
Price-to-Cash Flow	10.3–83.2	63.2
Price-to-Sales	1.9–18.7	14.14
Return on Equity	16.6–34.7%	30.7%
Beta		1.55

Byrum's Comments

Based in Woodbury, New York, Comverse Technology is a leading supplier of telecommunications applications to a variety of customers, including fixed and wireless telephone network operators, government agencies, financial institutions, and call centers. The company offers a wide variety of products designed to enhance the telecommunications capabilities and services of its customers.

The product line can be distilled into two broad areas: message-processing products, which include voice mail, interactive voice response, short-message service, and integrated voice/fax/e-mail unified messaging; and digital monitoring systems, which include recording systems for call centers, financial institutions, and emergency 911 services providers, along with monitoring systems for law enforcement and intelligence agencies. Approximately 90 percent of the company's revenues come from sales of message-processing products. Comverse enjoys a healthy growth rate, especially for products positioned to serve wireless data networks. As such, its long-term performance is strongly linked to the growth rate of digital wireless subscriber growth.

Several factors lead to a favorable outlook for the company, including the strong growth trend of digital wireless services and continued sales momentum of the company's products. The company is experiencing a heightened demand from wireless operators to add innovative services to ensure customer loyalty. As a result, Comverse Technology's value-added products are gaining sales momentum. In addition, Comverse's new innovative products should be accepted with strong demand in the coming months.

Risk Factors

In response to the company's impressive ability to exceed expectations for earnings growth, Comverse Technology has commanded a high PE valuation. Any disappointment or slowdown in sales momentum will almost certainly weigh heavily on the share price. Key product growth is quite robust in relation to the growth of wireless data services. This is expected to continue. However, investors are advised to watch the trend closely and consider the affect of rapidly changing technologies on the company's product line.

CONTACT INFORMATION

Comverse Technology, Inc., 170 Crossways Park Drive, Woodbury, NY 11797-2048
(516) 677-7200
www.comverse.com

Comverse Technology (CMVT)

Price Action Chart

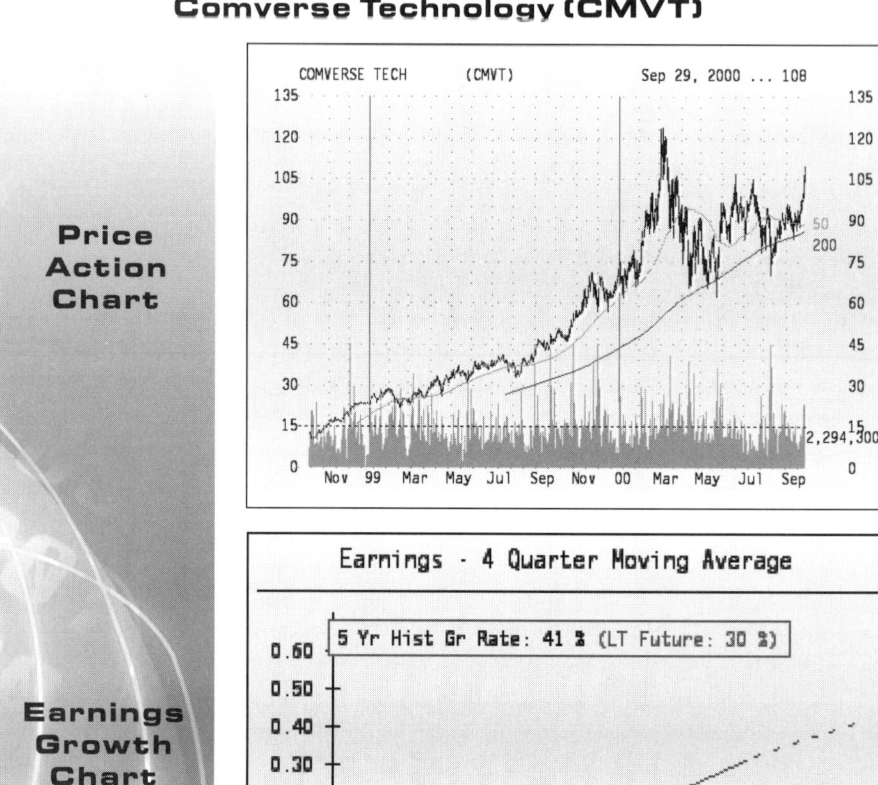

Earnings Growth Chart

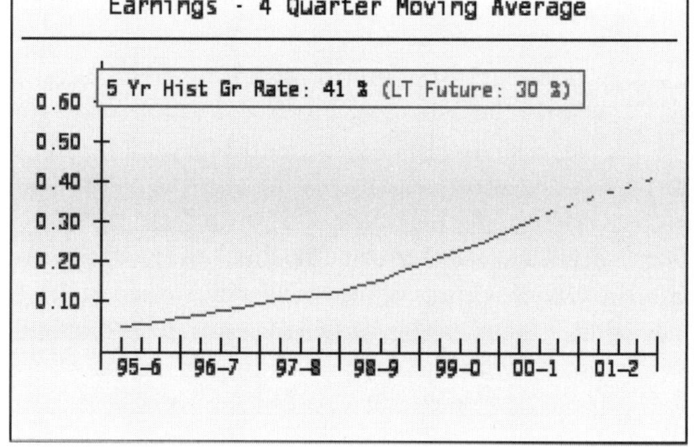

Revenue Growth Chart

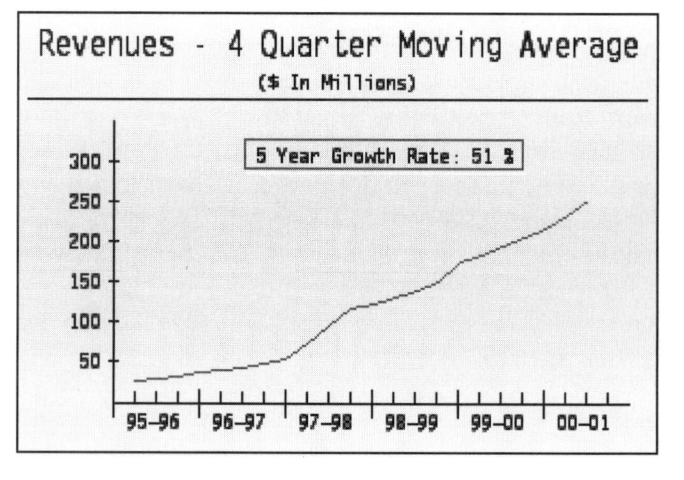

Charts provided by Baseline Financial Services.

7. INTEL

Symbol: INTC
Sector: Technology (Semiconductors)

COMPANY PROFILE

Intel designs and manufactures semiconductor chips. Best known for its Pentium family of microprocessors, the company also makes chipsets, flash memory devices, embedded processors and microcontrollers, networking and communications products, digital imaging and other PC-peripheral products, plus various component-level integrated circuits. Customers include manufacturers of personal computers, servers, telecommunications and data communications equipment, and peripherals; users of PCs and computing appliances; and businesses, schools, and state and local governments that are building or enhancing Internet data centers. In 2000, Intel agreed to buy Basis Communications, Kuck & Associates, Trillium Digital, Giga, and Ziatech.

EARNINGS

During the past 12 months, Intel earned $1.48 per share, up 39 percent from the previous year.

REVENUES

Revenues during the past 12 months totaled $31.9 billion, up 13 percent from a year earlier.

KEY RATIOS & MEASURES	5-YEAR RANGE	CURRENT
P/E	10–63	50.1
Price-to-Book	2.4–13.3	13
Price-to-Cash Flow	6.1–37.7	36.7
Price-to-Sales	1.9–16	15.54
Return on Equity	26.2–38.4%	31.8%
Beta		1.17

BYRUM'S COMMENTS

Intel is one of the world's most successful computer companies. It boasts a market share of more than 80 percent of the global market for microprocessors. While microchips remain the company's bread and butter, Intel has expanded its product line to include networking and wireless communication devices, as well as embedded processors, microcontrollers, flash memory devices, and graphics products.

Intel's revenues have surged along with the growth of the PC market and the seemingly insatiable consumer appetite for faster performance. However, chips are seen as a boom-or-bust business, with every innovation subject to quick replication by lower-cost producers. Intel proved its talent for marketing and engineering in this difficult environment, and has transformed its hard-working but invisible microprocessor into "Pentium," a widely recognized brand name.

Investors can't help but notice that Intel faces a number of challenges. Demand for PCs has already begun to slow, and foreign markets are unlikely to pick up the slack. Intel's future success depends on the continuous introduction of new products, each of which must fit perfectly with the latest trends in computer use and design. Still, PCs are here to stay, and Intel's skill at positioning its products for market dominance suggests that it will remain a significant player.

RISK FACTORS

Although Intel appears unlikely to lose its leadership position in the near future, its greatest long-term risk is that microchips will become low-margin commodities. Even small inroads by competitors (notably Advanced Micro Devices) could result in overcapacity and lower prices. In order to keep its Pentium line viable, Intel has to manage repeated migrations of computer architecture, and each new product introduction is subject to the risk of a high-profile failure.

CONTACT INFORMATION

Intel Corporation, 2200 Mission College Boulevard, Santa Clara, CA 95052-8119
(408) 765-8080
www.intel.com

Intel (INTC)

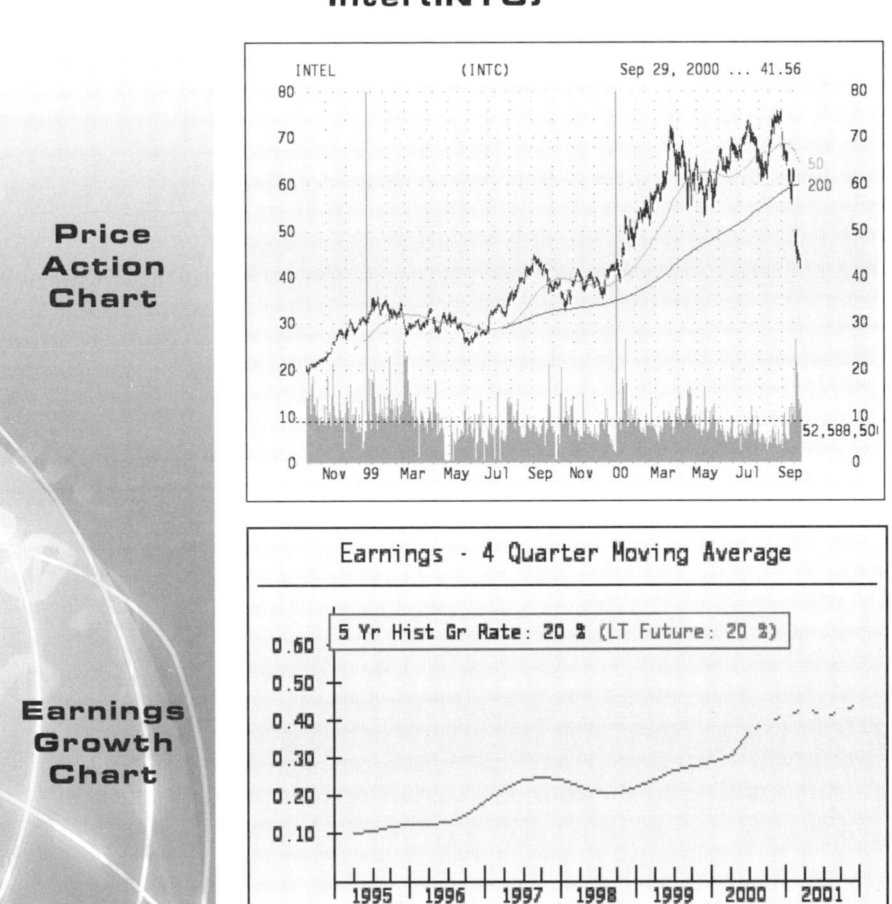

Revenue Growth Chart

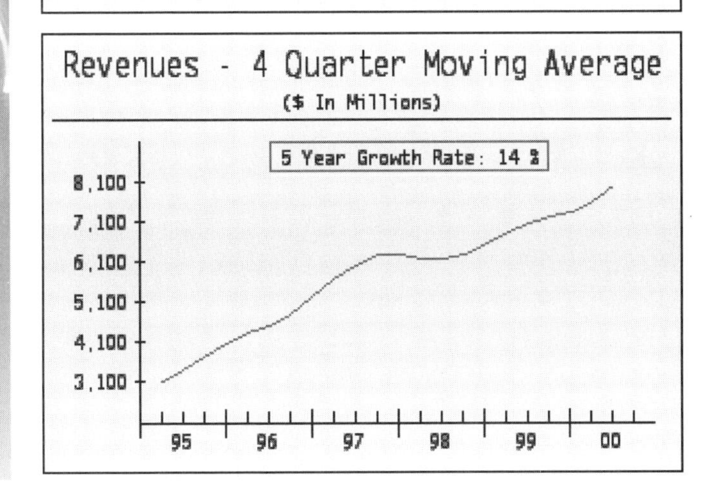

Charts provided by Baseline Financial Services.

8. JDS UNIPHASE

Symbol: JDSU
Sector: Technology (Communications Equipment)

COMPANY PROFILE

JDS Uniphase is a provider of advanced fiber-optic components and modules. It makes semiconductor lasers, high-speed external modulators, transmitters, amplifiers, couplers, multiplexers, circulators, tunable filters, optical switches, and isolators for fiber-optic applications. It also produces test instruments for system production applications and network installation. Furthermore, JDS Uniphase makes laser subsystems for a range of commercial applications. JDS Uniphase sells its products to telecommunications and cable television system providers worldwide, including Alcatel, Ciena, General Instrument, Lucent Technologies, Nortel, Pirelli, and others. The company was on a buying spree during 2000, gobbling up Optical Lab, Cronos Integrated Microsystems, Fujian Casix Laser, E-Tek Dynamics, and SDL.

EARNINGS

During the past 12 months, JDS Uniphase earned $0.41 per share, up 132 percent from the previous year.

REVENUES

Revenues during the past 12 months totaled $1.4 billion, up 406 percent from a year earlier.

KEY RATIOS & MEASURES	5-YEAR RANGE	CURRENT
P/E	21–557	300.2
Price-to-Book	0.6–13.3	10.7
Price-to-Cash Flow	19–361.8	277.9
Price-to-Sales	2.7–100	80.64
Return on Equity	3.1–10.3%	10.3%
Beta		1.65

Byrum's Comments

JDS Uniphase was formed in June 1999 as a product of the merger of Uniphase Corporation and JDS Fitel. The company is a market leader in the development, manufacture, and distribution of fiber-optic products for the telecommunications and cable television industries. JDS Uniphase supplies components for use in building fiber-optic networks, which enable the rapid transmission of large amounts of data over long distances via light waves.

The long-term success of JDS Uniphase is tied to aggressive capital expenditures by telecommunication companies as they migrate from electrical to optical networks over the next several years. Telecommunication companies are being forced to optimize and enhance data networks to meet the insatiable demand for bandwidth resulting from the explosion of Internet traffic. JDS Uniphase's broad product line of optical components is well suited to assist its customers in building the "next generation" network.

To date, the company has aggressively pursued its strategic vision to create a comprehensive group of products to serve customer needs, improve time to market, and increase internal manufacturing to meet growing demand. An aggressive acquisition strategy has provided key technologies for building a solid product line, although management is challenged to increase the scale of its manufacturing capacity over the next 12 to 18 months.

The outlook for JDS Uniphase should be quite favorable due to strong demand for optical networks, which in turn leads to strong demand for optical components. This trend makes the company a key part of the value chain in building the next generation of telecommunication networks.

Risk Factors

As part of its current strategic vision, JDS Uniphase is focused on ramping up manufacturing capacity to meet demand for optical components. Corporate plans call for increasing the output of key components fourfold over the next year and a half. There is a risk that the company could fall short on its plans to increase capacity, which may lead to slower growth than the industry average. Additionally, the proposed merger with SDL, while strengthening its product line and technology base, will pose significant challenges in integrating operations.

CONTACT INFORMATION

JDS Uniphase Corporation, 163 Baypointe Parkway, San Jose, CA 95134-1622
(408) 434-1800
www.jdsunph.com

JDS Uniphase (JDSU)

Price Action Chart

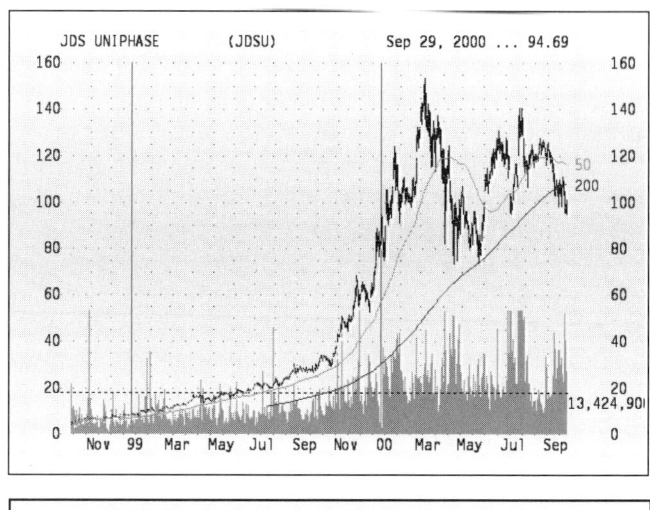

Earnings Growth Chart

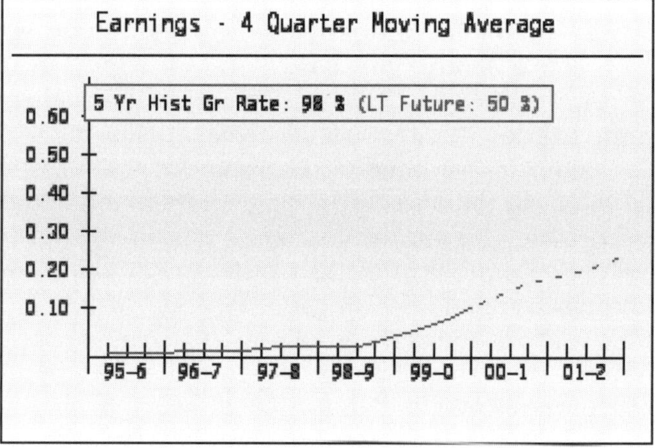

Revenue Growth Chart

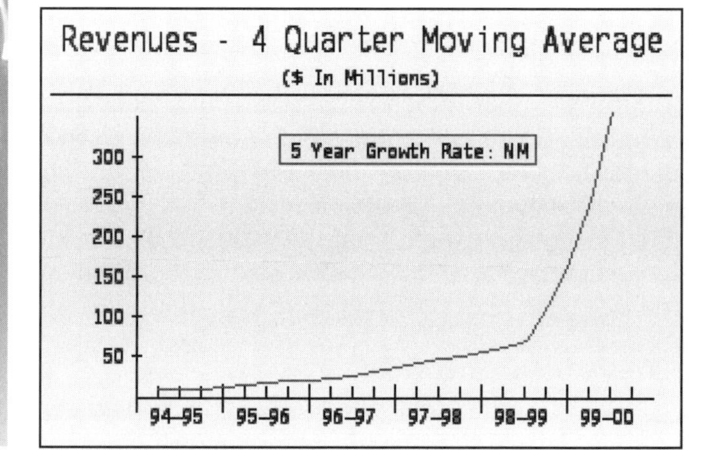

Charts provided by Baseline Financial Services.

9. LEVEL 3 COMMUNICATIONS

Symbol: LVLT
Sector: Services (Communications Services)

COMPANY PROFILE

Level 3 Communications is a communications and information services company. The company is building an international advanced facilities-based Internet-protocol network, to be completed in three to five years. The company provides a comprehensive range of services over its Level 3 network, including private line, long distance, colocation, Internet access, and managed modem services. Subsidiary PKSIS offers computer operations outsourcing and systems integration services to customers throughout the United States and abroad, including information system design and engineering, networking, and multiphase services. Level 3 also has investments in a telephone company, an Internet service provider, a cable television operator, three coal mines, and a toll road in California.

EARNINGS

During the past 12 months, Level 3 Communications lost $2.55 per share, down 166 percent from the previous year.

REVENUES

Revenues during the past 12 months totaled $718 million, up 75 percent from a year earlier.

KEY RATIOS & MEASURES	5-YEAR RANGE	CURRENT
P/E	NM	NM
Price-to-Book	2–15.8	10.2
Price-to-Cash Flow	NA	NM
Price-to-Sales	9.4–67.6	43.94
Return on Equity	NA	NM
Beta		1.37

NM, Not Meaningful; NA, Not Applicable

BYRUM'S COMMENTS

Armed with "good team of people, sufficient capital, and a blank sheet of paper," Level 3 Communications's driven and tenacious CEO, Jim Crowe, plans to build his vision of the next great communications company from scratch. Crowe wants to take advantage of a fundamental change in the communications industry: There is a move taking place from traditional circuit-switched networks, designed primarily for voice communications, to newer packet-switched networks using Internet protocol. The latter makes it possible to move data and voice transmissions with greater efficiency and higher capacity. Level 3's plan calls for building this advanced, highly efficient phone and data network in the United States, Europe, and Asia.

Level 3 was launched in 1997 with $4 billion in the company coffers, making it one of the best-funded start-ups in history. With the capital-raising dilemma out of the way, the company has focused its efforts entirely on the strategic planning and implementation of its corporate vision. If successful, Level 3 will lead the communications industry into the world of broadband data transmissions capabilities and revolutionize the industry, providing vast opportunities for growth in the years ahead.

RISK FACTORS

"Speculative" would be an appropriate word to describe Level 3 Communications. While revenue growth is significant, the company has yet to post a profit. As a result, investors must look several years into the future to predict value. In many ways, investors are betting on CEO Jim Crowe's vision and previous track record when purchasing shares of Level 3. Another concern is that while Level 3 is building the network of the future, it is also subject to the risk of rapidly changing technologies, such as the affect of wireless data networking, which may impact its ultimate profitability.

CONTACT INFORMATION

Level 3 Communications, Inc., 1025 Eldorado Boulevard, Broomfield, CO 80021
(720) 888-1000
www.level3.com

Level 3 Communications (LVLT)

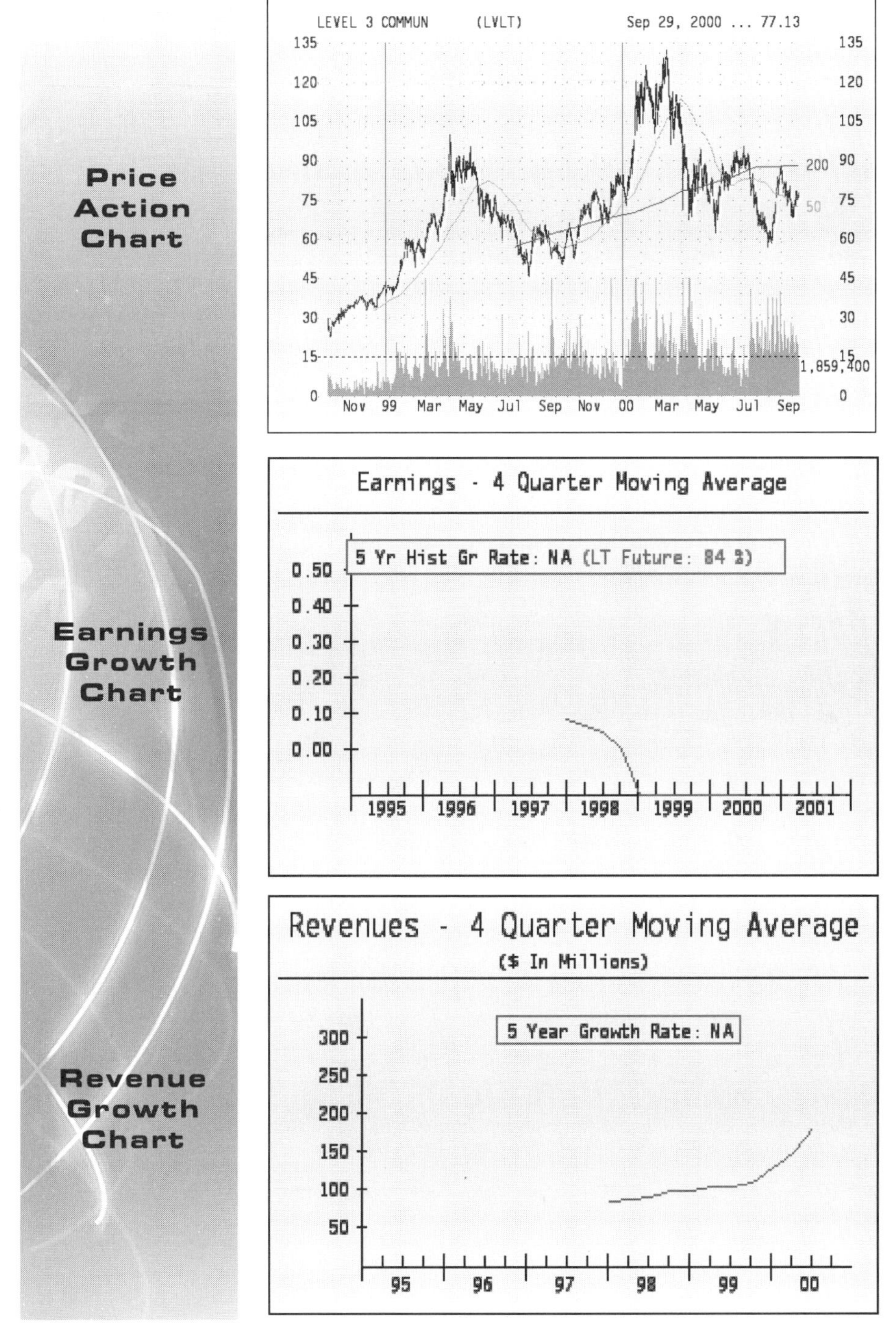

Charts provided by Baseline Financial Services.

10. LINEAR TECHNOLOGY

Symbol: LLTC
Sector: Technology (Semiconductors)

COMPANY PROFILE

Linear Technology designs, manufactures, and markets a broad line of standard high-performance linear (analog) integrated circuits. The company makes amplifiers, voltage regulators, voltage references, interface circuits, buffers, data converters, comparators, sample-and-hold devices, and switched capacitor filters. These products are used in a number of appliances, including notebook and desktop computers, video and multimedia systems, computer peripherals, cellular telephones, satellites, network and factory automation products, and industrial process controls. The company, which has manufacturing facilities in the United States, Malaysia, and Singapore, sells its products to more than 15,000 original equipment manufacturers.

EARNINGS

During the past 12 months, Linear Technology earned $0.88 per share, up 44 percent from the previous year.

REVENUES

Revenues during the past 12 months totaled $706 million, up 39 percent from a year earlier.

KEY RATIOS & MEASURES	5-YEAR RANGE	CURRENT
P/E	12–96	82.9
Price-to-Book	3.6–20	19.5
Price-to-Cash Flow	11.7–78.7	76.7
Price-to-Sales	4.3–33	32.14
Return on Equity	23.4–35.8%	27%
Beta		1.52

Byrum's Comments

As its name suggests, Linear Technology manufactures high-performance linear integrated circuits. Linear, or analog, circuits are designed to address a number of real-world phenomena that are linear in nature, such as temperature, speed, light, and pressure. In today's increasingly electronic world, Linear Technology's semiconductor chips are used in a wide variety of applications within the industrial automation, communications, computer, military, and satellite industries. In fact, the company currently produces more than 5,000 products to serve these markets. An important characteristic of Linear Technology's strategic plan is targeting the high-performance segment of the integrated circuit market, which has served as a profitable niche.

Since its incorporation in 1981, Linear Technology has enjoyed rapid growth, becoming a leading analog chip company. Its broad product line and diverse customer base have been key drivers for the company's success to date. Looking forward, several factors favor the company's outlook, including strong growth in demand for its high-performance chips and a solid management team with a proven track record for leading corporate strategy. According to Robert H. Swanson, chairperson and CEO, "These continue to be great times for a high-performance analog company. Opportunities in Internet infrastructure, wireless communication, and mobile computing fuel our growth in communications, computers, and industrial applications." High marks are deserved for Linear Technology's management team and its ability to generate solid revenues and consistently improve profit margins.

Risk Factors

Given its high volatility, Linear Technology is well-suited for the more aggressive investor willing and able to take on a higher-than-average level of risk. Despite the company's relatively consistent and stable growth, shares of Linear Technology are highly influenced by the cyclical nature of investor sentiment toward the semiconductor industry.

CONTACT INFORMATION

Linear Technology Corporation, 1630 McCarthy Boulevard, Milpitas, CA 95035-7417
(408) 432-1900
www.linear-tech.com

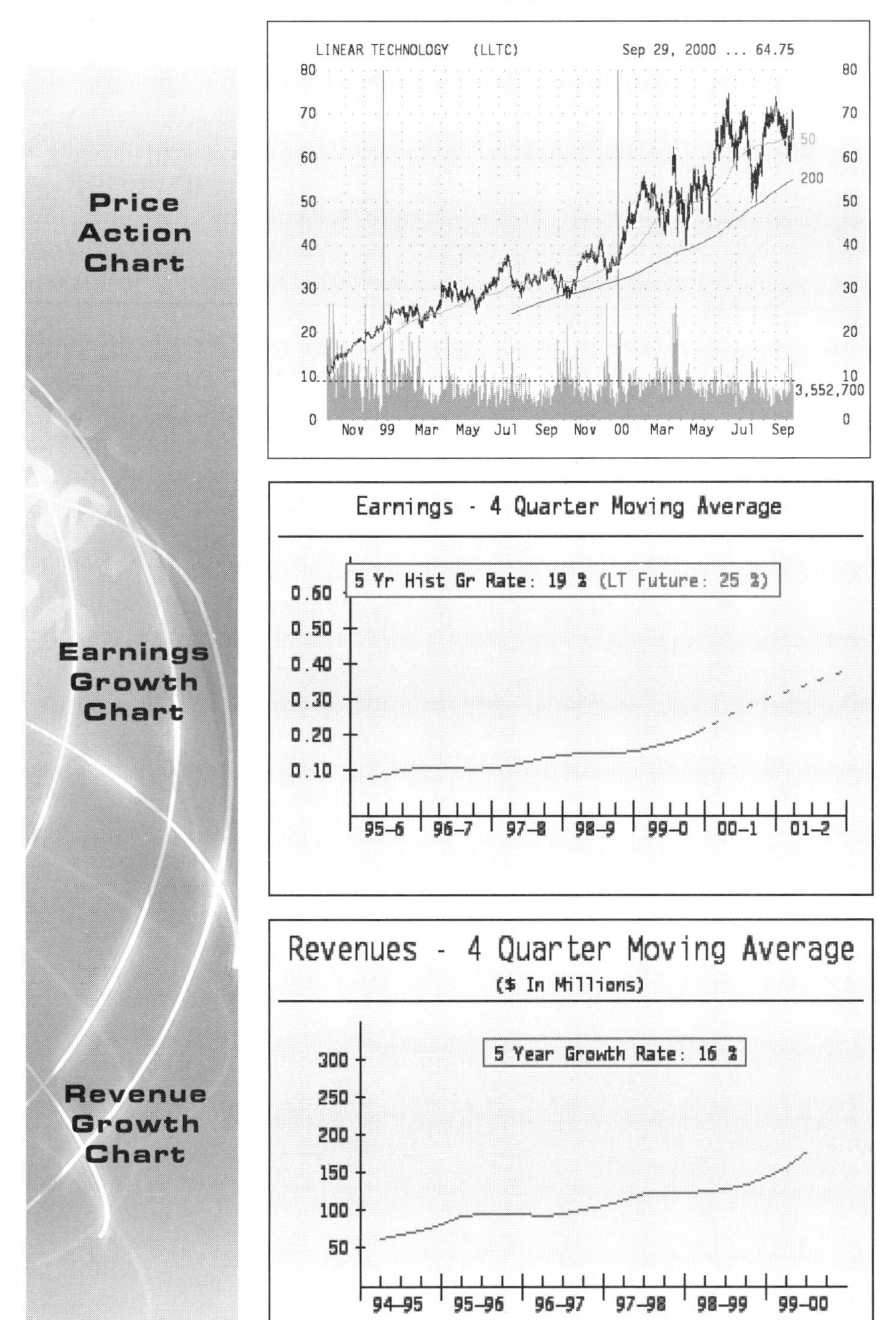

Charts provided by Baseline Financial Services.

11. McLEODUSA

Symbol: MCLD
Sector: Services (Communications Services)

COMPANY PROFILE

McLeodUSA provides communications services to business and residential customers in the midwestern and Rocky Mountain regions of the United States. The company offers local, long-distance, Internet access, data, voice-mail, and paging services over more than 397,600 local lines in 269 cities and towns across ten states. In most of its markets, McLeodUSA competes with the incumbent local phone company by leasing its lines and switches. In other markets (primarily in east central Illinois and southeast South Dakota), the company operates its own lines and switches. McLeodUSA provides long-distance services both by using its own communications network facilities and by leasing capacity from long-distance and local communications providers. During 2000, McLeodUSA acquired Splitrock Services, which also provides telecommunications and data services nationwide.

EARNINGS

During the past 12 months, McLeodUSA lost $0.67 per share, down 57 percent from the previous year.

REVENUES

Revenues during the past 12 months totaled $1.1 billion, up 57 percent from a year earlier.

KEY RATIOS & MEASURES	5-YEAR RANGE	CURRENT
P/E	NM	NM
Price-to-Book	2.1–18.5	8.5
Price-to-Cash Flow	NA	NM
Price-to-Sales	2.1–25.2	8.54
Return on Equity	NA	NM
Beta		1.49

NM, Not Meaningful; NA, Not Applicable

BYRUM'S COMMENTS

McLeodUSA provides local and long-distance telephone service to business and residential customers in the Midwest, Rocky Mountain, and Pacific Northwestern states. Founded in 1991 as a provider of fiber-optic maintenance services for the Iowa Communications Network, the company continues to provide system maintenance, as well as sales, leasing, and installation of telephone equipment. McLeodUSA also publishes White and Yellow Page telephone directories, provides computer-networking solutions, and offers direct marketing and telemarketing services.

McLeodUSA operates in direct competition with the Baby Bells and other telephone providers, but its healthy mix of revenue sources has made it a consistent performer. Although profit margins for voice long-distance have been dropping throughout the industry, McLeodUSA's strategy has been to bundle long distance together with local telephone and data services. This has worked particularly well for small and medium-sized business, many of which are willing to sign long-term contracts.

The acquisition of CapRock Communications has strengthened McLeodUSA's position, expanding its size and scope in a business that is considered to require a large footprint. It also greatly increased McLeodUSA's data capabilities. Because many investors worried that McLeodUSA would make a dilutive acquisition, the stock-for-stock deal removed a cloud of uncertainty from the company's shares.

RISK FACTORS

The telecommunications industry is characterized by cutthroat competition, and technological advances have repeatedly altered the shape of the market. In this environment, giant rivals could easily dwarf McLeodUSA. The company has chosen a slow-but-sure approach, quietly building its revenue quarter by quarter. Further development of the high-margin consultative aspects of its business may be the key to McLeodUSA's future prosperity.

CONTACT INFORMATION

McLeodUSA, Inc., 6400 C Street SW, P.O. Box 3177, Cedar Rapids, IA 52406-3177
(319) 364-0000
www.mcleodusa.com

McLeodUSA (MCLD)

Price Action Chart

Earnings Growth Chart

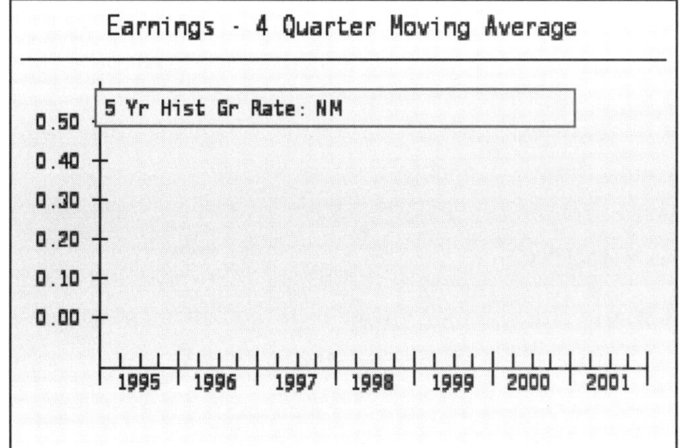

Revenue Growth Chart

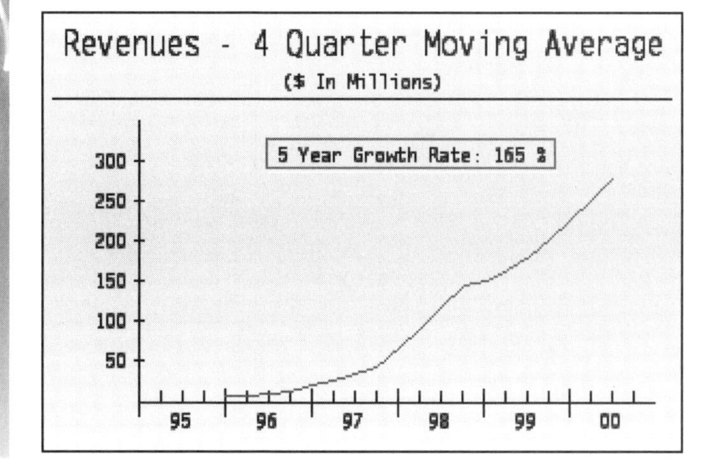

Charts provided by Baseline Financial Services.

12. MEDIMMUNE

Symbol: MEDI
Sector: Healthcare (Biotechnology and Drugs)

COMPANY PROFILE

Biotechnology company MedImmune develops and markets products for infectious diseases, autoimmune diseases, cancer, and for use in transplantation medicine. The company's Synagis monoclonal antibody is approved for sale in the United States for the prevention of respiratory syncytial virus (RSV), the leading cause of pneumonia and bronchiolitis in infants and children. MedImmune also markets CytoGam, used for the treatment of cytomegalovirus, and RespiGam, another drug for the prevention of RSV. The company has a marketing alliance with Abbott Laboratories to commercialize Synagis, and a manufacturing alliance with German-based Boehringer Ingelheim Pharma KG to supplement its own production capacity. Over the past year, MedImmune acquired U.S. Bioscience and renamed it MedImmune Oncology.

EARNINGS

During the past 12 months, MedImmune earned $0.47 per share, up 213 percent from the previous year.

REVENUES

Revenues during the past 12 months totaled $438 million, up 61 percent from a year earlier.

KEY RATIOS & MEASURES	5-YEAR RANGE	CURRENT
P/E	92–244	177.1
Price-to-Book	3.4–29.9	29.1
Price-to-Cash Flow	42.4–429.6	168.7
Price-to-Sales	3.3–40.8	39.67
Return on Equity	19.6–44.9%	19.6%
Beta		0.98

Byrum's Comments

MedImmune is a first-tier biotechnology company focused on developing and marketing vaccines, antibodies, and drugs for infectious diseases, cancer, and transplantation medicine. Several fundamental factors place MedImmune in a favorable position within the exciting, rapidly growing biotechnology industry.

The primary driver of MedImmune's earnings and growth potential is Synagis, a monoclonal antibody for the prevention of respiratory syncitial virus (RSV) infection in children. MedImmune launched the antibody in 1998, and with sales exceeding expectations, it quickly drove the company to profitability. The drug has the potential to reach near blockbuster status, with a potential market of $1 billion.

With sales of Synagis driving profits, MedImmune is in a unique position to commit additional resources toward developing new drugs to bring to market. As a result, MedImmune has a growing pipeline with a focus on cancer, infectious disease, and inflammation.

The acquisition of U.S. Biosciences in 1999 expanded the company's infrastructure in clinical development and manufacturing. That, coupled with the recent explosion of genomic data and technologies that can improve the drug development process, argues favorably for MedImmune's strong growth potential.

To effectively promote Synagis, and accelerate the market penetration of the drug, MedImmune has formed a marketing alliance with Abbott Laboratories. By leveraging strong marketing partners, MedImmune has been quite effective at achieving rapid market penetration of its products.

Risk Factors

The primary risk to MedImmune's continued growth is related to its current reliance on Synagis for sales revenue. Although the market for Synagis remains healthy, it will become increasingly important for the company to get another drug successfully to market. With several drugs in various stages of development, it is likely that MedImmune will succeed in keeping its pipeline gap to a minimum.

CONTACT INFORMATION

MedImmune, Inc., 35 West Watkins Mill Road, Gaithersburg, MD 20878-4024
(301) 417-0770
www.medimmune.com

MedImmune (MEDI)

Price Action Chart

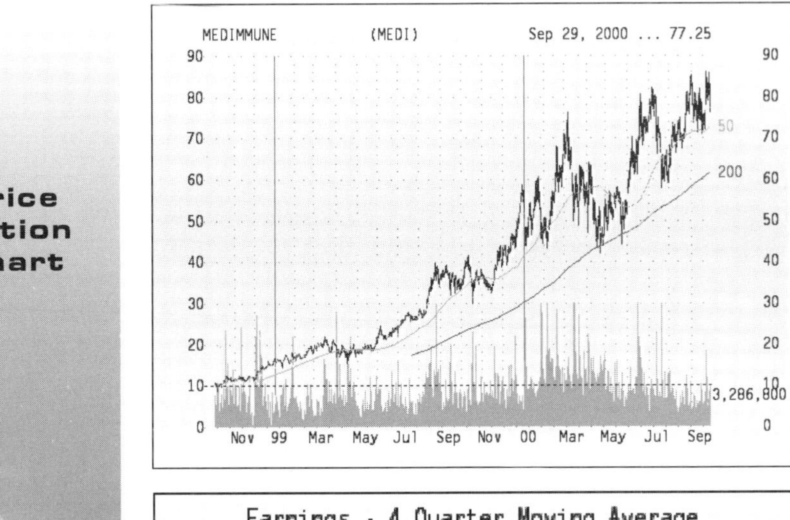

Earnings Growth Chart

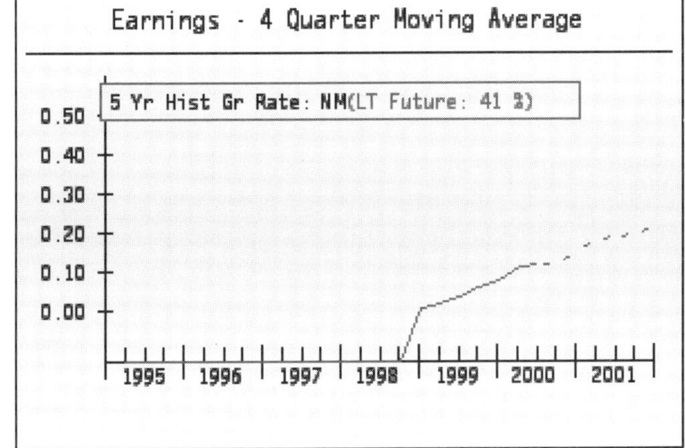

Revenue Growth Chart

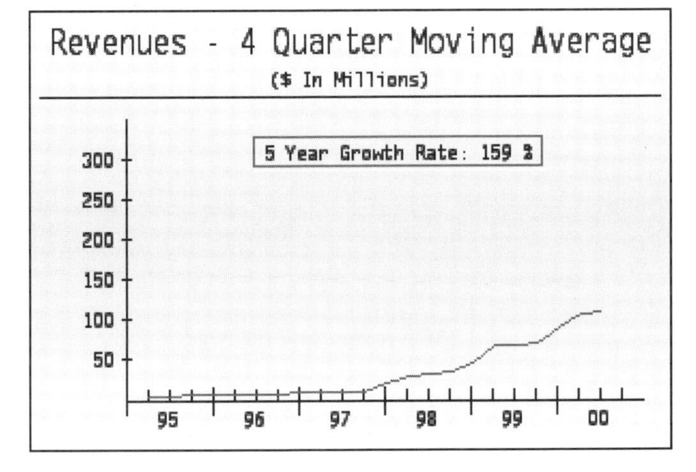

Charts provided by Baseline Financial Services.

13. METROMEDIA FIBER NETWORK

Symbol: MFNX
Sector: Services (Communications Services)

COMPANY PROFILE

Metromedia Fiber Network provides an advanced high-bandwidth, fiber-optic communications infrastructure to communications carriers, corporations, and governments. The company's intracity networks cover more than 1,000 route miles in the first 11 metropolitan areas, and its intercity network covers 255 route miles between New York City and Washington, D.C. Together with Viatel and Carrier 1 Holdings, Metromedia plans to build a dark-fiber intercity network between selected cities in Germany. When completed, the network will cover more than 1,450 route miles connecting 14 major cities. Metromedia Company and its partners control about 62 percent of the company's outstanding voting power.

EARNINGS

During the past 12 months, Metromedia Fiber Network lost $0.45 per share.

REVENUES

Revenues during the past 12 months totaled $112 million, up 70 percent from a year earlier.

KEY RATIOS & MEASURES	5-YEAR RANGE	CURRENT
P/E	NM	NM
Price-to-Book	2.1–22.9	11
Price-to-Cash Flow	175.7–1742.9	NM
Price-to-Sales	10–254.1	187.91
Return on Equity	NA	NM
Beta		2.36

NM, Not Meaningful; NA, Not Applicable

BYRUM'S COMMENTS

Metromedia Fiber Network is a provider of dedicated fiber-optic, high-bandwidth communications infrastructure and services to corporate and government customers in the United States and Europe. Through its subsidiaries, AboveNet Communications and PAIX.NET, the company provides connectivity services to facilitate e-commerce and advanced Internet applications. Metromedia Fiber Network's business is focused on serving local exchange carriers, long-distance and cable companies, wireless communications and Web-hosting service providers, and e-commerce initiatives. The company has built and continues to expand both intracity and intercity networks in 51 major markets in the U.S. and 16 in cities across Europe.

There are two primary sources of revenue for Metromedia Fiber Network. First, the company receives approximately 25 percent of total revenue from optical infrastructure services for communications carriers. Metromedia Fiber Network receives the remaining 75 percent of its revenue from Internet infrastructure services for a wider range of customers. Metromedia added to its ability to provide connectivity services with its acquisition of SiteSmith, a leading provider of Internet infrastructure management services.

Metromedia's sales and earnings growth continue to be strong, though capital expenditure and acquisition charges have made turning a profit difficult. The company appears to be financially sound and capable of continuing its expansion efforts. In addition, the company is in good shape to capture revenue from the growing competitive local exchange carrier market.

RISK FACTORS

The tremendous build-up of high-bandwidth capacity and networks could affect revenues for fiber-optic equipment makers. Communications companies that have built their own fiber networks are having difficulty in acquiring customers for their networks and have seen their stock prices plunge. There has been a divergence of opinion among analysts as to whether those same profit challenges will translate to the makers of fiber-optic equipment. Fortunately, Metromedia Fiber Network has a diverse customer base and unique combination of product and service offerings in the market for dedicated fiber-optic networks, Internet services, and e-commerce.

CONTACT INFORMATION

Metromedia Fiber Network, Inc., 1 North Lexington Avenue, White Plains, NY 10601
(914) 421-6700
www.mmfn.com

Metromedia Fiber Network (MFNX)

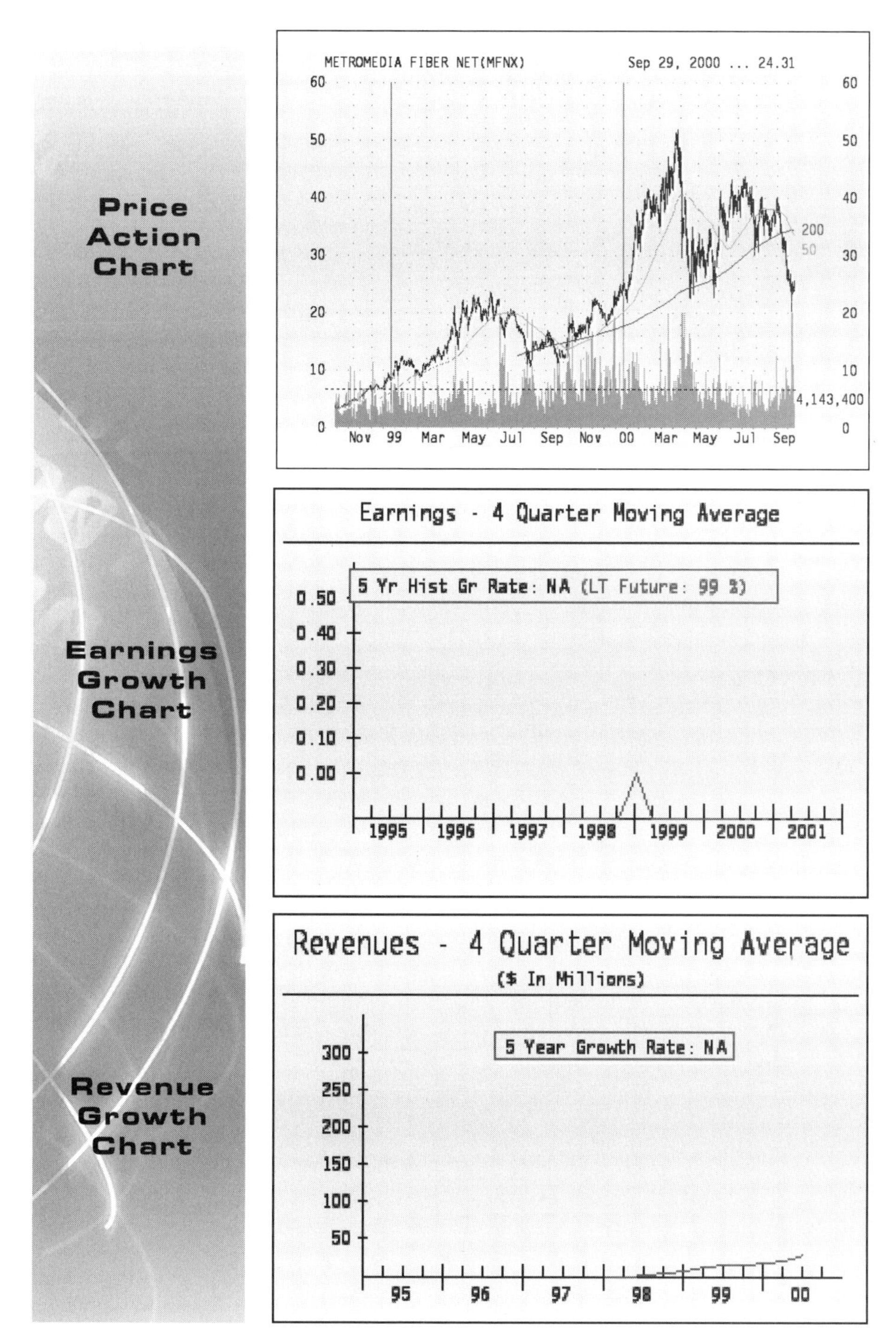

Charts provided by Baseline Financial Services.

14. MICROSOFT

Symbol: MSFT
Sector: Technology (Software and Programming)

COMPANY PROFILE

Microsoft develops, licenses, and supports a wide range of software items. Microsoft's products include operating systems for intelligent devices, personal computers, and servers (Windows 98/2000/NT/CE); server applications for client-server environments (Microsoft BackOffice); business productivity applications (Microsoft Office 2000); and software development tools (Microsoft Visual C++ and Visual Basic). Its MSN Portal business provides services on the Internet; its Internet Explorer Web browser offers an alternative to Netscape's Communicator. Microsoft also licenses consumer software; sells PC input devices; and trains and certifies system integrators. The company spun-off part of its Expedia travel reservations service and acquired Visio during 2000.

EARNINGS

During the past 12 months, Microsoft earned $1.72 per share, up 24 percent from the previous year.

REVENUES

Revenues during the past 12 months totaled $23 billion, up 16 percent from a year earlier.

KEY RATIOS & MEASURES	5-YEAR RANGE	CURRENT
P/E	27–84	40.8
Price-to-Book	6.8–22.9	9.9
Price-to-Cash Flow	18.8–75.7	36.7
Price-to-Sales	4.9–28.4	16.09
Return on Equity	28.1–39.1%	28.1%
Beta		1.17

Byrum's Comments

Microsoft Corporation is the world's largest software company. Its primary focus is on the development, manufacture, and distribution of operating system software, business and consumer application software, and software development tools. Microsoft is the dominant player in the PC software market. Its operating systems run approximately 90 percent of the PCs currently in use. Over the past decade, Microsoft's Windows software, through its ease-of-use graphical interface, has propelled the PC revolution.

Microsoft came under significant selling pressure in 2000 as a result of slower projected growth of the PC market and an antitrust suit brought by the U.S. Justice Department. In April 2000, Microsoft was found to have violated the Sherman Antitrust Act by exhibiting monopoly power over industry competitors. The ruling was followed by an order to break up the company. Although the ruling was against Microsoft, the appeals process is expected to be quite lengthy and will give Microsoft the opportunity to present a solid case.

Against the backdrop of the antitrust trial, Microsoft has unveiled its strategic vision to reposition the company for new growth as the PC market matures. The company's .Net platform encompasses Microsoft's foray into providing products to power Internet appliances, as well as hand-held and mobile devices. This represents a major shift for the Redmond, Washington-based company. Tapping into this fast-growing space is critical to its long-term success. If successful, Microsoft will be able to establish itself as a leading provider of software and services in the Internet era.

Risk Factors

The major risks associated with Microsoft in the near term include the uncertainty associated with the antitrust case currently underway, and the potential for slower-than-expected growth of PC demand. Over the long term, we need to keep an eye on the company's ability to shift its business model to capitalize on the trend toward Internet appliances and applications. Possible disruptions may include the longer-than-expected rollout of its .Net platform and the reluctance of corporate users to adopt its new software products.

CONTACT INFORMATION

Microsoft Corporation, 1 Microsoft Way, Building 8N, #2211, Redmond, WA 98052-6399
(425) 882-8080
www.microsoft.com

Microsoft (MSFT)

Price Action Chart

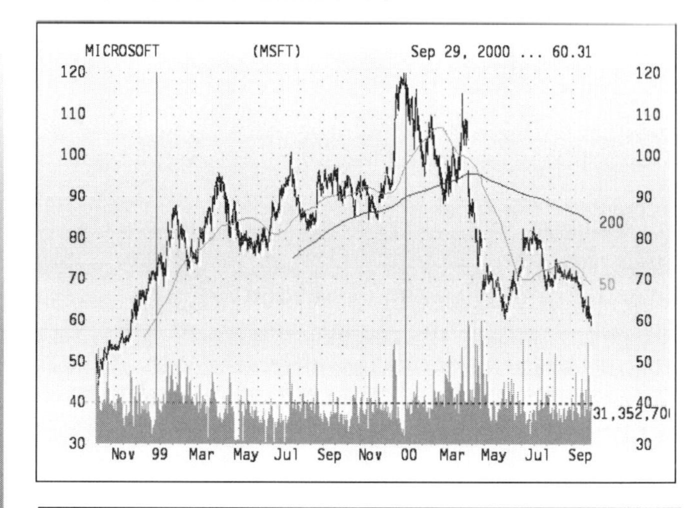

Earnings Growth Chart

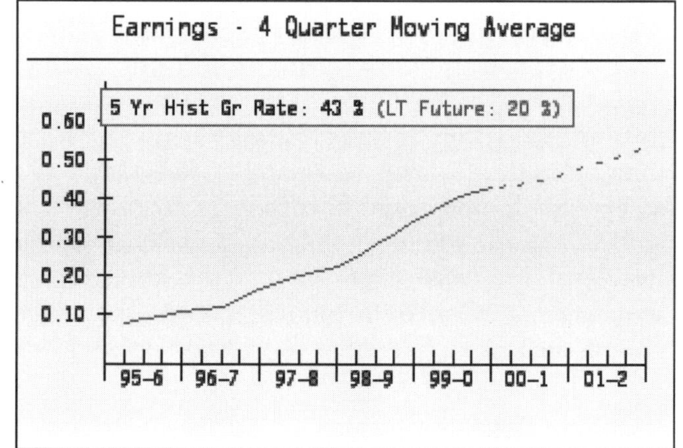

Revenue Growth Chart

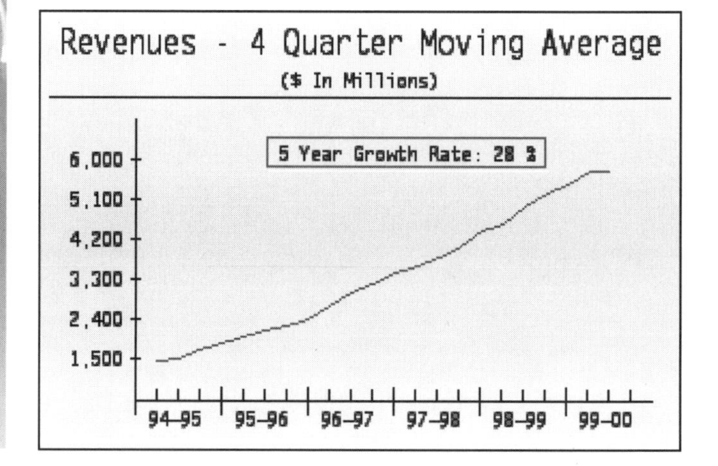

Charts provided by Baseline Financial Services.

15. Network Appliance

Symbol: NTAP
Sector: Technology (Computer Networks)

Company Profile

Network Appliance makes and supports network data-storage devices designed to provide fast, reliable file service for data-intensive networks. Products consist of filers and proxy caching solutions developed to address the specific needs of network environments and the World Wide Web. The company's filers make use of a software kernel optimized to perform the file service task. By using its proprietary software architecture, Network Appliance is able to use standard hardware components rather than specialized hardware. There are products for small workgroups, large departments, and enterprise class filers. All products include Data ONTAP, which modularizes and administrates data. Its NetCache 3.4 product offers corporate Intranet/Internet access and advanced security features.

Earnings

During the past 12 months, Network Appliance earned $0.26 per share, up 102 percent from the previous year.

Revenues

Revenues during the past 12 months totaled $707 million, up 111 percent from a year earlier.

Key Ratios & Measures	5-Year Range	Current
P/E	30–709	440
Price-to-Book	3.2–80.8	71.1
Price-to-Cash Flow	24.2–394.9	367.8
Price-to-Sales	2.4–53.5	49.74
Return on Equity	0.6–29.9%	20.6%
Beta		1.54

BYRUM'S COMMENTS

Network Appliance is a pioneer in the fast-growing server application market. It is strategically positioned to be a leader in Internet content delivery and data management. The company is involved in the manufacturing, distribution, and support for network data storage devices and Web-caching products. Currently, the vast majority of the company's sales come from network-attached storage (NAS) devices. The recent success of Network Appliance relates to the explosive growth of data and demand for storage capacity due to the ever-increasing use of the Internet. Key factors that favor Network Appliance over the next several years include the rapid growth of the market for its products, its strong product line of leading technology solutions, and its development and acquisition of new technologies.

Clearly, Network Appliance's core products have benefited from the rapid growth of the Internet. The company hit the nail on the head by offering products that addressed the issue of managing vast amounts of online data, and it is poised to profit from the ongoing demand for higher bandwidth. Internet usage is expected to continue to grow rapidly. This should lead to further strong growth in Network Appliance's target market. Being a pioneer in the development of network-attached storage has given Network Appliance a significant head start among its competition. Its products are well-positioned and more advanced than other offerings. Given the rapid development of specialized devices used on networks, Network Appliance is investing heavily, mainly through acquisition, in new technologies designed to extend its product reach. This will potentially propel the company from a niche player offering specialized products to a more well-rounded storage application company.

RISK FACTORS

The main areas of risk are those generally associated with young rapidly growing technology companies. Careful consideration should be given to the company's valuation in relation to its growth potential. Given its higher-than-average long-term growth prospects, the company can easily sustain a high PE ratio. However, lower-than-expected revenue growth can severely affect the company share price. In addition, competition may become an issue as new entrants target this attractive growth segment. To counter the increased competition, Network Appliance will need to build a solid customer relationship with its ever-expanding list of customers. Customer support will be important to maintain customer loyalty as new products designed to compete with the company's offerings enter the marketplace.

CONTACT INFORMATION

Network Appliance, Inc., 495 East Java Drive, Sunnyvale, CA 94089
(408) 822-6000
www.netapp.com

Network Appliance (NTAP)

Price Action Chart

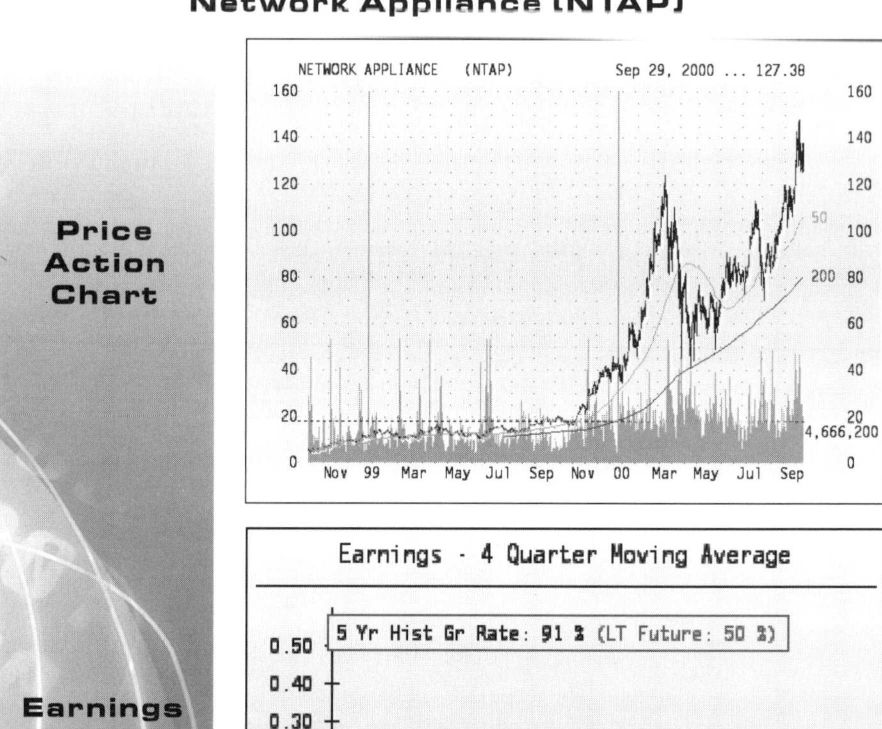

Earnings Growth Chart

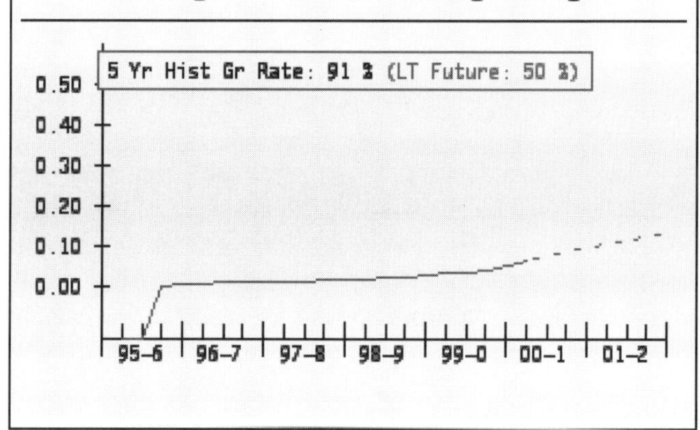

Revenue Growth Chart

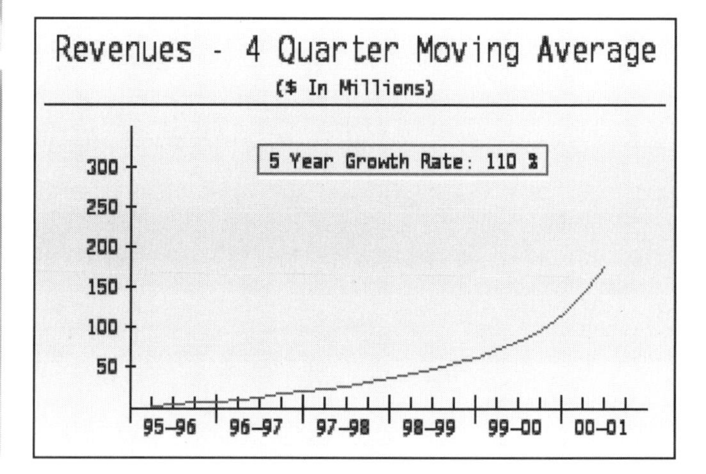

Charts provided by Baseline Financial Services.

16. Nextel Communications

Symbol: NXTL
Sector: Services (Communications Services)

Company Profile

Nextel Communications offers digital wireless communications services throughout the United States. More than 4.5 million users subscribe to its digital wireless communications product, which provides coverage in 94 of the nation's top 100 metropolitan statistical areas. Nextel also plans to offer customers access to the Internet and new digital two-way mobile data services through its Nextel Online service. The company's Nextel International subsidiary operates or has investments in international wireless companies in Latin America, Asia, and Canada that provide service to more than 1.2 million subscribers. Motorola, which owns about 15 percent of Nextel, provides the infrastructure and subscriber handsets used in Nextel's domestic and international operations.

Earnings

During the past 12 months, Nextel Communications lost $1.77 per share, up 38 percent from the previous year.

Revenues

Revenues during the past 12 months totaled $4.2 billion, up 65 percent from a year earlier.

Key Ratios & Measures	5-Year Range	Current
P/E	NM	NM
Price-to-Book	1.1–36.1	23.3
Price-to-Cash Flow	401.6–889.2	573.5
Price-to-Sales	2.3–16.5	9.64
Return on Equity	NA	NM
Beta		1.36

NM, Not Meaningful; NA, Not Applicable

BYRUM'S COMMENTS

Reston, Virginia-based Nextel Communications is a nationwide provider of digital broadband wireless voice and data services. It is the only national operator of integrated cellular and dispatch services. Nextel currently serves more than 4.5 million domestic digital subscribers. It is one of only three nationwide providers of digital broadband wireless services, and soon expects to cover nearly all potential users in the United States.

Nextel Communications's key value propositions include a strong focus on the business segment, integrated push-to-talk connectivity, nationwide digital wireless service, and the recent introduction of wireless data applications. What makes Nextel unique among its competitors is its "direct connect" service, a dispatch-type feature that allows a user to talk to one or many designated individuals simultaneously and instantaneously in a conference-call format.

Within the wireless sector, the key driver of success has shifted from the rate at which subscribers are being added to the rate at which companies can distribute Internet-based information and services. Due to its large customer base and record for innovative service delivery, Nextel is favorably positioned to take advantage of the growth opportunities associated with the wireless data sector. Working aggressively to promote new wireless data services, Nextel has established the "Nextel Developers Program," which currently consists of more than 200 organizations qualified to develop wireless applications. A rapid rollout of these new services will keep Nextel's record of innovative service intact and provide tremendous upside potential for the company.

RISK FACTORS

The main risk to Nextel's solid franchise is that competition may increase as other carriers bolster their national presence. Industry consolidation, combined with AT&T's aggressive posture to extend its wireless footprint, should further intensify the competitive landscape. Still, Nextel is well-positioned to capture additional share, given its differentiated feature set and strong focus on the business segment. Other areas to watch closely include the size of the target market, which remains unclear, and the substantial expansion of capacity in the industry, which may further reduce expected average revenue per user (ARPU). Nextel can offset this trend by focusing on the business segment and emphasizing its differentiated service offerings, which should support the company's ability to charge a premium over commoditized wireless voice services.

CONTACT INFORMATION

Nextel Communications, Inc., 80 29th Street, Reston, VA 20191
(703) 433-4000
www.nextel.com

Nextel Communications (NXTL)

Price Action Chart

NEXTEL COMMUNICATNS (NXTL) Sep 29, 2000 ... 46.75

90 80 70 60 50 40 30 20 10 0

200 50 8,838,000

Nov 99 Mar May Jul Sep Nov 00 Mar May Jul Sep

Earnings Growth Chart

Earnings - 4 Quarter Moving Average

5 Yr Hist Gr Rate: NM(LT Future: 25 %)

0.50 0.40 0.30 0.20 0.10 0.00

1995 1996 1997 1998 1999 2000 2001

Revenue Growth Chart

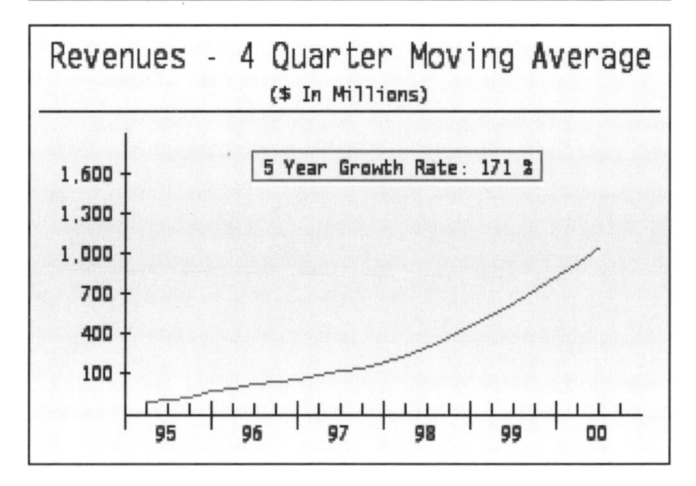

Charts provided by Baseline Financial Services.

17. ORACLE

Symbol: ORCL
Sector: Technology (Software and Programming)

COMPANY PROFILE

Oracle is a supplier of software for information management. The company develops and markets computer software that helps corporations manage and grow their businesses. Oracle's systems software is a complete Internet platform to develop and deploy applications on the Internet and corporate Intranets, and includes database management software and development tools. Internet business applications software automates the performance of data-processing functions for financial management, procurement, project management, human resources management, and supply chain management. In addition, Oracle offers a range of consulting, education, and support services for its customers. During 2000, the company acquired Carleton and approved the spinoff and launch of Oraclemobil.com.

EARNINGS

During the past 12 months, Oracle earned $0.69 per share, up 57 percent from the previous year.

REVENUES

Revenues during the past 12 months totaled $10.1 billion, up 15 percent from a year earlier.

KEY RATIOS & MEASURES	5-YEAR RANGE	CURRENT
P/E	18–184	134.2
Price-to-Book	5.8–44	40.3
Price-to-Cash Flow	13.5–112.3	111.9
Price-to-Sales	2.1–26.1	25.95
Return on Equity	30.5–39.2%	38.6%
Beta		1.63

BYRUM'S COMMENTS

Oracle Corporation was founded in 1977. Over the years it has grown to become a leading independent software company with more than 40,000 employees worldwide and revenues exceeding $10 billion. Oracle is primarily focused on supplying e-business software solutions for Internet commerce and Web-based applications. The company's software runs on a wide variety of platforms including PCs, workstations, mainframes, personal digital assistants (PDAs), and set-top boxes.

In recent years, Oracle has undergone a major transition to better align its products and services with today's increasingly Web-based and e-commerce-driven economy. To spark this transition, CEO Larry Ellison ordered the "Internctization" of the company in 1998. This significantly enhanced its core database technology, allowing Oracle's software to better integrate into a company's Web infrastructure. As a result, Oracle's database products have become the de facto standard for B2B commerce, a market expected to grow to well more than $1.3 trillion by 2003, according to Forrester Research. Oracle's swift response to position its products to help its customers handle the explosion of Internet traffic and e-commerce has greatly enhanced the company's prospects going forward. Oracle is truly more than just a database software vendor; it's a premier B2B e-commerce company.

Going forward, key positive factors driving the company's growth include continued operating margin expansion, by leveraging the effectiveness of the Internet, and strong product demand. Oracle is well positioned to tap the tremendous opportunity in the enterprise application market as corporations attempt to convert to an e-business operating model.

RISK FACTORS

To the extent that Oracle has already achieved optimal efficiency using its Web-based database software, the improvements in operating margins may diminish over time. Although most industry observers, as well as Oracle's management, feel that further cost reductions are possible, this may become a negative factor in the coming years. In addition, competitive pressures in the enterprise application space, from well-established companies like Peoplesoft and SAP, may cut into Oracle's market share.

CONTACT INFORMATION

Oracle Corporation, 500 Oracle Parkway, Redwood City, CA 94065
(650) 506-7000
www.oracle.com

Oracle (ORCL)

Price Action Chart

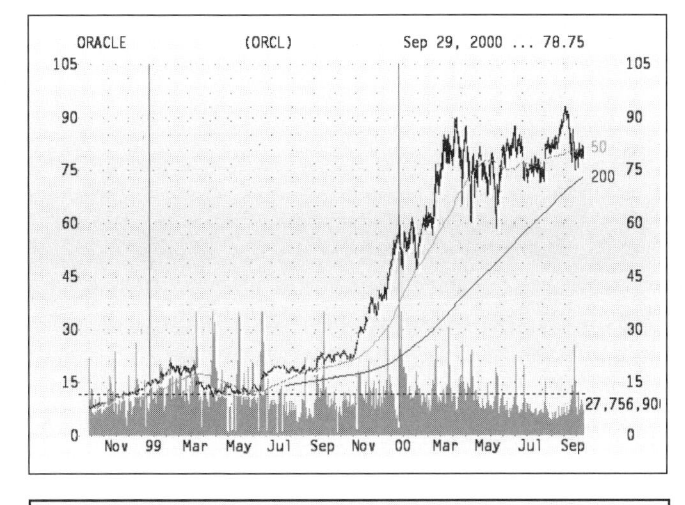

Earnings Growth Chart

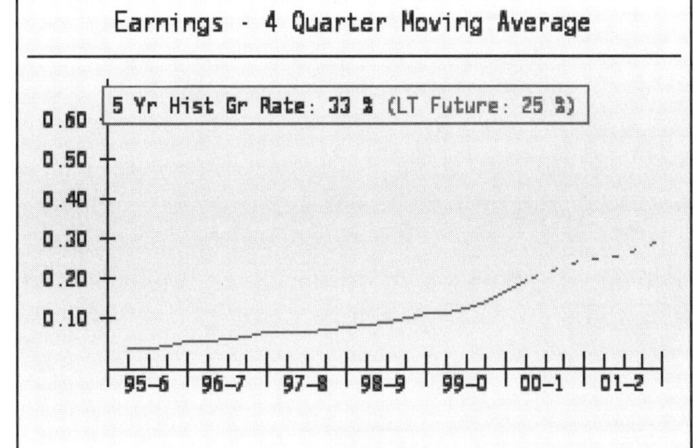

Revenue Growth Chart

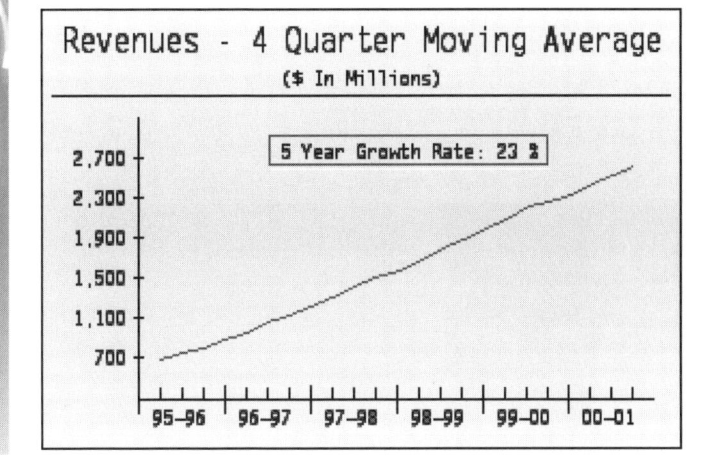

Charts provided by Baseline Financial Services.

18. PAYCHEX

Symbol: PAYX
Sector: Services (Business Services)

COMPANY PROFILE

Paychex provides payroll, human resources, and employee benefit outsourcing solutions for small- to medium-sized businesses. The company's payroll segment provides payroll processing and payroll tax-preparation services to more than 351,000 businesses in the United States. Other products include preparation of payroll checks; internal accounting records; annual W-2 forms; federal, state, and local tax returns; and new hire reporting. The company's TAXPAY service provides automatic payment of payroll taxes and filing of quarterly and annual payroll tax returns. The employee pay services unit gives employers the option of paying employees by Direct Deposit, Access Card, a check drawn on a Paychex account, or a check drawn on the employer's account.

EARNINGS

During the past 12 months, Paychex earned $0.51 per share, up 36 percent from the previous year.

REVENUES

Revenues during the past 12 months totaled $1.5 billion, up 24 percent from a year earlier.

KEY RATIOS & MEASURES	5-YEAR RANGE	CURRENT
P/E	34–95	86.3
Price-to-Book	10.9–31.5	28.9
Price-to-Cash Flow	28.7–78.8	72.3
Price-to-Sales	3.2–12.2	11.13
Return on Equity	31.6–37.7%	37.7%
Beta		0.77

Byrum's Comments

Paychex enables small- and medium-sized businesses to outsource a number of their thorniest recurring tasks. Founded in 1979, Paychex provides computerized calculation of tax withholding and other deductions; preparation of earnings statements for the employee and the IRS; generation of journals, earnings histories, and other accounting records; and transmittal of payments to employees by check or direct deposit. Paychex also prepares monthly, quarterly, and annual payroll tax returns as required by federal, state, and local governments. Through a separate division, the company offers "a la carte" personnel services, including employee handbooks, management manuals and personnel forms, and the administration of 401(k) plans, flexible spending accounts, and other benefit programs.

The company's marketing plan has been consistently clever. Paychex was among the first to tailor payroll services for the smaller businesses that are most in need of assistance in this complex area. Marketing efforts have been aimed at independent accountants, who are easily reached through their professional associations, and who are often among the first to spot new and growing businesses in their regions. Finally, Paychex has wisely developed its nonpayroll services, which have improved the bottom line through higher profit margins.

Paychex enjoys the dominant position in its small business market, which appears to be nowhere near the saturation point. In addition to an admirable growth record and good prospects, Paychex has appealed to shareowners for the consistency of its earnings, and it has proved more resilient than many Nasdaq issues during periods when investors flee to quality.

Risk Factors

Investors may perceive Paychex to be an all-weather stock, but its small business clients would be particularly vulnerable during an economic downturn. Not only would an increase in bankruptcies exacerbate client attrition, but a slower rate of new company formation would result in a slower replenishment of the pool of potential clients. Paychex could also be a victim of its own success, because its combination of growth and consistency sometimes commands unsustainably lofty valuations.

CONTACT INFORMATION

Paychex, Inc., 911 Panorama Trail South, Rochester, NY 14625-0397
(716) 385-6666
www.paychex.com

Paychex (PAYX)

Price Action Chart

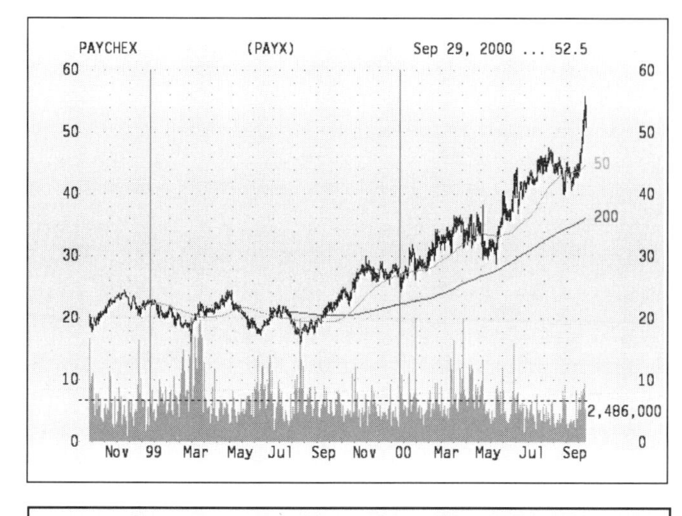

Earnings Growth Chart

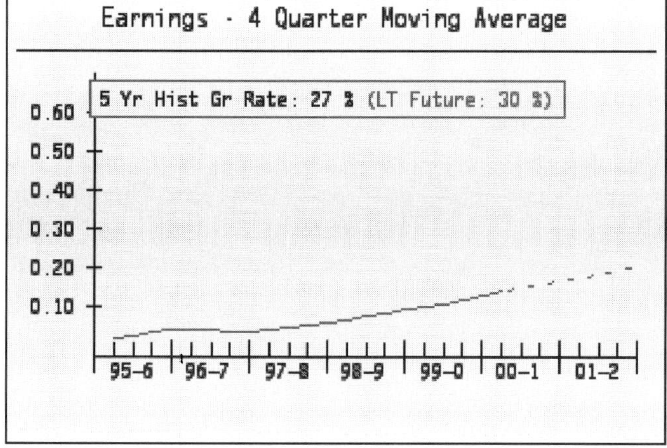

Revenue Growth Chart

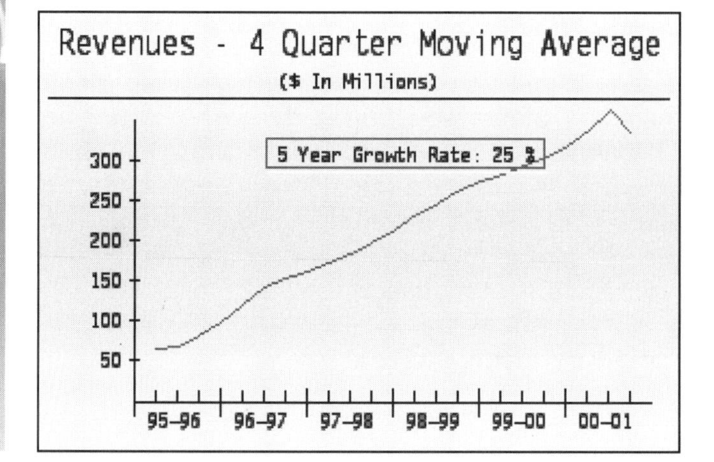

Charts provided by Baseline Financial Services.

19. PMC-SIERRA

Symbol: PMCS
Sector: Technology (Semiconductors)

COMPANY PROFILE

PMC-Sierra develops high-performance semiconductor networking products for the international telecommunications market. It makes wide area network (WAN) remote access equipment (frame relay access devices and switches, access multiplexers, wireless base stations, digital loop carriers, and others); WAN transmission and switching equipment (edge and core switches, routers, digital cross-connects, and add-drop and terminal multiplexers); and local area network (LAN) switches, routers, and network interface cards. PMC-Sierra's components are used in equipment based on Asynchronous Transfer Mode, Synchronized Optical Network, Synchronized Digital Hierarchy, T1/E1/J1 and T3/E3/J2 access transmission, and Ethernet protocols. In 2000, PMC-Sierra acquired both Extreme Network Devices and Quantum Effect Devices.

EARNINGS

During the past 12 months, PMC-Sierra earned $0.68 per share, up 91 percent from the previous year.

REVENUES

Revenues during the past 12 months totaled $389 million, up 98 percent from a year earlier.

KEY RATIOS & MEASURES	5-YEAR RANGE	CURRENT
P/E	6–541	363
Price-to-Book	4.5–120.4	115.4
Price-to-Cash Flow	6.1–305.4	292.8
Price-to-Sales	1.1–95.8	91.86%
Return on Equity	38–49.8%	38%
Beta		1.97

Byrum's Comments

PMC-Sierra was formed in 1992 when Sierra Semiconductor made its initial investment in Pacific Microelectronics Centre. Sierra later purchased Pacific Microelectronics's remaining shares and changed its name to PMC-Sierra in 1997. Self-described as "enabling the world's broadband communications revolution," the company is a leading supplier of high-speed semiconductor architectural solutions. PMC-Sierra has positioned itself as an important part of the broadband build-out by supplying semiconductors that are designed to handle high-speed digital data transmission. PMC-Sierra's core products include asynchronous transfer mode (ATM) switches, digital cross connects, and synchronous optical networking (SONET) solutions.

The company is an important link in the broadband food chain. Demand for PMC-Sierra's products results from the trend of communications equipment providers—such as Cisco Systems, Lucent Technologies, and Nortel Networks—to outsource chip development and manufacturing. PMC-Sierra designs the chips and in turn outsources manufacturing to large semiconductor foundries such as Taiwan Semiconductor and Chartered Semiconductor. The value that PMC brings to the table includes key design and development techniques, and overall product support. It comes as no surprise that most of the company's efforts surround protecting its technology franchise either through its strong commitment to research and development or through the acquisition of key technologies. Recent acquisitions have strengthened its technology capabilities, including Abrizio, a developer of broadband switch chip fabrics, and Switch On Networks, a developer of next-generation IP equipment.

Riding the wave of several strong business trends, including sales momentum and excess demand for its products, the company continues to deliver better-than-expected top line growth. With its diverse customer base and broad product line contributing to revenues, PMC-Sierra should enjoy strong growth going forward.

Risk Factors

Over the past few years, PMC-Sierra has performed spectacularly riding the wave of two significant trends: the rapid growth of networking infrastructure and the trend of original equipment manufacturers (OEMs) to outsource semiconductor design and manufacturing.

Although these trends seem intact for the foreseeable future, slower-than-expected growth or a shift in the outsourcing trend could affect the company's growth potential. In addition, prospective investors should give careful consideration to PMC-Sierra's traditionally rich stock price valuation relative to its growth potential.

CONTACT INFORMATION

PMC-Sierra, Inc., 8555 Baxter Place, #105, Burnaby, BC, V5A 4V7 CANADA
(604) 415-6000
www.pmc-sierra.com

PMC-Sierra (PMCS)

Price Action Chart

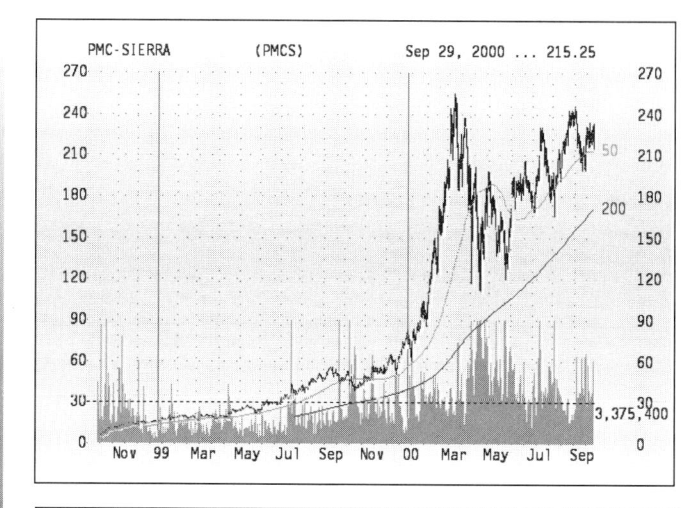

Earnings Growth Chart

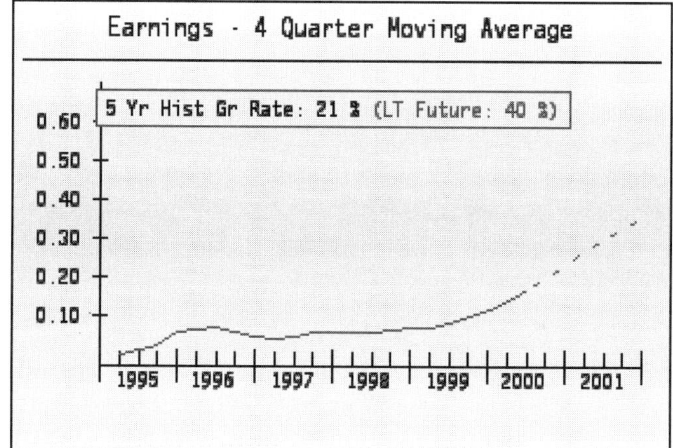

Revenue Growth Chart

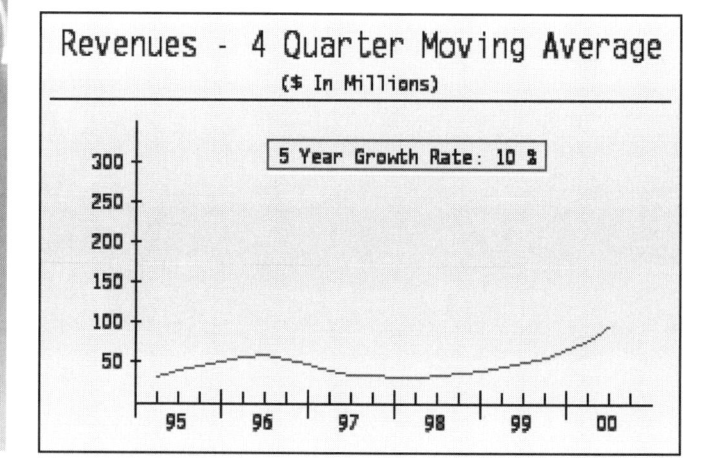

Charts provided by Baseline Financial Services.

20. SANMINA

Symbol: SANM
Sector: Technology (Electronic Instruments and Controls)

COMPANY PROFILE

Sanmina provides customized integrated electronic manufacturing services to original equipment manufacturers (OEM) in the electronics industry. The company's electronics manufacturing services consist of the manufacture of complex printed circuit board assemblies using surface-mount and pin-through-hole interconnection technologies, backplane assemblies, complex multilayered printed circuit boards, and testing and assembly of completed systems. Its turnkey manufacturing management also provides procurement and materials management, and consultation on printed circuit board design and manufacturing. Its subsidiary Sanmina Cable Systems manufactures custom cable and wire harness assemblies. In 2000, Sanmina acquired Hadco, a maker of electronic interconnection products.

EARNINGS

During the past 12 months, Sanmina earned $1.30 per share, up 42 percent from the previous year.

REVENUES

Revenues during the past 12 months totaled $2.4 billion, up 112 percent from a year earlier.

KEY RATIOS & MEASURES	5-YEAR RANGE	CURRENT
P/E	13–93	89.3
Price-to-Book	2.7–18.9	18.3
Price-to-Cash Flow	9.4–74.7	72.2
Price-to-Sales	0.8–7.5	7.26
Return on Equity	18.2–32.9%	18.2%
Beta		1.49

BYRUM'S COMMENTS

Investors and consumers alike are familiar with the high-tech products of IBM, Compaq, Nokia, Lucent, Motorola, and Siemens. But few realize that these mammoth companies turn to Sanmina to handle key elements of the manufacturing process. Sanmina provides customized manufacturing services to original equipment manufacturers (OEMs) in the electronics industry. Sanmina's specialties include the manufacture of complex printed circuit board assemblies, custom-designed plane assemblies, and electronic enclosure systems. The company also offers testing of electronic subsystems, as well as procurement and materials management, and consultation on circuit board design and manufacturing.

Sanmina's success rides the crest of two waves: First is the dramatic growth of the computer and communications industries it serves. A less evident trend is that of outsourcing. Cutting-edge companies are not always equipped to manufacture what they design. OEMs rely with increasing frequency upon contract manufacturers such as Sanmina, which reproduce key components to strict specifications. Sanmina is well-positioned to serve this market. Its high degree of vertical integration and emphasis on turnkey delivery enable it to act as problem solver to OEMs in a wide variety of situations.

Although most of its income has come from North America, Sanmina's recent acquisitions can be seen as the building blocks of a global strategy. By purchasing Essex AB, for example, Sanmina acquired a significant foothold in the Nordic countries, home of such key customers as Nokia and Ericsson. Its purchase of Hadco gives Sanmina control of a large producer of high circuit boards, a component whose capacity problems have often created industry bottlenecks.

RISK FACTORS

In good times and bad, Sanmina's fortunes are tied to those of the electronics manufacturers it serves. Significant downturns in computers or cellular communications would make Sanmina's shares less attractive. In addition, like all companies on the cutting edge of technology, Sanmina will always be challenged to avoid visible missteps in the introduction of new products. Despite the volatility of its industry, however, Sanmina's large geographic reach and wide range of services may help insulate it during turbulent times.

CONTACT INFORMATION

Sanmina Corp., 2700 North 1st Street, San Jose, CA 95134
(408) 964-3500
www.sanmina.com

Sanmina (SANM)

Price Action Chart

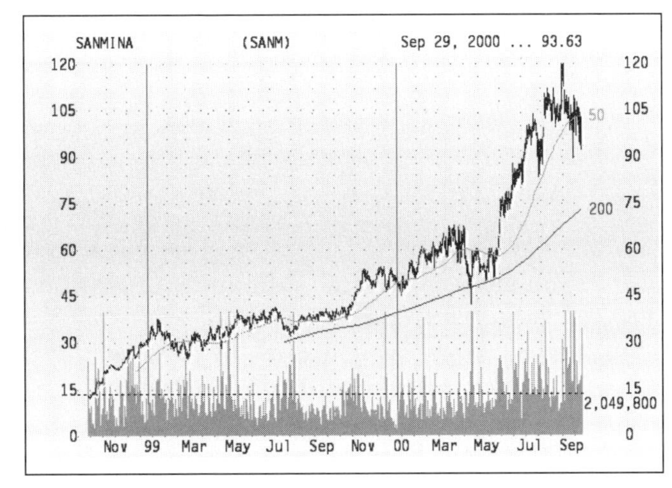

Earnings Growth Chart

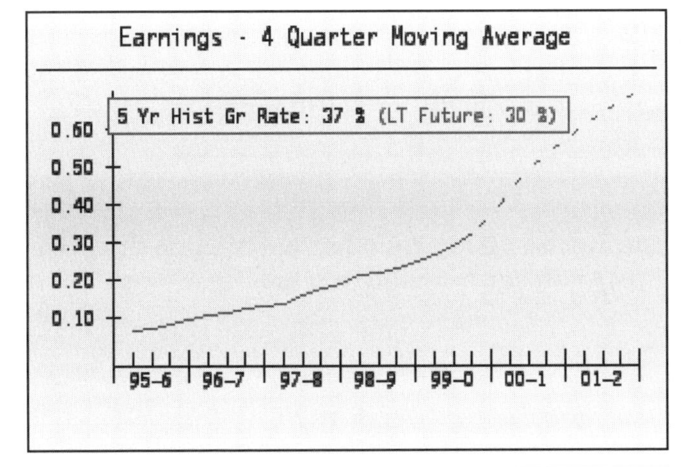

Revenue Growth Chart

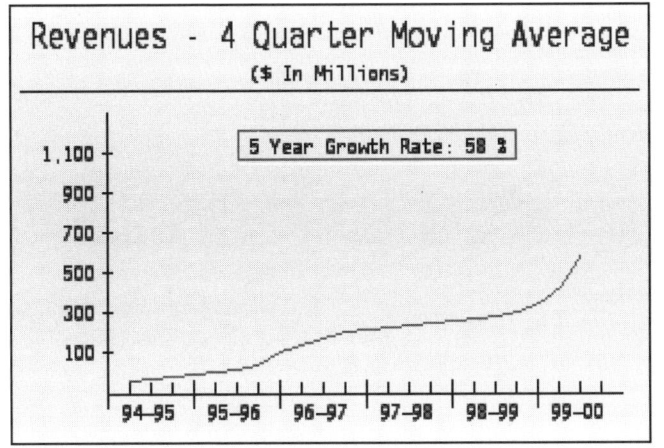

Charts provided by Baseline Financial Services.

21. SUN MICROSYSTEMS

Symbol: SUNW
Sector: Technology (Computer Hardware)

COMPANY PROFILE

Sun Microsystems provides products, services, and support for building and maintaining network computing environments. The company designs and manufactures a range of workstations, servers, storage systems, and network switches, as well as high-performance SPARC and Java microprocessors, board reference platforms, processor modules, chip sets, and logic products for Sun products and third-party customers. Sun's software lineup includes the Solaris Operating Environment, Java software, Chorus OS, software tools, and security products. Through its alliances with America Online and Netscape, Sun also develops and sells enterprise and e-commerce software. During 2000, the company agreed to buy both Innosoft International and Gridware.

EARNINGS

During the past 12 months, Sun Microsystems earned $1.03 per share, up 45 percent from the previous year.

REVENUES

Revenues during the past 12 months totaled $15.7 billion, up 34 percent from a year earlier.

KEY RATIOS & MEASURES	5-YEAR RANGE	CURRENT
P/E	10–136	125.5
Price-to-Book	2.9–31.4	31.2
Price-to-Cash Flow	8.6–91.1	90.6
Price-to-Sales	0.8–13.1	13
Return on Equity	21.8–30.5%	29.7%
Beta		1.54

Byrum's Comments

Founded in 1982, Sun Microsystems has built its business around the vision that "The Network is the Computer." This emphasizes the importance of open networks over proprietary stand-alone PCs. From the invention of the workstation (a type of computer offering a higher degree of power and graphics capability than ordinary PCs) to the more recent invention of the Java programming language (which enables developers to write applications once to run on any computer), Sun has led the industry with a number of breakthrough, forward-thinking ideas. Over the years, Sun has become a leading supplier of network-based products, including servers, storage devices, and workstations. All products are powered by its own line of software and high-speed microprocessors.

Given its forward-thinking leadership position, the opportunity for Sun Microsystems over the long term is quite favorable. Sun high-end servers and storage devices are specifically designed to support the build-out of the Internet's infrastructure. Sun Microsystems enjoys strong brand recognition, has demonstrated effective marketing and distribution to Internet service providers and dot-com companies, and has a history of continually improving its technology and services. In addition, the acquisition of Cobalt Networks appears to be strengthening Sun's position in the server appliance market, which will be a key growth area going forward. Overall, the company enjoys a strong competitive position in a rapidly growing market.

Risk Factors

Sun competes in a highly competitive segment of the market. Several other companies are jockeying to capitalize on the infrastructure build-out of the Internet. Competitors with specific niches and substantial resources are likely to create significant challenges to Sun's leadership position. What's more, companies like IBM and Hewlett-Packard are aggressively targeting the server market, which will force Sun to remain innovative. Other risks include the potential negative impact of Windows 2000 on Sun's workgroup server sales and a relatively high valuation that leaves little room for error.

CONTACT INFORMATION

Sun Microsystems, Inc., 901 San Antonio Road, Palo Alto, CA 94303
(650) 960-1300
www.sun.com

Sun Microsystems (SUNW)

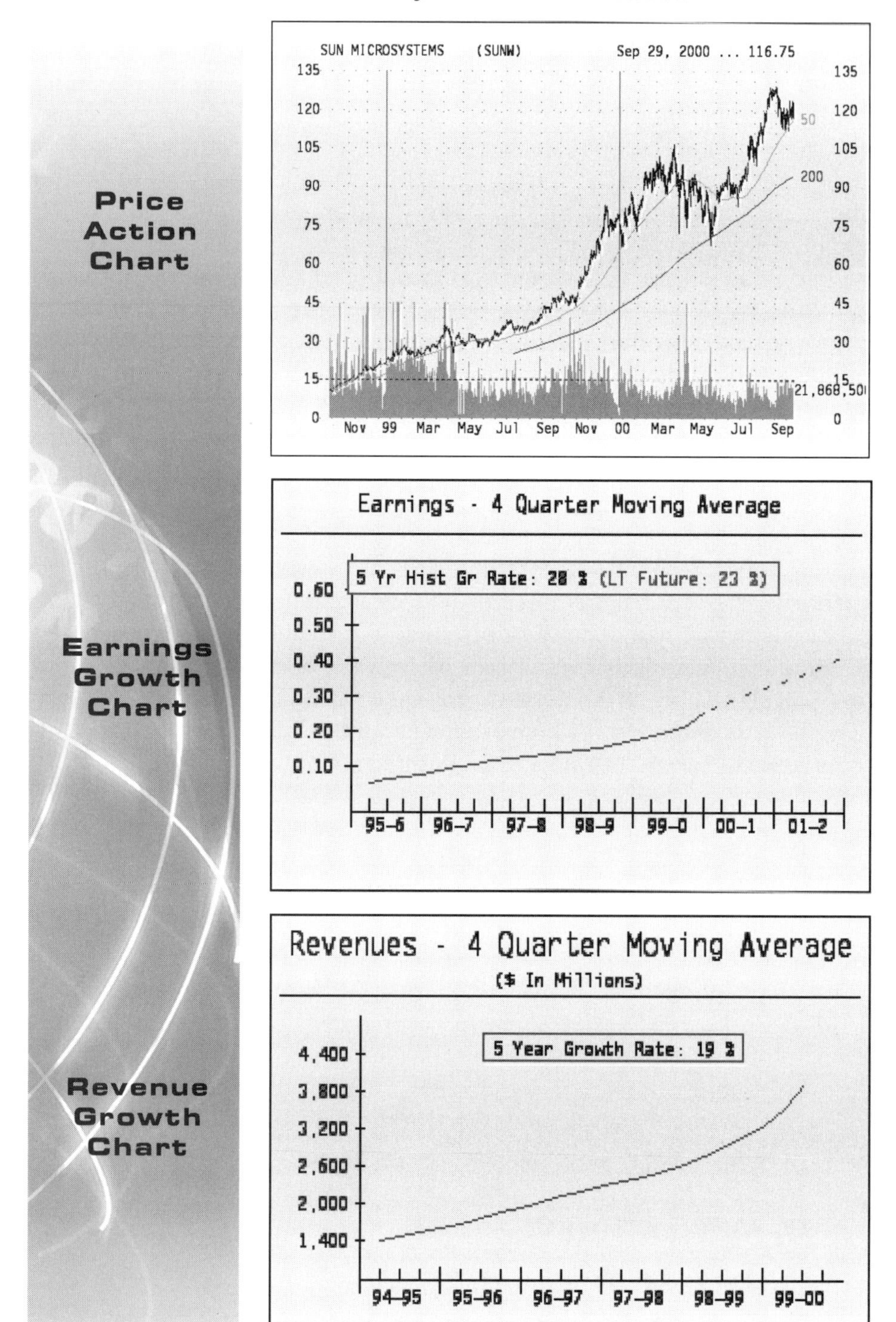

Charts provided by Baseline Financial Services.

22. USA NETWORKS

Symbol: USAI
Sector: Services (Broadcasting and Cable Television)

COMPANY PROFILE

USA Networks is a media and e-commerce powerhouse. The company operates the USA Network and Sci-Fi Channel cable networks, and produces and distributes television programming. Through its America's Store and Home Shopping Network, USA Networks sells items over the air. The company has ticketing operations, primarily through Ticketmaster and its online sibling, Ticketmaster.com. USA Networks's Hotel Reservations Network consolidates hotel rooms for consumer resale. The company provides various other Internet services, including its online retailing business—the Internet Shopping Network—and local city guides. USA Networks also owns and operates TV stations, and distributes and produces domestic theatrical films.

EARNINGS

During the past 12 months, USA Networks lost $0.23 per share, down 557 percent from the previous year.

REVENUES

Revenues during the past 12 months totaled $3.8 billion, up 31 percent from a year earlier.

KEY RATIOS & MEASURES	5-YEAR RANGE	CURRENT
P/E	67–251	NM
Price-to-Book	0.7–7.6	6.6
Price-to-Cash Flow	2.7–49.3	10.9
Price-to-Sales	0.8–21.4	2.44
Return on Equity	1–3.8%	NM
Beta		1.37

NM, Not Meaningful

BYRUM'S COMMENTS

USA Networks is one of the nation's fastest-growing media and entertainment companies. It provides advertisers access to a vast cable television audience through the Sci-Fi Channel and USA Network, and reaches directly for viewers' credit cards via the Home Shopping Network. The company owns 39 television stations, and produces its own shows at Studios USA. Those weary of TV can surf on the company's Internet Shopping Network, and couch potatoes ready for live entertainment are likely to book seats through Ticketmaster, the largest ticket retailer in the country. Even globetrotters generate income for USA Networks through yet another affiliate, Hotel Reservations Network.

USA Nctworks clearly has a wide reach. But investor enthusiasm is not based merely on diversification. It's also based on the company's creative use of both old and new media strategies. In addition to its strong position among traditional advertising-based media companies, USA Networks takes full advantage of the higher margins enjoyed through direct selling and fee-based services. The company has developed its own back-office systems for Home Shopping Network and Ticketmaster, allowing it to sell transaction processing capacity to other e-commerce vendors. Finally, a recent agreement to develop private label services for the National Basketball Association illustrates USA Networks's ability to find unique sources of new revenue.

RISK FACTORS

Much of USA Networks's success is attributable to CEO Barry Diller. Diller's penchant for acquisitions has resulted in rather confusing balance sheets, which makes the company difficult to value. USA Networks also carries the risks inherent in any enterprise whose success has relied on the performance of one key player. Finally, it remains to be seen how sensitive new media companies such as USA Networks will be to economic fluctuations.

CONTACT INFORMATION

USA Networks, Inc., 152 West 57th Street, New York, NY 10019
(212) 314-7300
www.usanetwork.com

USA Networks (USAI)

Price Action Chart

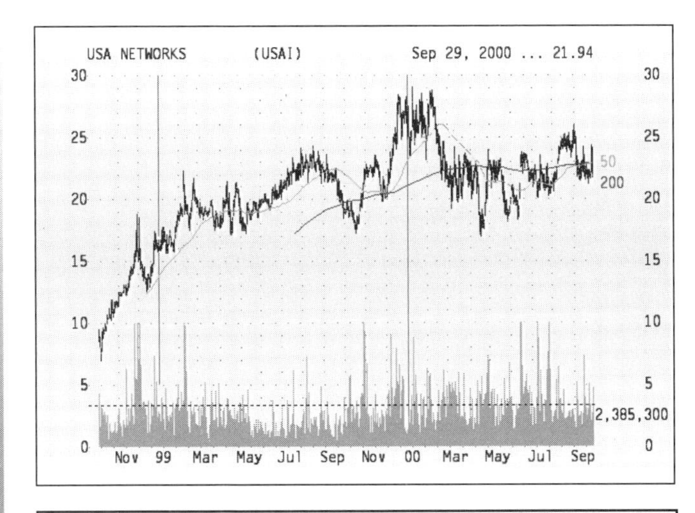

Earnings Growth Chart

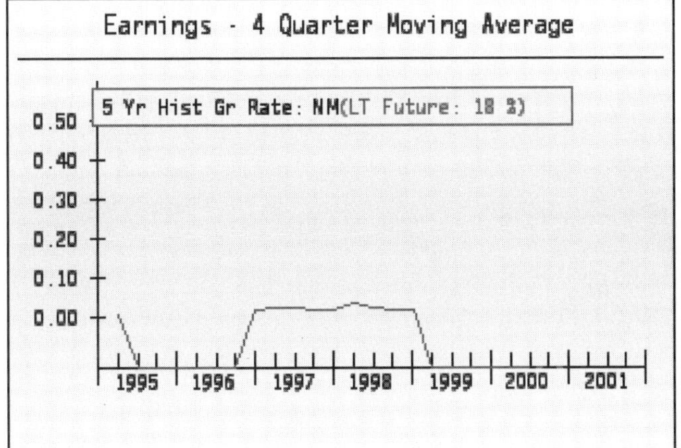

Revenue Growth Chart

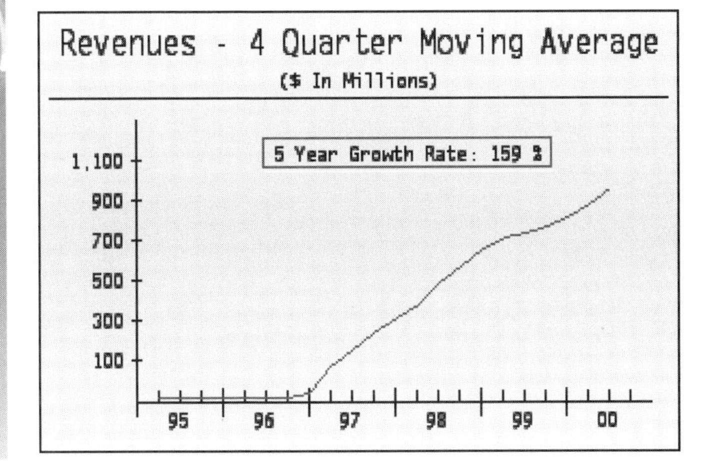

Charts provided by Baseline Financial Services.

23. XILINX

Symbol: XLNX
Sector: Technology (Semiconductors)

COMPANY PROFILE

Xilinx designs, develops, and markets complete programmable logic solutions. The company's products include advanced integrated circuits, software design tools, predefined system functions delivered as cores of logic, and field engineering support. Xilinx's programmable logic devices include field programmable gate arrays and complex programmable logic devices. These products are designed to provide high integration and quick time-to-market for electronic equipment manufacturers, primarily in the telecommunications, networking, computing, industrial, and consumer markets. Sales are carried out globally through a network of independent sales representatives and distributors. Xilinx owns more than 400 U.S.-issued patents in the areas of software, integrated circuit architecture, and design.

EARNINGS

During the past 12 months, Xilinx earned $0.87 per share, up 77 percent from the previous year.

REVENUES

Revenues during the past 12 months totaled $1.2 billion, up 62 percent from a year earlier.

KEY RATIOS & MEASURES	5-YEAR RANGE	CURRENT
P/E	15–137	106.2
Price-to-Book	3.9–17.3	15.4
Price-to-Cash Flow	13.2–98.1	91.6
Price-to-Sales	3.1–26.9	25.13
Return on Equity	18.1–25.7%	20.3%
Beta		1.67

Byrum's Comments

Xilinx designs and builds advanced integrated circuits, software design tools, and predefined system functions for electronic equipment manufacturers. Founded in 1984, the company's software design tool solutions allow customers to implement their specific design needs into its Programmable Logic Devices, or PLDs. These devices allow for a high degree of customization through software programming. The PLD is a hybrid of the application-specific integrated circuit. It can meet a customer's specific requirements without designing and fabricating an entirely new chip. Xilinx serves customers in computing, telecommunications, networking, and industrial markets including defense and aerospace.

Xilinx is a leader in Field Programmable Gate Array (FPGA) technology and competes directly with Altera Corporation and Lattice Semiconductor Corporation. Xilinx's objective is to capture the market for PLDs by providing standardized parts at a low cost and with high-performance characteristics. The company concentrates its efforts on designing new products and tools, while outsourcing the actual manufacturing of its products.

Xilinx has adopted two key initiatives for building and protecting market share. First, it is increasing its ability to upgrade products in the field. This should extend the time-in-market of its products and is in line with its low-cost strategy. Second, it is using the Web to assist customers, provide support, and make software available for programmers and developers at no cost.

Risk Factors

Although Xilinx is a leader in a niche market, the company faces increased competition due to new entrants and developments in technology. Xilinx's revenue is strongly tied to the demand of the communications, computing, and networking end-markets. The extent to which it can meet the needs and serve these markets will determine its near-term profitability. This requires effective inventory management and anticipating shifts in demand among business as well as geographic sectors.

CONTACT INFORMATION

Xilinx, Inc., 2100 Logic Drive, San Jose, CA 95124-3450
(408) 559-7778
www.xilinx.com

Xilinx (XLNX)

Price Action Chart

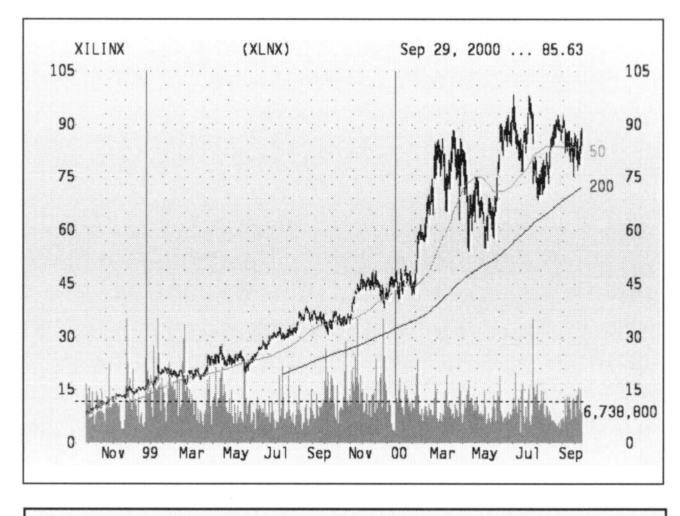

Earnings Growth Chart

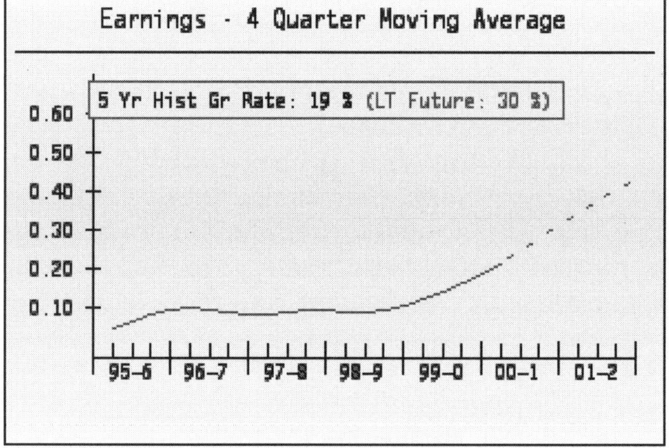

Revenue Growth Chart

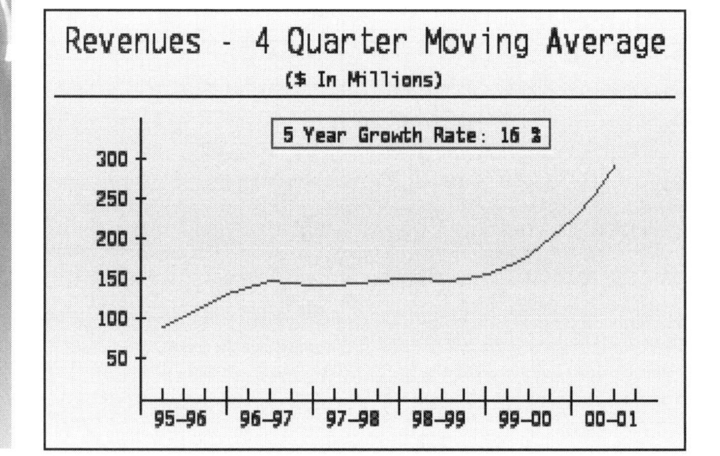

Charts provided by Baseline Financial Services.

24. XO COMMUNICATIONS

Symbol: XOXO
Sector: Services (Communications Services)

COMPANY PROFILE

XO Communications (formerly NEXTLINK) provides telecommunication services to small- and medium-sized businesses. The company currently owns and operates 31 high-bandwidth, or broadband, local networks in 19 states. XO Communications offers a variety of voice services, plus high-speed Internet access. Through its interactive subsidiary, the company also provides a number of voice-response, speech-recognition, and e-commerce services. The company's Digital Subscriber Line (DSL) technology, which is increasing in popularity, meets high-bandwidth needs. XO Communications has also begun to install Internet Protocol routers, which will enable the company to carry Internet traffic more efficiently and to offer more data services. In addition, XO Communications acquired Concentric Network Corporation in 2000.

EARNINGS

During the past 12 months, XO Communications lost $3.05 per share, down 51 percent from the previous year.

REVENUES

Revenues during the past 12 months totaled $412 million, up 116 percent from a year earlier.

KEY RATIOS & MEASURES	5-YEAR RANGE	CURRENT
P/E	NM	NM
Price-to-Book	14–21.1	NM
Price-to-Cash Flow	NA	NM
Price-to-Sales	4.1–44.2	24.17
Return on Equity	NA	NM
Beta		1.61

NM, Not Meaningful; NA, Not Applicable

BYRUM'S COMMENTS

XO Communications, founded in September of 1994 as NEXTLINK, has become a leading provider of broadband and telecommunications services to commercial customers. The company owns and operates 31 broadband local networks in 19 states and continues to expand its network holdings. XO Communications provides local and long-distance communication services, putting it in direct competition with a vast array of local exchange carriers. However, the company is in a strong position to deliver enhanced communications services, especially following its acquisition of Concentric Network, an internet hosting and Web service provider.

In addition to the company's significant local network assets, XO Communications also has large license holdings for access to fixed wireless spectrum in 30 U.S. cities. This fits in with the company's strategy of circumventing access from local carriers by connecting customers directly via fiber-optic extensions from either its proprietary networks or through wireless means. XO Communications is taking advantage of its networks and equipment to bundle services—such as local, long distance, and Internet DSL—to business customers. XO Communications's primary competitors are the growing number of carriers that continue to build their presence in a growing local exchange market.

RISK FACTORS

XO Communications is in a period of high capital expenditure, corporate acquisition, and research and development. This means earnings probably won't turn positive until 2005. The company has a solid balance sheet and is under no financial pressure at this time, but there are some concerns. First, there is growing competition in the local exchange market. This could affect margins and increase the cost of customer acquisitions. Second, with the large number of players currently racing to lay fiber-optic cable, an overcapacity of bandwidth could develop, further eroding profits. XO Communications has proven its ability to execute a high-growth strategy. It is important that the company continue to be effective in marketing its services to businesses, while strengthening its competitive advantage in reaching its customers through a proprietary infrastructure.

CONTACT INFORMATION
XO Communications, 1505 Farm Credit Drive, McLean, VA 22102
(703) 547-2000
www.XO.com

XO Communications (XOXO)

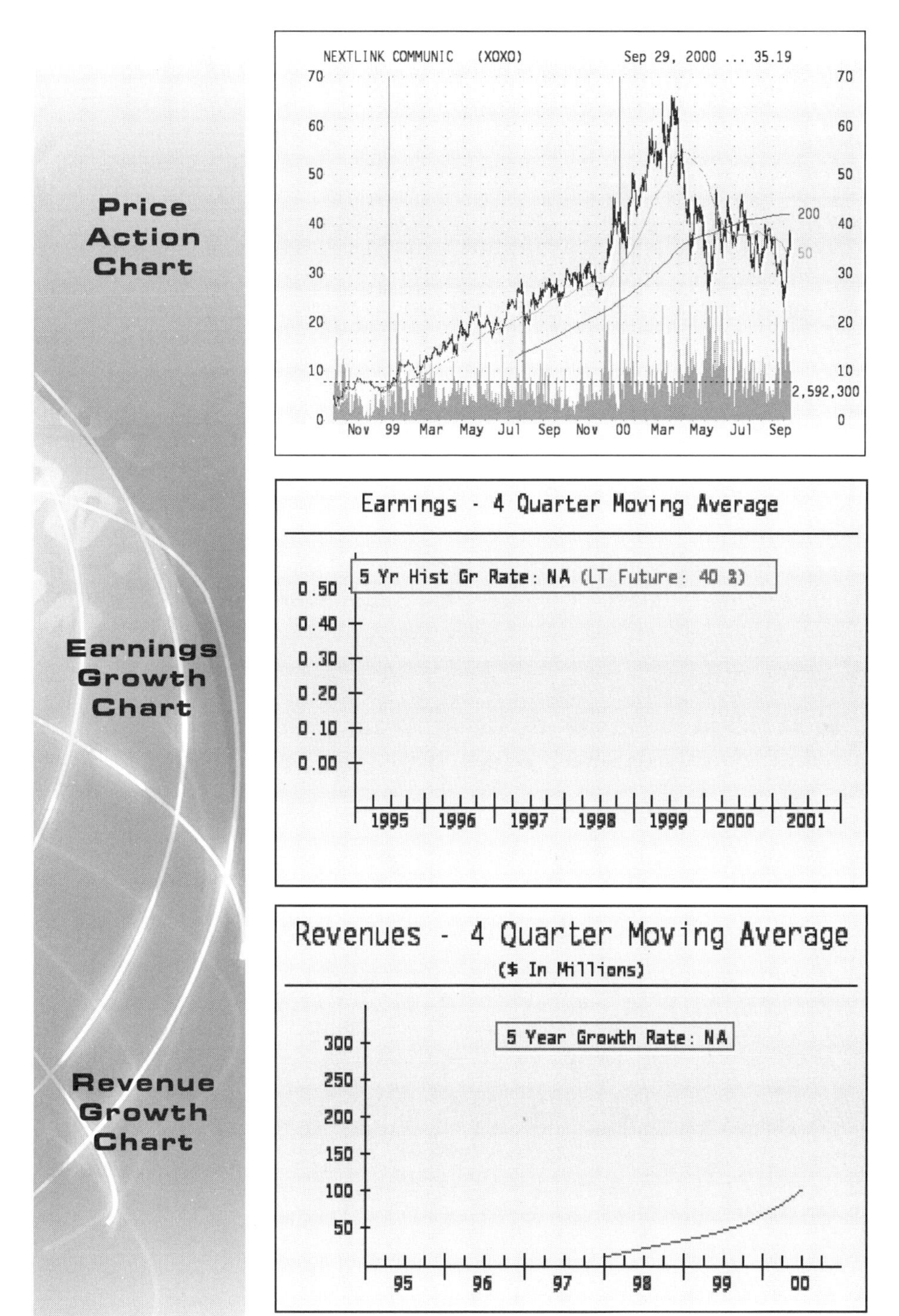

Charts provided by Baseline Financial Services.

25. YAHOO!

Symbol: YHOO
Sector: Technology (Computer Services)

COMPANY PROFILE

Yahoo! is a global Internet communications, commerce, and media company that offers a comprehensive branded network of services. Its flagship product, www.yahoo.com, provides a subject-based directory of Web sites that enables users to locate and access information and services through various hypertext links. Yahoo! also incorporates current and reference information from outside content providers, and organizes links to Web sites featuring current events, issues of interest, Yellow Pages, classifieds, and maps. In addition, Yahoo! provides an array of online business services, including audio and video streaming, store hosting and management, and Web site tools and services. It has offices in Europe, Asia Pacific, Latin America, Canada, and throughout the United States. Yahoo! serves more than 120 million users each month.

EARNINGS

During the past 12 months, Yahoo! earned $0.39 per share, up 271 percent from the previous year.

REVENUES

Revenues during the past 12 months totaled $855 million, up 119 percent from a year earlier.

KEY RATIOS & MEASURES	5-YEAR RANGE	CURRENT
P/E	NM	292.1
Price-to-Book	4–96.7	44
Price-to-Cash Flow	112–1760	243.5
Price-to-Sales	7.6–200.2	72.42
Return on Equity	6.8–16.7%	16.7%
Beta		1.69

NM, Not Meaningful

Byrum's Comments

Founded in 1994 as the first online navigational guide, Yahoo! has become one of the most recognizable and popular Internet brand names. Yahoo! currently delivers online media, Web navigation, communication services, and commerce to more than 166 million individuals throughout the world. Its Web site, www.yahoo.com, is one of the most trafficked addresses on the Internet.

Over the past few years, due to positive earnings surprises and significant gains in user traffic, Yahoo!'s stock has outperformed the market. Because it doesn't charge users for its services, much of Yahoo!'s revenues are derived from the sale of advertisements on its Web site. Yahoo! also generates revenue from business services, e-commerce transactions, and sales of corporate sponsorship agreements. The company has positioned itself as a leading online media provider and is set to provide rich interactive content to users as broadband access becomes more pervasive.

Yahoo!'s strengths include a large and growing user base. One-third of its users reside outside the United States. More recently, a significant online presence enabling e-commerce transactions has been fueling growth. According to a recent Yahoo! press release, the company enabled more than $3 billion in online transactions during the first nine months of 2000, leading to growth of approximately 300 percent in e-commerce transactions over the past year. Yahoo! has also been aggressive at extending its reach to mobile devices, such as the Palm Pilot and cellular phones with Internet access. Yahoo! has signed agreements with both Sprint and Motorola to expand its wireless services.

Risk Factors

Of primary concern to Yahoo! investors is whether the company is in a position to challenge other powerful Web portals with substantial online media capabilities, deep content, and strong brand recognition. The AOL/Time Warner merger, which combines Time Warner's traditional media properties with AOL's popular online content, is a notable competitor. This combined company will have a powerful, broad menu of content to provide its user base. Additional strong competitors include Microsoft's MSN.com portal and Disney's Go.com portal, both of which have significant resources behind them. Another concern is a possible cutback in Web advertising by Yahoo!'s major advertising clients, many of which are struggling dot-com's. That could severely diminish the company's cash flow and revenue stream.

CONTACT INFORMATION

Yahoo! Inc., 3420 Central Expressway, Santa Clara, CA 95051-0703
(408) 731-3300
www.yahoo.com

Yahoo! (YHOO)

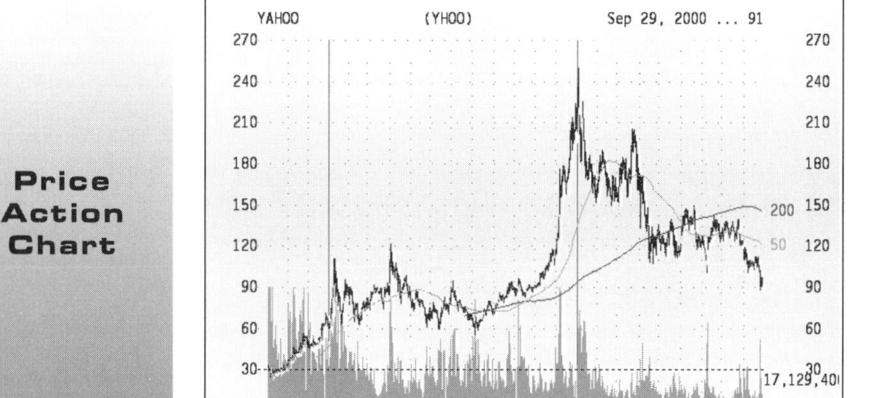

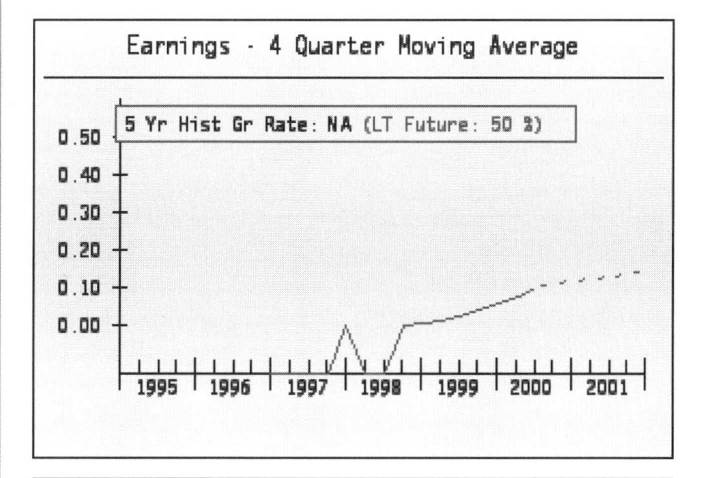

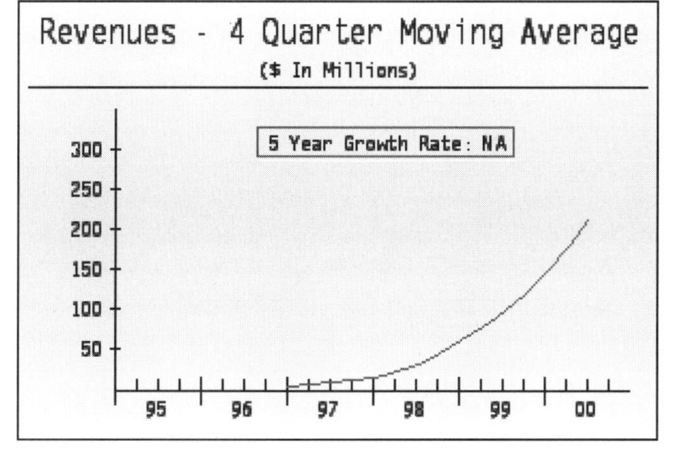

Charts provided by Baseline Financial Services.

5

THE REST OF THE NASDAQ-100

26. Abgenix
27. Adelphia Communications
28. Adobe Systems
29. Amazon.com
30. Apple Computer
31. Applied Micro Circuits
32. Atmel
33. BEA Systems
34. Bed, Bath & Beyond
35. Biogen
36. Biomet
37. BMC Software
38. BroadVision
39. Check Point Software Technologies
40. Chiron
41. CIENA
42. Cintas
43. Citrix Systems
44. CMGI
45. CNET Networks
46. Comcast
47. Compuware
48. Concord EFS
49. Conexant Systems
50. Costco Wholesale
51. Dell Computer
52. eBay
53. EchoStar Communications
54. Electronic Arts
55. Excite@Home
56. Exodus Communications
57. Fiserv
58. Flextronics International
59. Gemstar-TV Guide Intl.
60. Genzyme General
61. Human Genome Sciences
62. IDEC Pharmaceuticals
63. Immunex
64. Inktomi
65. Intuit
66. i2 Technologies
67. Juniper Networks
68. KLA-Tencor

69. LM Ericsson Telephone ADR
70. Lycos*
71. Maxim Integrated Products
72. Mercury Interactive
73. Microchip Technology
74. Millennium Pharmaceuticals
75. Molex
76. Novell
77. NTL*
78. PACCAR
79. Palm
80. PanAmSat
81. Parametric Technology
82. PeopleSoft
83. QLogic
84. QUALCOMM
85. Rational Software
86. RealNetworks
87. RF Micro Devices
88. SDL
89. Siebel Systems
90. Smurfit-Stone Container
91. Staples
92. Starbucks
93. Tellabs
94. TMP Worldwide
95. 3Com
96. VeriSign
97. VERITAS Software
98. Vitesse Semiconductor
99. VoiceStream Wireless
100. WorldCom

*Lycos and NTL were replaced by Broadcom and Ariba as this book went to press.

26. ABGENIX

Symbol: ABGX
Sector: Healthcare (Biotechnology and Drugs)

COMPANY PROFILE

Abgenix is a biopharmaceutical company that develops antibody therapeutic products designed to treat or prevent various diseases. These diseases include inflammatory and autoimmune disorders, transplant-related diseases, cardiovascular disease, and cancer. The company's XenoMouse technology is designed to generate high-affinity antibodies against any diseases amenable to treatment by antibody therapy. Abgenix has four antibody product candidates under development, including ABX-CBL (a treatment for transplant-rejection disorders) and ABX-ILB (a treatment for psoriasis). Both of these products are in human clinical trials. Abgenix has development and commercialization arrangements with Pfizer, Genetech, Millennium, Chiron, and others.

EARNINGS

During the past 12 months, Abgenix lost $0.12 per share, up 65 percent from the previous year.

REVENUES

Revenues during the past 12 months totaled $20.3 million, up 416 percent from a year earlier.

KEY RATIOS & MEASURES	5-YEAR RANGE	CURRENT
P/E	NM	NM
Price-to-Book	1.5–53.8	42
Price-to-Cash Flow	NA	NM
Price-to-Sales	13.7–306.1	239.5
Return on Equity	NA	NM
Beta		1.96

NM, Not Meaningful; NA, Not Applicable

CONTACT INFORMATION

Abgenix, Inc., 7601 Dumbarton Circle, Fremont, CA 94555
(510) 608-6500
www.abgenix.com

Abgenix (ABGX)

Price Action Chart

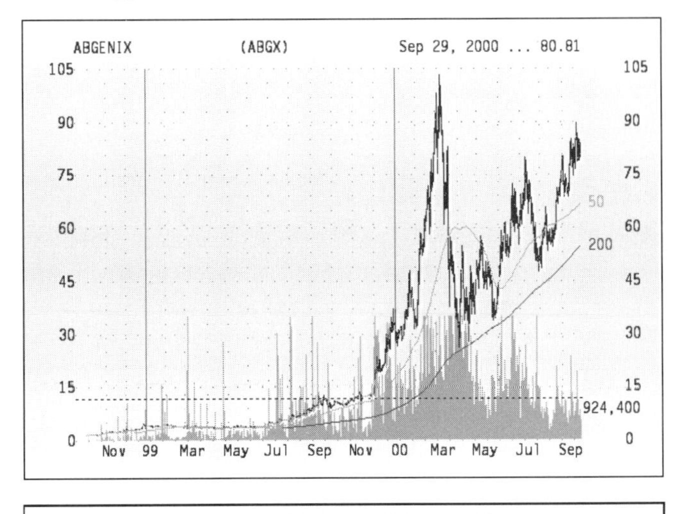

Earnings Growth Chart

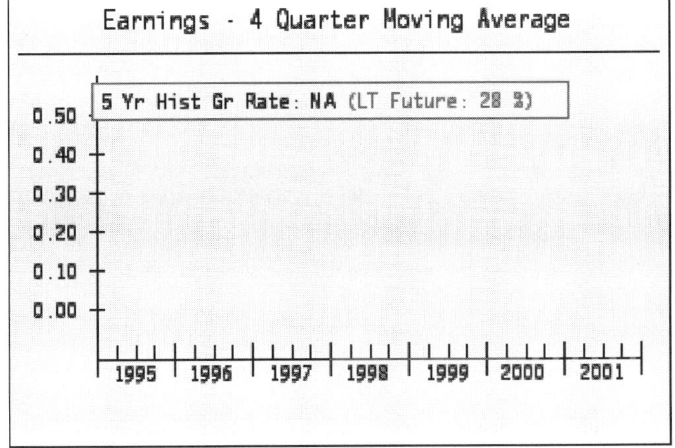

Revenue Growth Chart

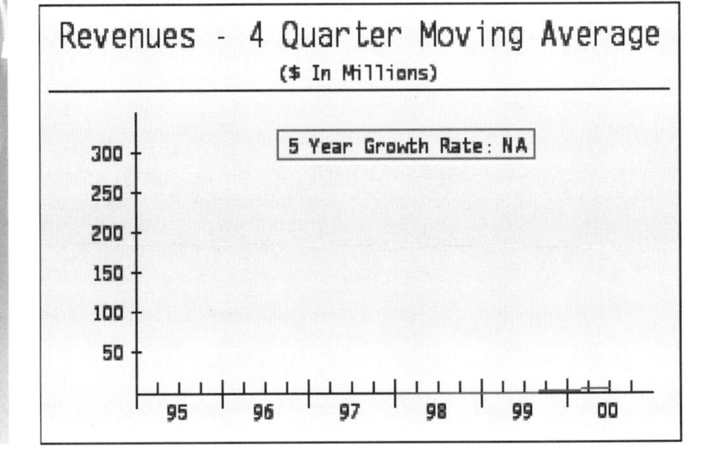

Charts provided by Baseline Financial Services.

27. ADELPHIA COMMUNICATIONS

Symbol: ADLAC
Sector: Services (Broadcasting and Cable Television)

COMPANY PROFILE

Adelphia Communications offers services for the telecommunications and cable television industries. The company owns or manages cable systems in more than 10 states nationwide, including New York, Pennsylvania, Virginia, New Jersey, and Ohio. Together, these systems serve more than 1.5 million basic subscribers, mostly in the suburban areas of large- and mid-sized cities. Adelphia also owns a 50-percent interest in Olympus Communications, a joint venture that operates a cable system in Florida. The company offers telecommunications and local telephone services through its majority-owned subsidiary Hyperion Telecommunication, plus high-speed Internet access through its Power Link high-speed data cable modem service. In the past year, the company agreed to buy cable TV firms FrontierVision Partners and Century Communications.

EARNINGS

During the past 12 months, Adelphia Communications lost $3.57 per share, up 8 percent from the previous year.

REVENUES

Revenues during the past 12 months totaled $1.8 billion, up 127 percent from a year earlier.

KEY RATIOS & MEASURES	5-YEAR RANGE	CURRENT
P/E	NM	NM
Price-to-Book	1–2.9	1.2
Price-to-Cash Flow	18.5–36	NM
Price-to-Sales	0.2–6.2	2.71
Return on Equity	NA	NM
Beta		1.02

NM, Not Meaningful; NA, Not Applicable

CONTACT INFORMATION

Adelphia Communications Corporation, 1 North Main Street, Coudersport, PA 16915-1141
(814) 274-9830
www.adelphia.net

Adelphia Communications (ADLAC)

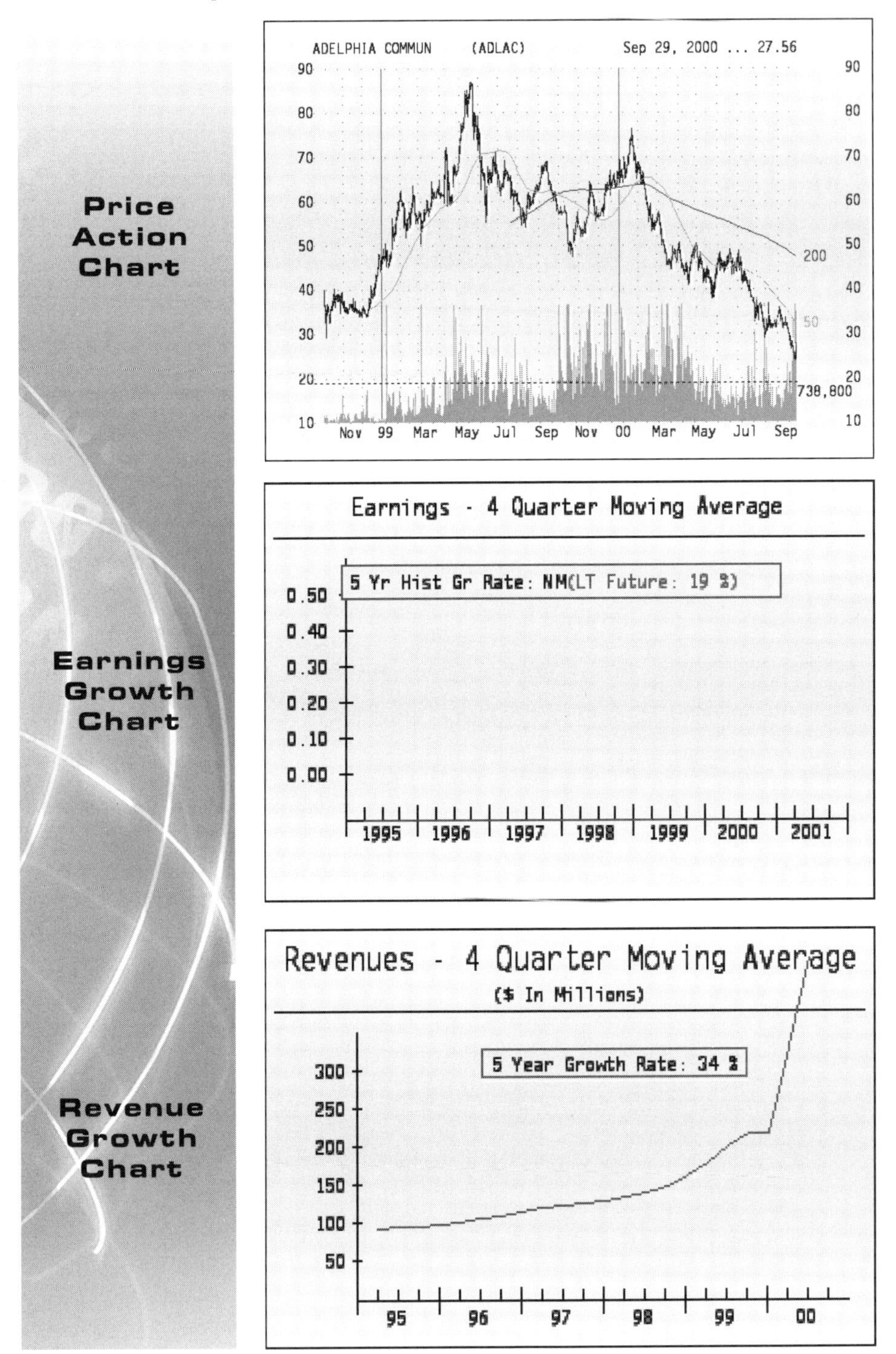

Charts provided by Baseline Financial Services.

28. ADOBE SYSTEMS

Symbol: ADBE
Sector: Technology (Software and Programming)

COMPANY PROFILE

Adobe Systems develops graphic design, publishing, and imaging software for Web and print production. Adobe offers a market-leading line of application software and type products for creating and distributing visually-rich communication materials. It licenses its industry-standard technologies to major hardware manufacturers, software developers, and service providers. Plus, it offers integrated software solutions to businesses of all sizes. Adobe's software runs on Microsoft Windows, Apple Macintosh, Linux, and UNIX platforms. Adobe distributes its products through a network of original equipment manufacturers, distributors, dealers, value-added resellers, and system integrators. Adobe has operations in Europe, Asia, Latin America, and the United States.

EARNINGS

During the past 12 months, Adobe Systems earned $1.84 share, up 50 percent from the previous year.

REVENUES

Revenues during the past 12 months totaled $1.1 billion, up 19 percent from a year earlier.

KEY RATIOS & MEASURES	5-YEAR RANGE	CURRENT
P/E	12–79	73.5
Price-to-Book	2.7–27.3	25.8
Price-to-Cash Flow	8.6–63.3	59.8
Price-to-Sales	1.7–15.3	14.4
Return on Equity	17.1–46.2%	37.4%
Beta		1.15

CONTACT INFORMATION

Adobe Systems, Inc., 345 Park Avenue, San Jose, CA 95110-2704
(408) 536-6000
www.adobe.com

Adobe Systems (ADBE)

Price Action Chart

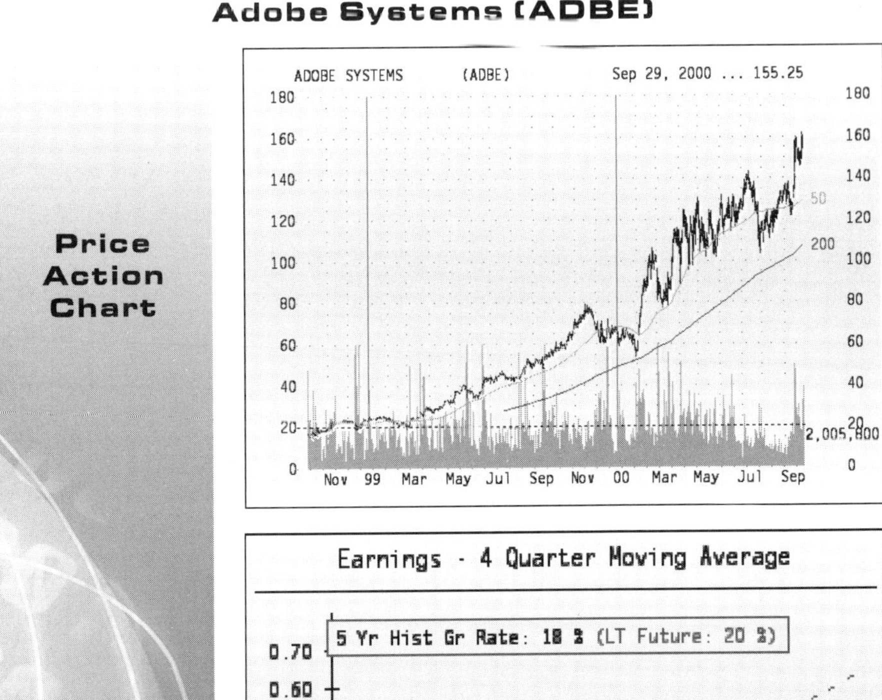

Earnings Growth Chart

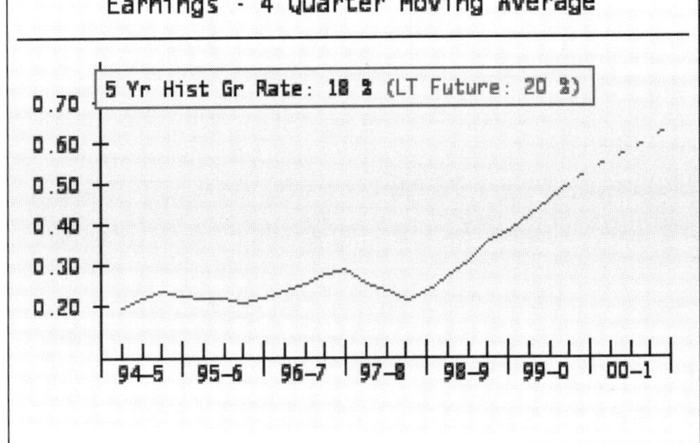

Revenue Growth Chart

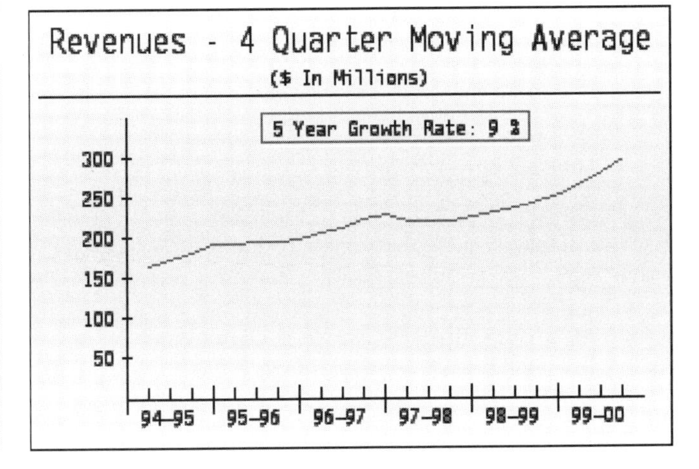

Charts provided by Baseline Financial Services.

29. AMAZON.COM

Symbol: AMZN
Sector: Services (Specialty Retail)

COMPANY PROFILE

Amazon.com isn't just a bookstore any more. The company offers books, music, DVDs, videos, electronics, toys, software, video games, and home-improvement products through its popular Web site at www.amazon.com. Customers can also purchase gift certificates, conduct searches, browse highlighted selections, view bestseller lists, read and post reviews, register for personalized services, participate in promotions, and check the status of an order. Amazon.com offers a streamlined ordering process using its patented 1-Click technology. This enables users to place an order by clicking one button, and is designed to encourage frequent return visits. The company's Amazon.com Auctions, zShops, and sothebys.amazon.com Web-based marketplaces allow buyers and sellers to conduct transactions for a wide range of products. But, so far, earnings for this company remain a distant thought.

EARNINGS

During the past 12 months, Amazon.com lost $1.49 per share, down 186 percent from the previous year.

REVENUES

Revenues during the past 12 months totaled $2.2 billion, up 115 percent from a year earlier.

KEY RATIOS & MEASURES	5-YEAR RANGE	CURRENT
P/E	NM	NM
Price-to-Book	9.5–994.6	451.1
Price-to-Cash Flow	NA	NM
Price-to-Sales	2.1–31.5	6.76
Return on Equity	NA	NM
Beta		2.15

NM, Not Meaningful; NA, Not Applicable

CONTACT INFORMATION

Amazon.com, Inc., 1200 12th Avenue South, #1200, Seattle, WA 98144-2734
(206) 266-1000
www.amazon.com

Amazon.com (AMZN)

Price Action Chart

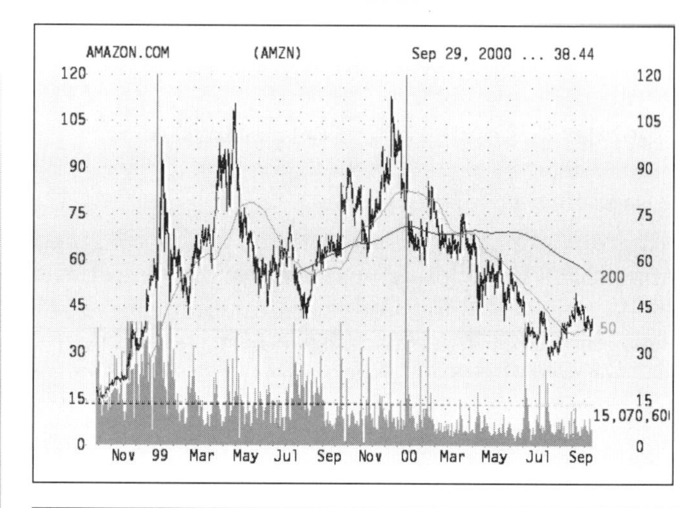

Earnings Growth Chart

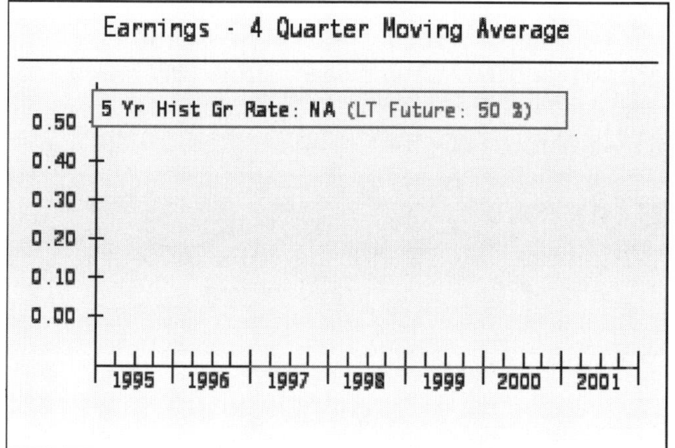

Revenue Growth Chart

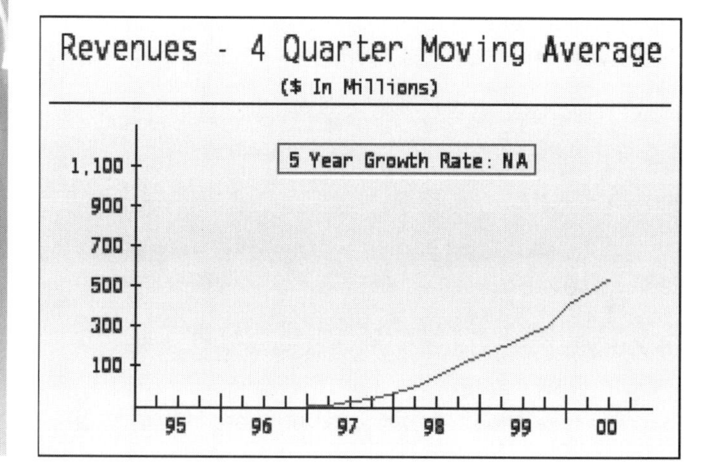

Charts provided by Baseline Financial Services.

30. APPLE COMPUTER

Symbol: AAPL
Sector: Technology (Computer Hardware)

COMPANY PROFILE

Apple Computer designs, makes, and markets microprocessor-based personal computers and related computing products and solutions. Most of the company's net sales come from the sale of its Apple Macintosh line. These computers are characterized by their ease of use; built-in multimedia, networking, and graphics capabilities; and unique PowerPC microprocessors. Apple's operating system software, Mac OS, provides its PCs with a consistent, easy-to-navigate user interface. The company also develops and markets AppleWorks, an integrated suite of software applications that combines word-processing, database, spreadsheet, communications, and drawing modules into one package for both MAC OS and Windows. Apple sells its products primarily to the education, creative, consumer, business, and government markets.

EARNINGS

During the past 12 months, Apple Computer earned $1.65 per share, up 20 percent from the previous year.

REVENUES

Revenues during the past 12 months totaled $7.4 billion, up 17 percent from a year earlier.

KEY RATIOS & MEASURES	5-YEAR RANGE	CURRENT
P/E	9–54	38.6
Price-to-Book	0.9–7.2	6
Price-to-Cash Flow	4.9–39.5	33.3
Price-to-Sales	0.2–3.3	2.77
Return on Equity	15.6–25.3%	15.6%
Beta		0.87

CONTACT INFORMATION

Apple Computer, Inc., 1 Infinite Loop, Cupertino, CA 95014-6299
(408) 996-1010
www.apple.com

Apple Computer (AAPL)

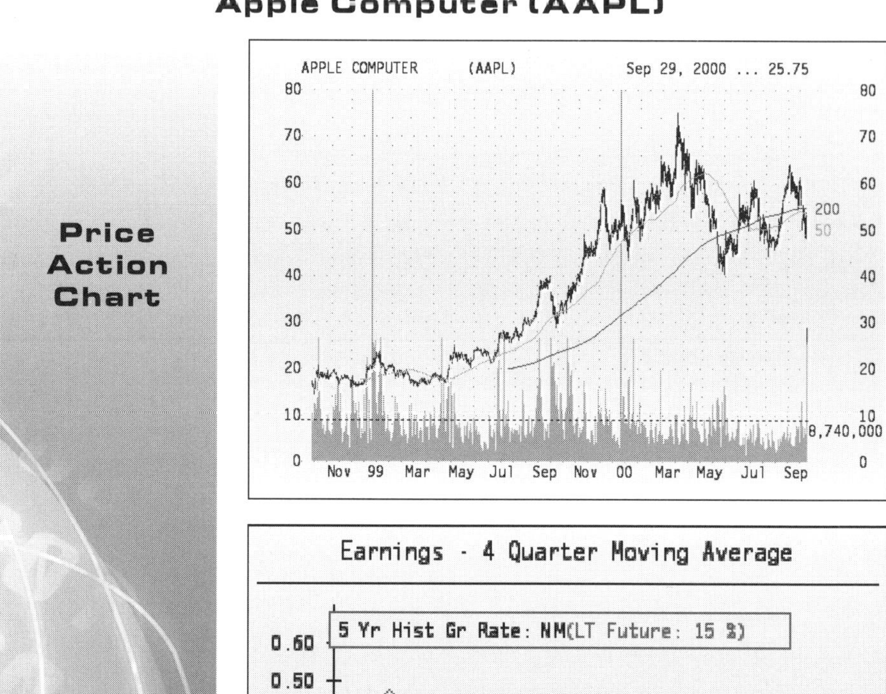

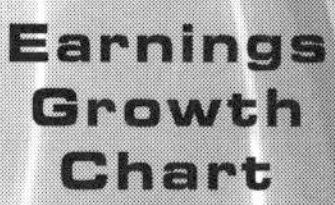

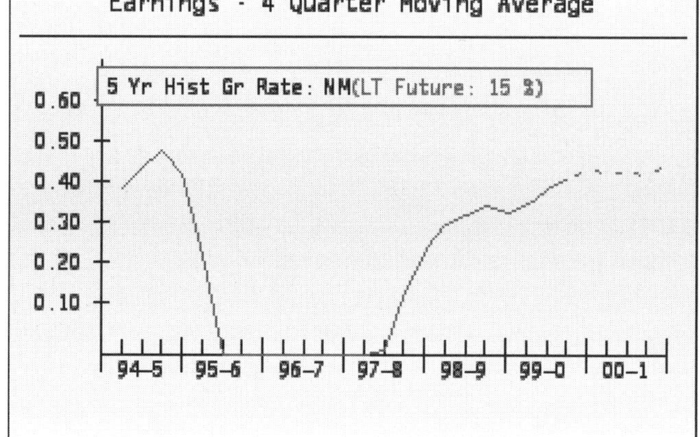

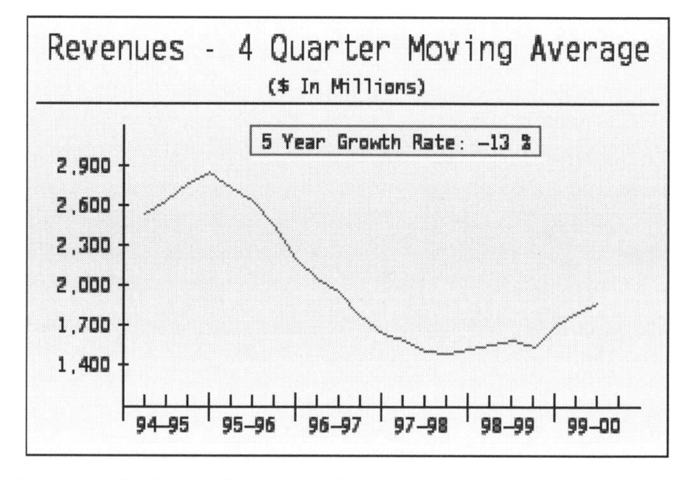

Charts provided by Baseline Financial Services.

31. APPLIED MICRO CIRCUITS

Symbol: AMCC
Sector: Technology (Semiconductors)

COMPANY PROFILE

Applied Micro Circuits designs and manufactures integrated circuits. Its products are used in the wide area network (WAN) markets and address the SONET/SDH and ATM transmission standards. The company also makes products for the fiber-optic-based portions of local area network (LAN) markets that address the Gigabit Ethernet and Fibre Channel transmission standards. Products include transceivers, crosspoint switches, clock recovery and synthesis units, amplifiers and laser drivers, framers, and mappers. In addition, Applied Micro Circuits provides solutions for the ATV, broadcast HDTV, high-speed computing, and military markets. Customers include 3Com, Alcatel, Cisco Systems, Lucent Technologies, Nortel, and Raytheon Systems. In 2000, the company agreed to buy both YuniNetworks and MMC Networks.

EARNINGS

During the past 12 months, Applied Micro Circuits earned $0.56 per share, up 155 percent from the previous year.

REVENUES

Revenues during the past 12 months totaled $215 million, up 92 percent from a year earlier.

KEY RATIOS & MEASURES	5-YEAR RANGE	CURRENT
P/E	39–539	367.9
Price-to-Book	3–56.2	23.9
Price-to-Cash Flow	12.6–336.7	0
Price-to-Sales	2.8–122.8	119.22
Return on Equity	8.6–25.5%	10.2%
Beta		2.02

CONTACT INFORMATION

Applied Micro Circuits Corporation, 6290 Sequence Drive, San Diego, CA 92121
(858) 450-9333
www.amcc.com

Applied Micro Circuits (AMCC)

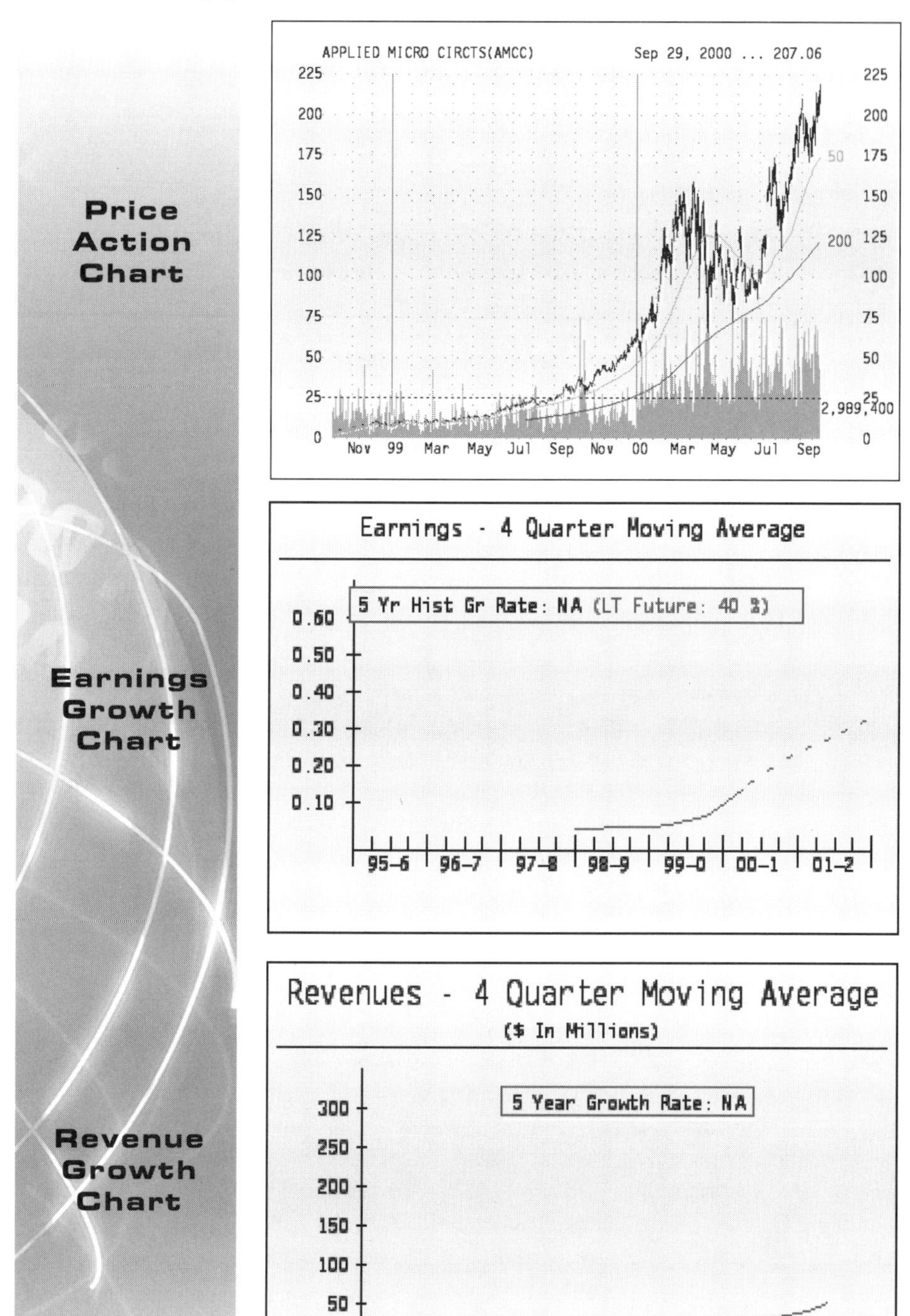

Charts provided by Baseline Financial Services.

32. ATMEL

Symbol: ATML
Sector: Technology (Semiconductors)

COMPANY PROFILE

Atmel Corporation designs, manufactures, and markets high-performance, nonvolatile memory and logic integrated circuits. The company's nonvolatile memory products consist primarily of erasable programmable read-only memories, electrically erasable programmable read-only memories, and flash memories. Its logic products include microcontrollers, erasable programmable logic devices, and field programmable gate arrays. Atmel also makes application-specific integrated circuits (ASICs) and cell-based integrated circuits. The company's products are used for networking, telecommunications, computing, and automotive and consumer electronics applications, among others. In 2000, Atmel contracted to acquire Thomson-CSF's ASIC-manufacturing business.

EARNINGS

During the past 12 months, Atmel earned $0.35 per share, up 289 percent from the previous year.

REVENUES

Revenues during the past 12 months totaled $1.6 billion, up 41 percent from a year earlier.

KEY RATIOS & MEASURES	5-YEAR RANGE	CURRENT
P/E	9–222	59.5
Price-to-Book	0.8–13.9	9.4
Price-to-Cash Flow	2.5–38.3	25.9
Price-to-Sales	0.5–8.4	5.64
Return on Equity	0.2–29.3%	12.7%
Beta		1.67

CONTACT INFORMATION
Atmel Corporation, 2325 Orchard Parkway, San Jose, CA 95131-2032
(408) 441-0311
www.atmel.com

Atmel (ATML)

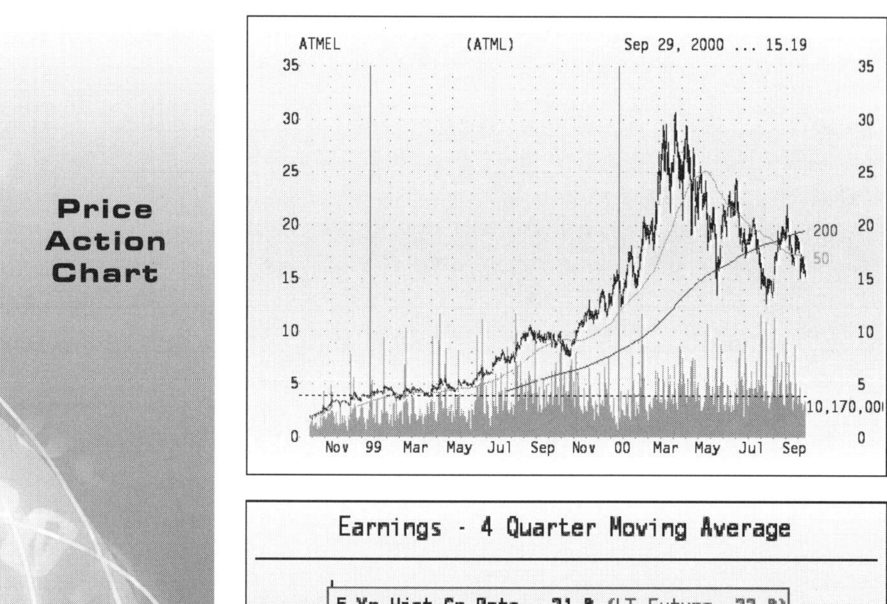

Earnings Growth Chart

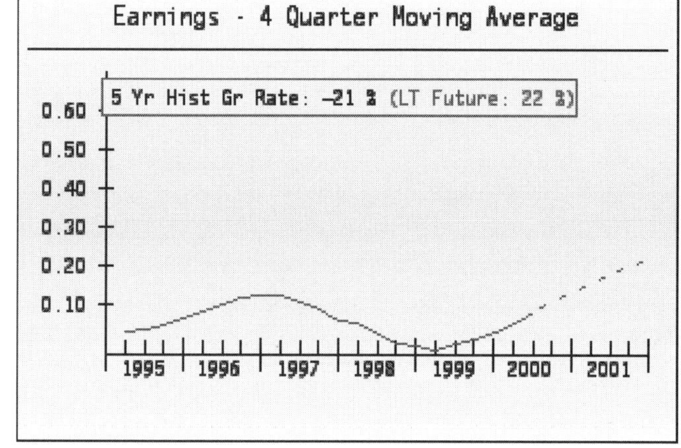

Revenue Growth Chart

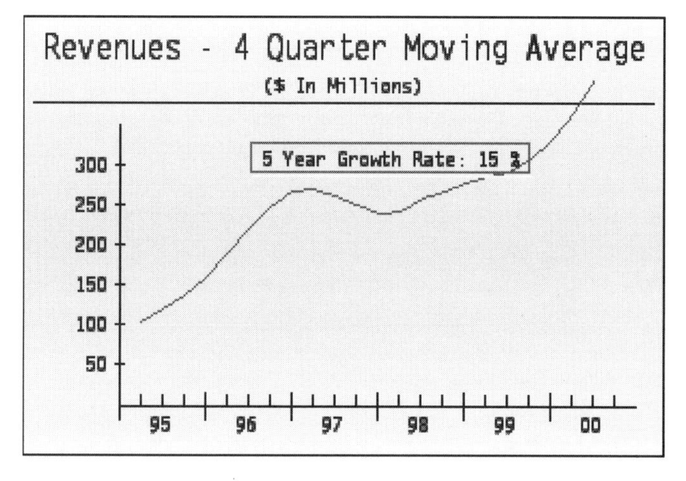

Charts provided by Baseline Financial Services.

33. BEA SYSTEMS

Symbol: BEAS
Sector: Technology (Software and Programming)

COMPANY PROFILE

BEA Systems provides e-commerce infrastructure software designed to help businesses build integrated e-commerce solutions that extend capabilities of existing computer systems. BEA's products serve as a platform or integration tool for applications such as billing; provisioning; customer service; electronic funds transfers; ATM networks; securities trading; Web-based banking; Internet sales; supply chain management; scheduling and logistics; and hotel, airline, and rental car reservations. BEA's solutions are used by more than 4,000 licensees worldwide in varied industries including banking and finance, telecommunications, manufacturing, retail, and transportation.

EARNINGS

During the past 12 months, BEA Systems earned $0.16 per share, up 158 percent from the previous year.

REVENUES

Revenues during the past 12 months totaled $615 million, up 75 percent from a year earlier.

KEY RATIOS & MEASURES	5-YEAR RANGE	CURRENT
P/E	32–752	502.4
Price-to-Book	2.2–62	59.5
Price-to-Cash Flow	6.4–265.6	254.9
Price-to-Sales	2.3–50.2	48.1
Return on Equity	NA	21%
Beta		1.38

NA, Not Applicable

CONTACT INFORMATION

BEA Systems, Inc., 2315 North 1st Street, San Jose, CA 95131
(408) 570-8000
www.bea.com

BEA Systems (BEAS)

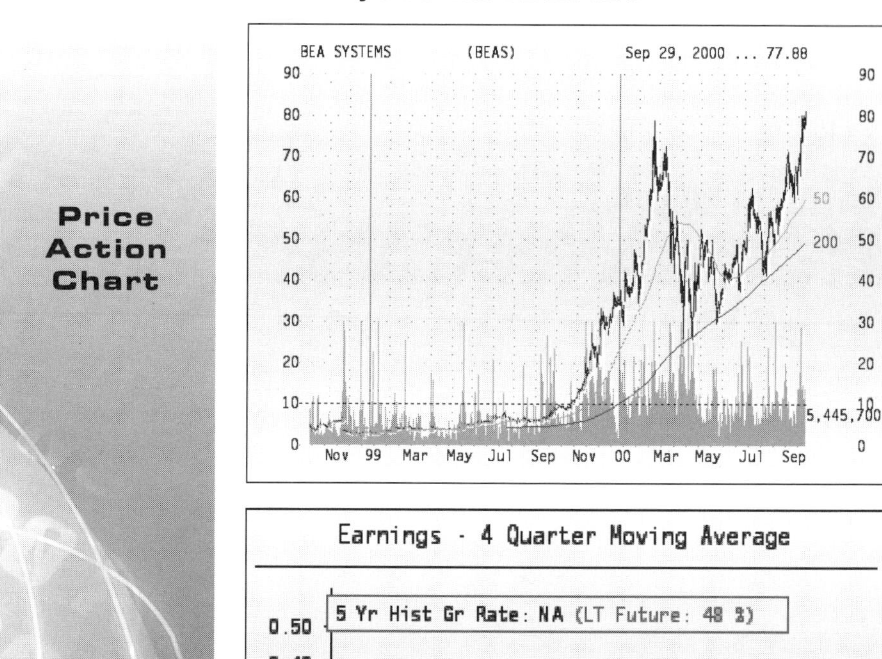

Earnings Growth Chart

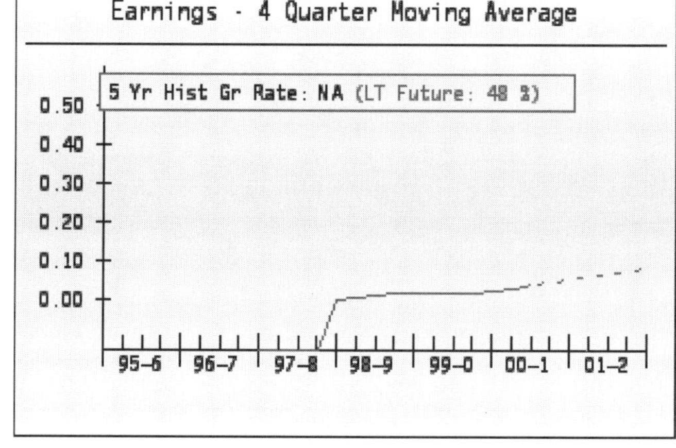

Revenue Growth Chart

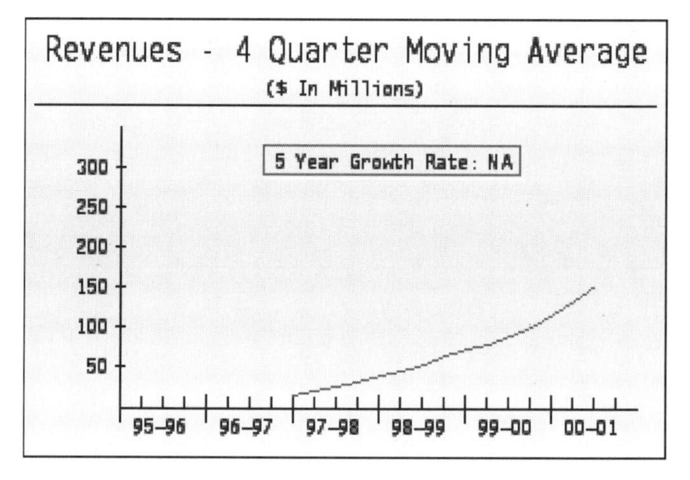

Charts provided by Baseline Financial Services.

34. BED, BATH & BEYOND

Symbol: BBBY
Sector: Services (Specialty Retail)

COMPANY PROFILE

Bed, Bath & Beyond sells home furnishings and domestic merchandise. The company's ever-growing domestic lineup includes bed linens and related items, kitchen textiles, and bath items. Its home furnishings include kitchen and tabletop items, basic housewares, and general home furnishings. The stores carry such brand names as Wamsutta, Martex, Fieldcrest, J.A. Henckels, Krups, Cannon, Croscill, Laura Ashley, Calphalon, All-Clad, Portmeirion, Rubbermaid, Black & Decker, Springs, Braun, Kitchenaid, Cuisinart, Hoover, Brita, Conair, Pillowtex, Mikasa, and Waverly. Bed, Bath & Beyond maintains everyday low prices that are generally comparable to or below department store sale prices. The company operates over 240 superstores in approximately 40 states throughout the United States.

EARNINGS

During the past 12 months, Bed, Bath & Beyond earned $0.48 per share, up 34 percent from the previous year.

REVENUES

Revenues during the past 12 months totaled $2 billion, up 33 percent from a year earlier.

KEY RATIOS & MEASURES	5-YEAR RANGE	CURRENT
P/E	20–62	37.6
Price-to-Book	5.5–16.5	8.6
Price-to-Cash Flow	18.7–54.5	30.4
Price-to-Sales	1.4–3.9	2.53
Return on Equity	25.8–30.1%	25.8%
Beta		1.18

CONTACT INFORMATION

Bed, Bath & Beyond, Inc., 650 Liberty Avenue, Union, NJ 07083
(908) 688-0888
www.bedbath.com

Bed, Bath & Beyond (BBBY)

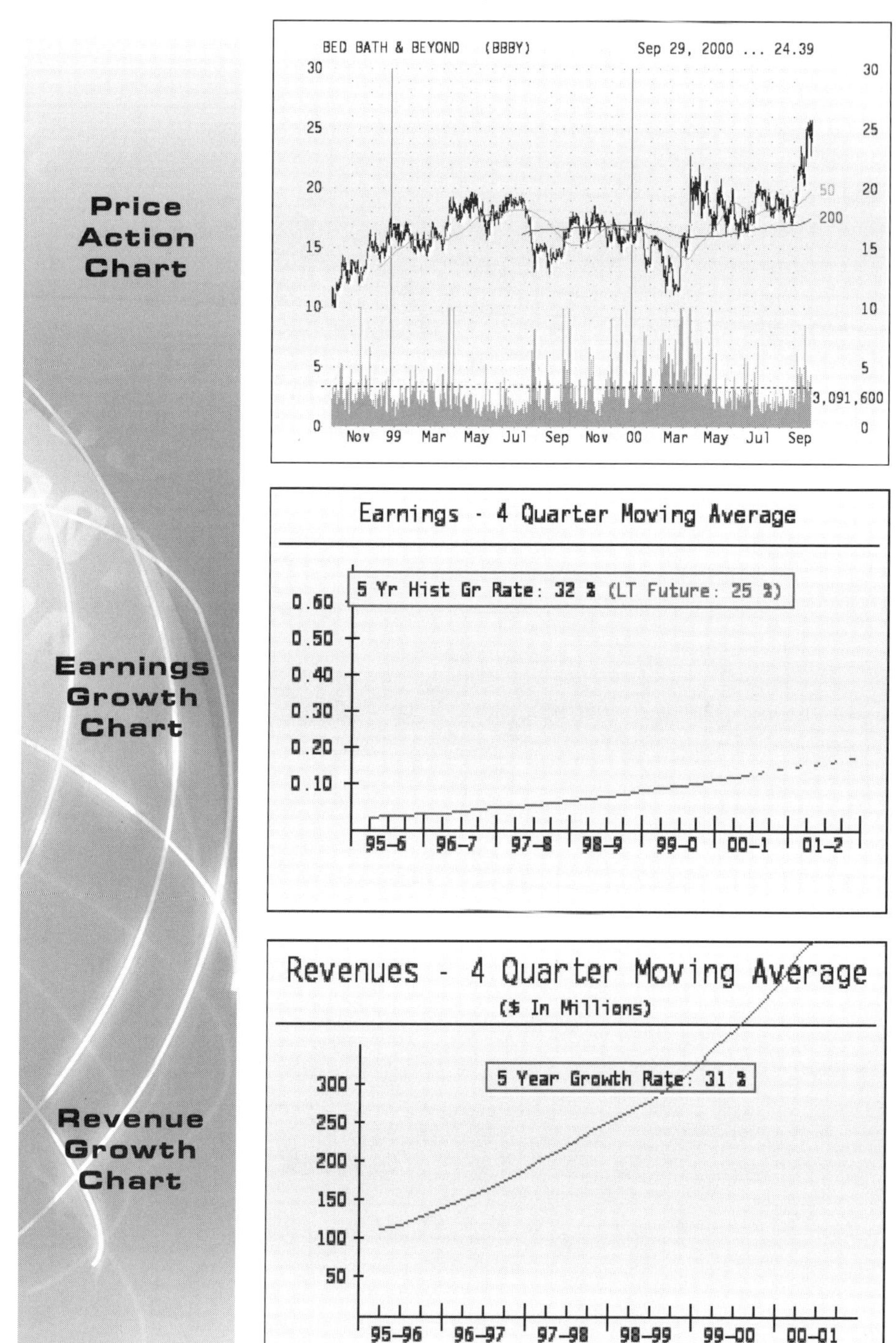

Charts provided by Baseline Financial Services.

35. BIOGEN

Symbol: BGEN
Sector: Healthcare (Biotechnology and Drugs)

COMPANY PROFILE

Biogen is a biopharmaceutical company that develops, manufactures, and markets drugs for human healthcare. Biogen's core product, AVONEX, is used for the treatment of relapsing forms of multiple sclerosis. The company markets AVONEX in more than 50 countries throughout North and South America, Europe, Asia, Africa, and Australia. Biogen also focuses its research and development efforts on inflammatory and cardiovascular diseases, kidney diseases and disorders, developmental biology, and gene therapy. Biogen has completed early-stage clinical trials of several product candidates, including AMEVIVE for psoriasis, and BG9719, a potential treatment for congestive heart failure. Biogen halted clinical trials on ANTOVA, a drug for ideopathic thrombocytopenic purpura, some two years ago.

EARNINGS

During the past 12 months, Biogen earned $1.69 per share, up 45 percent from the previous year.

REVENUES

Revenues during the past 12 months totaled $861 million, up 31 percent from a year earlier.

KEY RATIOS & MEASURES	5-YEAR RANGE	CURRENT
P/E	23–89	41
Price-to-Book	3.3–17.6	9.3
Price-to-Cash Flow	15.2–68.7	36.4
Price-to-Sales	4.3–21.8	11.54
Return on Equity	9.3–26.5%	26.5%
Beta		1.24

CONTACT INFORMATION

Biogen, Inc., 14 Cambridge Center, Cambridge, MA 02142-1481
(617) 679-2000
www.biogen.com

Biogen (BGEN)

Price Action Chart

Earnings Growth Chart

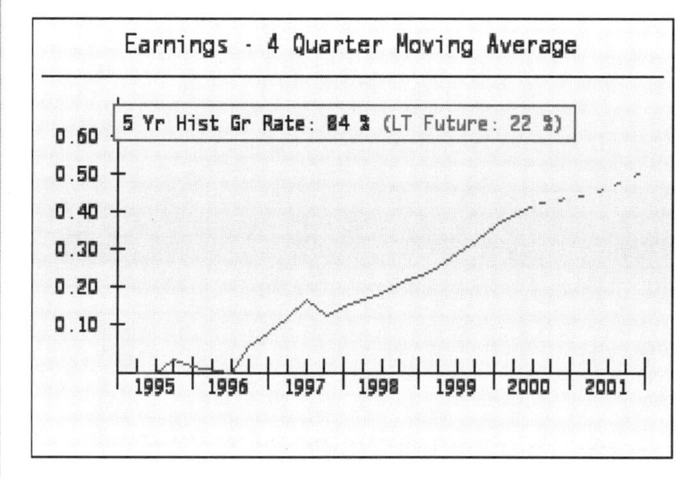

Revenue Growth Chart

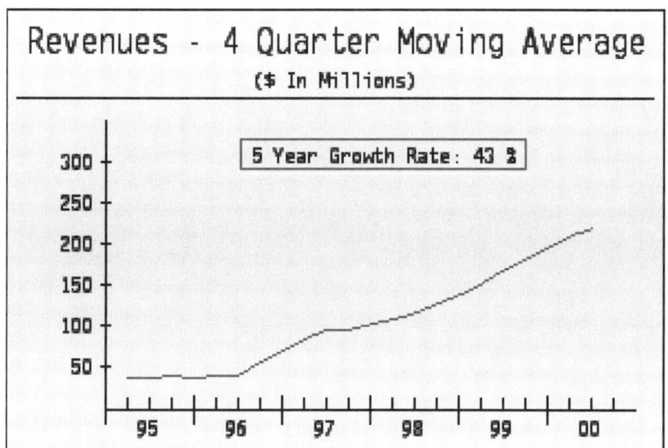

Charts provided by Baseline Financial Services.

36. BIOMET

Symbol: BMET
Sector: Healthcare (Medical Equipment and Supplies)

COMPANY PROFILE

Biomet and its subsidiaries design, manufacture, and market products used primarily by musculoskeletal medical specialists in both surgical and nonsurgical therapy. The company's products include reconstructive and fixation devices, electrical bone-growth stimulators, orthopedic support devices, operating room supplies, spinal implants, general surgical instruments, arthroscopy products, craniomaxillofacial implants, and craniomaxillofacial instruments. Biomet and its subsidiaries operate office and manufacturing facilities in more than 40 locations worldwide. The company's products are marketed in various countries internationally, including Australia, Canada, Austria, Sweden, Mexico, New Zealand, Norway, and Portugal.

EARNINGS

During the past 12 months, Biomet earned $1.01 per share, up 18 percent from the previous year.

REVENUES

Revenues during the past 12 months totaled $921 million, up 11 percent from a year earlier.

KEY RATIOS & MEASURES	5-YEAR RANGE	CURRENT
P/E	15–39	32.9
Price-to-Book	2.7–7	6.3
Price-to-Cash Flow	12.5–31	27
Price-to-Sales	2.6–6.8	6.43
Return on Equity	16.1–20.9%	20.9%
Beta		0.84

CONTACT INFORMATION

Biomet, Inc., Airport Industrial Park, Warsaw, IN 46581-0587
(219) 267-6639
www.biomet.com

Biomet (BMET)

Price Action Chart

BIOMET (BMET) Sep 29, 2000 ... 35

Earnings Growth Chart

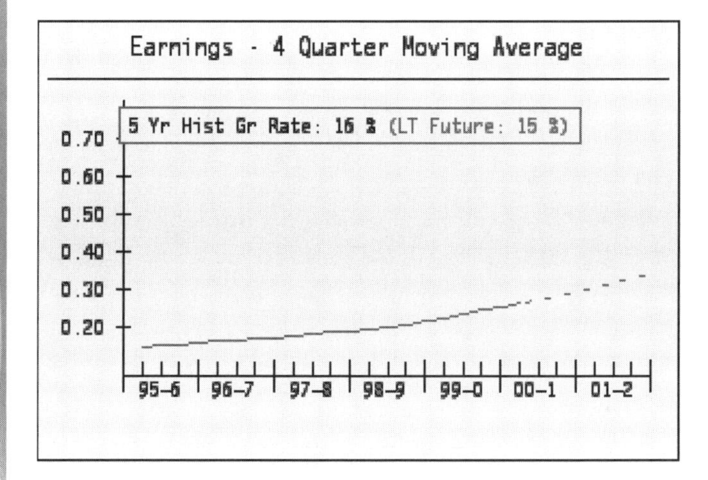

Revenue Growth Chart

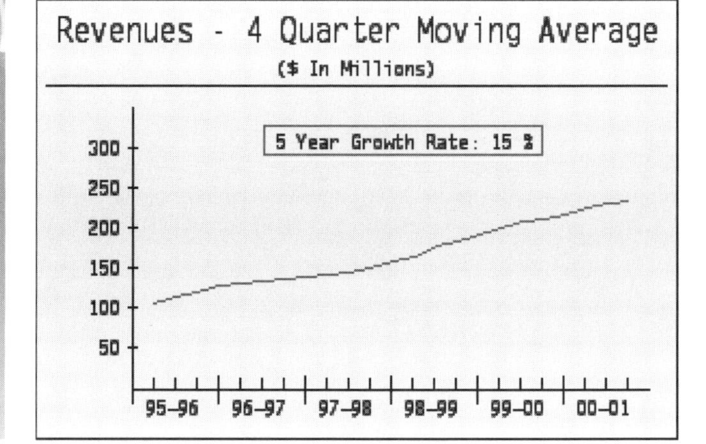

Charts provided by Baseline Financial Services.

37. BMC SOFTWARE

Symbol: BMCS
Sector: Technology (Software and Programming)

COMPANY PROFILE

BMC Software is an independent software vendor that delivers comprehensive software-management solutions. The company provides products that enhance the availability, performance, and recoverability of customers' business-critical applications. This helps them to better manage their businesses. BMC's products include PATROL, an application service-management product. It also offers Enterprise Data Availability solutions, plus a variety of OS/390 products that provide performance enhancements for batch and online processing functions, mainframe networks, and other specialized subsystems. Additionally, BMC offers professional consulting services and education programs. BMC acquired OptiSystems Solutions in 2000, and boasts such clients as Federal Express, Boeing, and the United States Postal Service.

EARNINGS

During the past 12 months, BMC Software earned $1.54 per share, down 8 percent from the previous year.

REVENUES

Revenues during the past 12 months totaled $1.7 billion, up 19 percent from a year earlier.

KEY RATIOS & MEASURES	5-YEAR RANGE	CURRENT
P/E	10–52	18.5
Price-to-Book	2.2–16.4	3.8
Price-to-Cash Flow	6.4–44.6	11.4
Price-to-Sales	2.3–12.6	4.12
Return on Equity	15.6–35.3%	23.5%
Beta		1.36

CONTACT INFORMATION
BMC Software, Inc., 2101 City West Boulevard, Houston, TX 77042-2827
(713) 918-8800
www.bmc.com

BMC Software (BMCS)

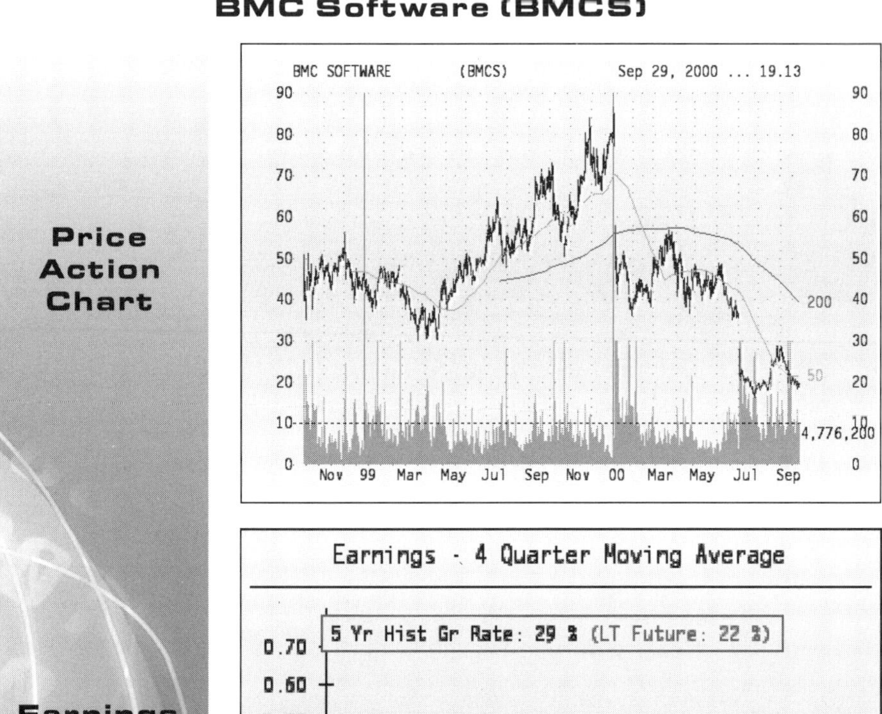

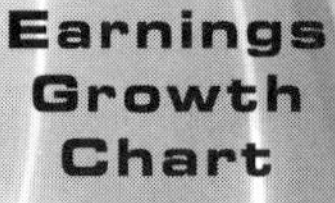

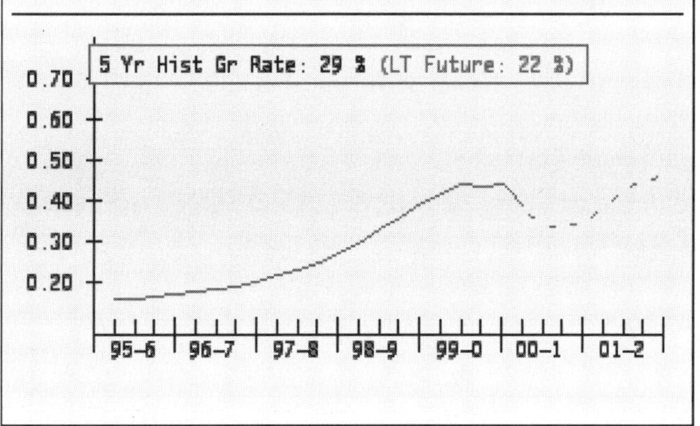

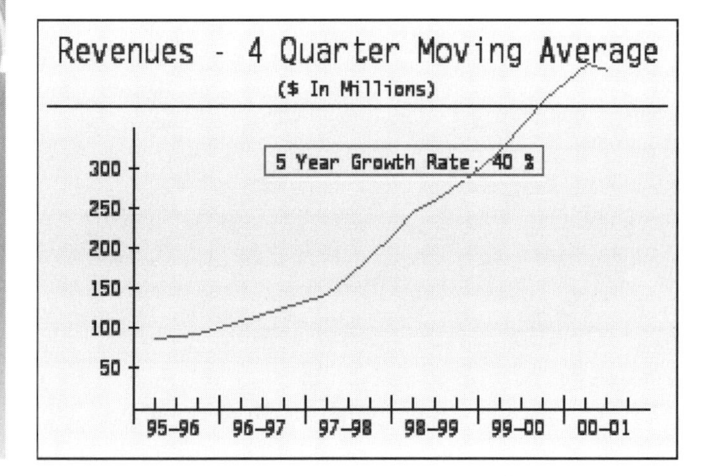

Charts provided by Baseline Financial Services.

38. BROADVISION

Symbol: BVSN
Sector: Technology (Software and Programming)

COMPANY PROFILE

BroadVision develops software applications that enable businesses to use the Internet as a platform for conducting commerce; offering online financial services; providing self-service; and delivering targeted information to their customers, suppliers, distributors, and employees. The BroadVision One-to-One product family allows companies to tailor Web site content to the needs and interests of individual users by personalizing each visit on a real-time basis. BroadVision's One-to-One applications interactively capture Web site visitor profile information, organize the enterprise's content, target that content to each visitor based on easily constructed business rules, and execute transactions. In 2000, BroadVision acquired Interleaf, a maker of management software.

EARNINGS

During the past 12 months, BroadVision earned $0.13 per share, up 200 percent from the previous year.

REVENUES

Revenues during the past 12 months totaled $230 million, up 223 percent from a year earlier.

KEY RATIOS & MEASURES	5-YEAR RANGE	CURRENT
P/E	NM	308.4
Price-to-Book	1.8–62.7	26.2
Price-to-Cash Flow	20.7–627.5	262.7
Price-to-Sales	2.9–122.8	42.37
Return on Equity	5.2–8.8%	5.2%
Beta		1.79

NM, Not Meaningful

CONTACT INFORMATION

BroadVision, Inc., 585 Broadway Street, Redwood City, CA 94063-3122
(650) 261-5100
www.broadvision.com

BroadVision (BVSN)

Price Action Chart

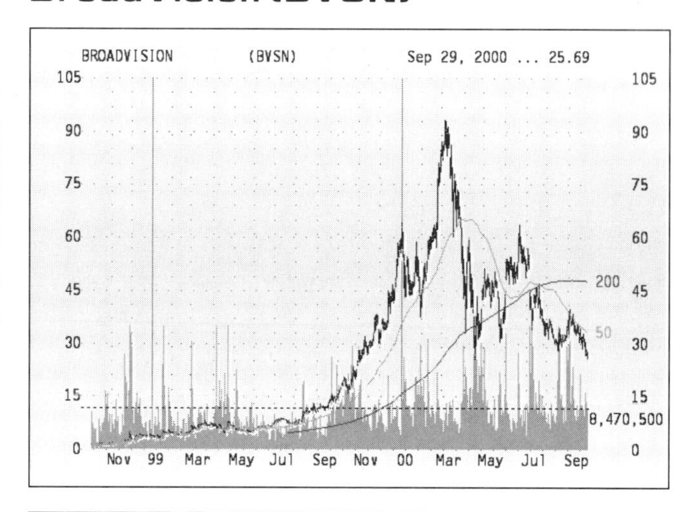

Earnings Growth Chart

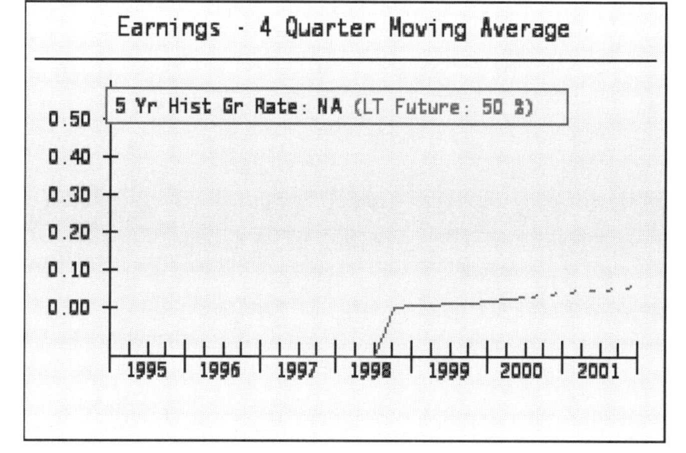

Revenue Growth Chart

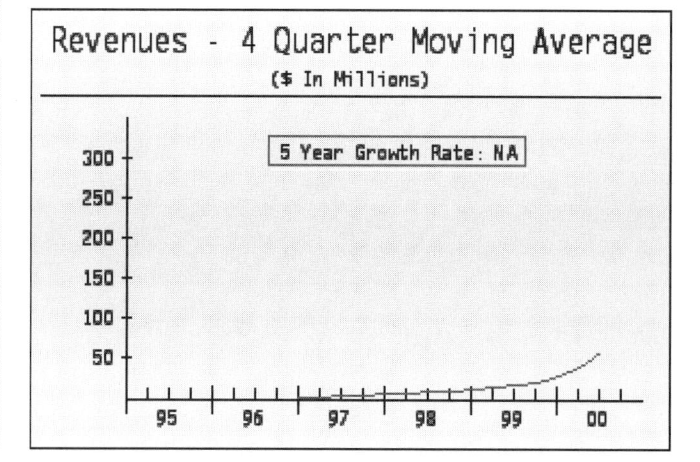

Charts provided by Baseline Financial Services.

39. CHECK POINT SOFTWARE TECHNOLOGIES

Symbol: CHKP
Sector: Technology (Software and Programming)

COMPANY PROFILE

Check Point Software Technologies develops, markets, and supports policy-based network security software for enterprise networks, including virtual private networks (VPNs), firewalls, intranet and extranet security, and managed service provider (MSP) management. The company's solutions, including its Check Point Firewall-1 enterprise suite and VPN-1 family of VPN software, enable secure, reliable, and manageable business-to-business communications over virtually any Internet Protocol (IP) network. Check Point Software also offers traffic control and quality-of-service and IP address management software. The company's products provide for centralized management, distributed deployment, and comprehensive policy administration.

EARNINGS

During the past 12 months, Check Point Software Technologies earned $0.78 per share, up 60 percent from the previous year.

REVENUES

Revenues during the past 12 months totaled $295 million, up 74 percent from a year earlier.

KEY RATIOS & MEASURES	5-YEAR RANGE	CURRENT
P/E	6–255	203.2
Price-to-Book	2.2–68.8	66.3
Price-to-Cash Flow	5.7–204.6	197.2
Price-to-Sales	2.9–84.3	81.24
Return on Equity	26.4–51%	39%
Beta		1.66

CONTACT INFORMATION

Check Point Software Technologies Ltd., 3A Jabotinsky St., Diamond Tower, Ramat Gan, 52520, Israel
011-972-3-753-4555—U.S. Investor Contact: (650) 628-2000
www.checkpoint.com

Check Point (CHKP)

Price Action Chart

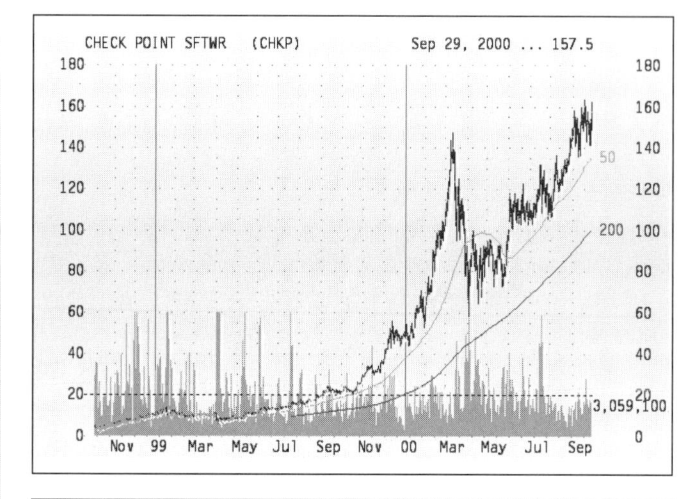

Earnings Growth Chart

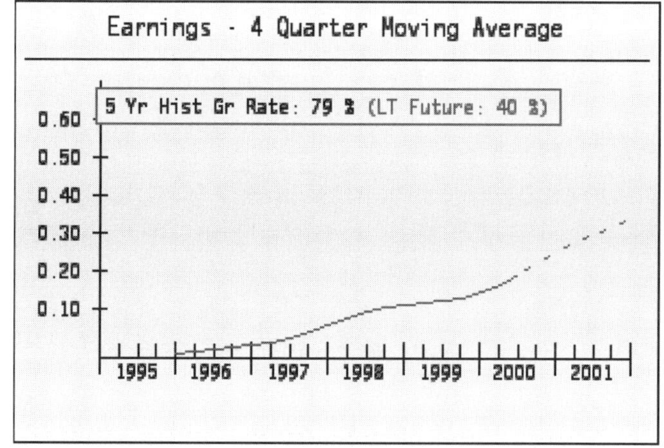

Revenue Growth Chart

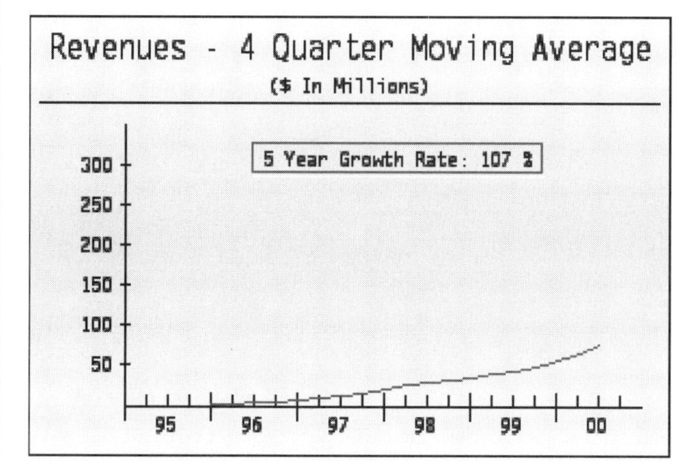

Charts provided by Baseline Financial Services.

40. CHIRON

Symbol: CHIR
Sector: Healthcare (Biotechnology and Drugs)

COMPANY PROFILE

Chiron is a biotechnology company that focuses primarily on infectious diseases, cancer, and cardiovascular diseases. Chiron's products include Proleukin, a treatment for certain metastatic skin and kidney cancers; a human-platelet-derived growth factor for the treatment of diabetic foot ulcers; Betaseron, a treatment for multiple sclerosis; and a line of adult and pediatric vaccines marketed in Europe, the Middle East, Africa, and Latin America. Chiron conducts part of its research and development effort in collaboration with third parties it feels can contribute significant enabling technologies and other resources to the development and commercialization of new products. Novartis AG owns 44 percent of the company's outstanding shares. In August 2000, Chiron agreed to acquire Pathogenesis.

EARNINGS

During the past 12 months, Chiron earned $0.81 per share, up 25 percent from the previous year.

REVENUES

Revenues during the past 12 months totaled $856 million, up 6 percent from a year earlier.

KEY RATIOS & MEASURES	5-YEAR RANGE	CURRENT
P/E	31–155	66.9
Price-to-Book	1.6–7.3	5.5
Price-to-Cash Flow	12.6–59.6	45.4
Price-to-Sales	2.5–15	11.38
Return on Equity	6.2–8.4%	8.4%
Beta		0.82

CONTACT INFORMATION
Chiron Corporation, 4560 Horton Street, Emeryville, CA 94608-2916
(510) 655-8730
www.chiron.com

Chiron (CHIR)

Price Action Chart

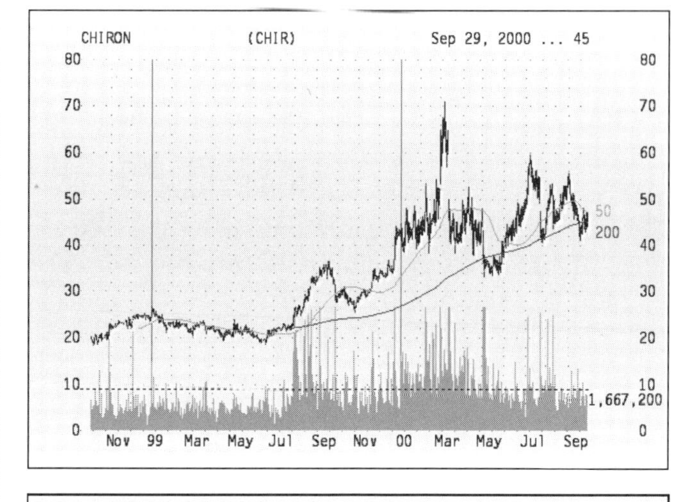

Earnings Growth Chart

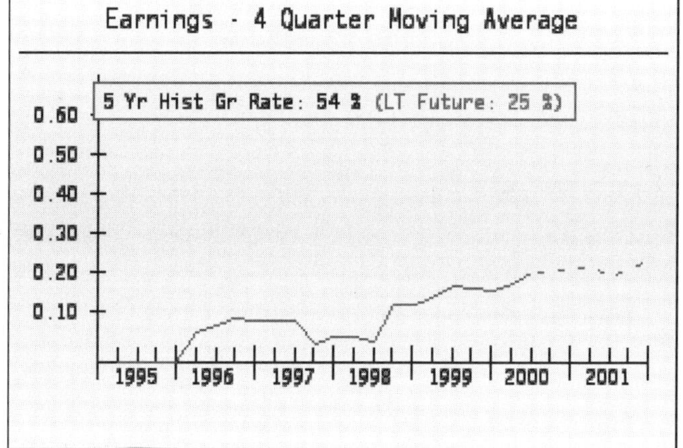

Revenue Growth Chart

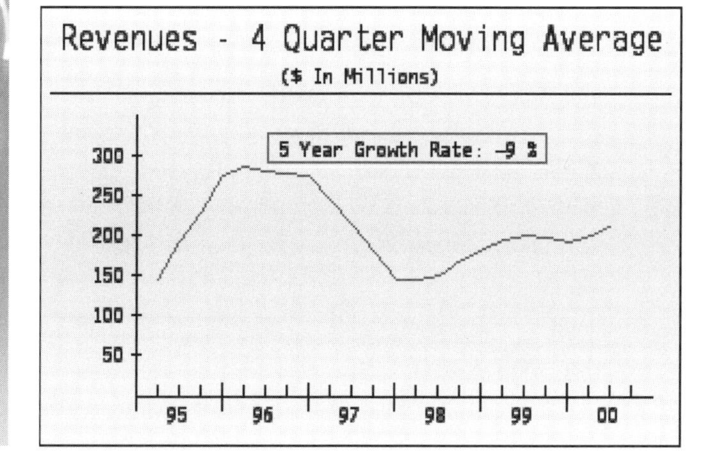

Charts provided by Baseline Financial Services.

41. CIENA

Symbol: CIEN
Sector: Technology (Communications Equipment)

COMPANY PROFILE

CIENA designs and manufactures optical networking equipment for telecommunications and data-communications service providers. Although CIENA earns the majority of its revenues from the sale of long-distance optical transport equipment (such as the MultiWave Sentry 4000 and MultiWave CoreStream systems), its comprehensive portfolio of products also includes intelligent switching and multiservice delivery systems that enable providers to provide, manage, and deliver high-bandwidth services to their customers. CIENA's clients include long-distance carriers, competitive local exchange carriers, Internet service providers, and wholesale carriers. To build its business, CIENA recently acquired both Lightera Networks and Omnia Communications.

EARNINGS

During the past 12 months, CIENA earned $0.20 per share.

REVENUES

Revenues during the past 12 months totaled $713 million, up 65 percent from a year earlier.

KEY RATIOS & MEASURES	5-YEAR RANGE	CURRENT
P/E	9–575.3	575.3
Price-to-Book	1.7–54.7	54.7
Price-to-Cash Flow	7.3–297.8	297.7
Price-to-Sales	1.8–45.3	45.20
Return on Equity	9.4–55.2%	9.4%
Beta		1.36

CONTACT INFORMATION

CIENA Corporation, 1201 Winterson Road, Linthicum, MD 21090
(410) 865-8500
www.ciena.com

CIENA (CIEN)

Price Action Chart

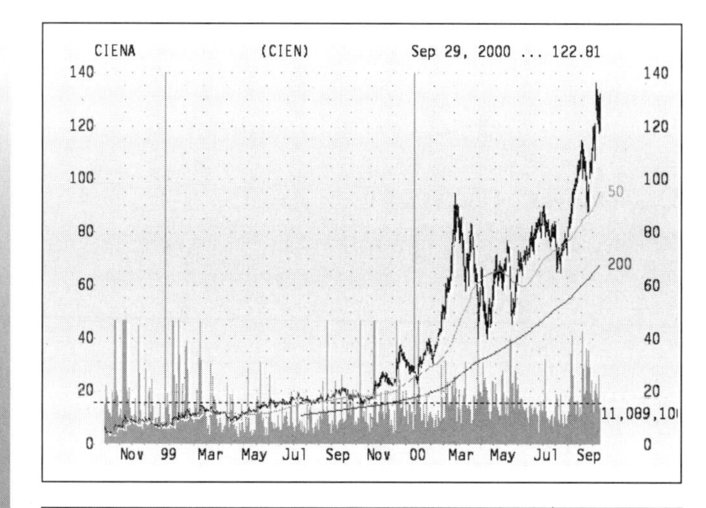

Earnings Growth Chart

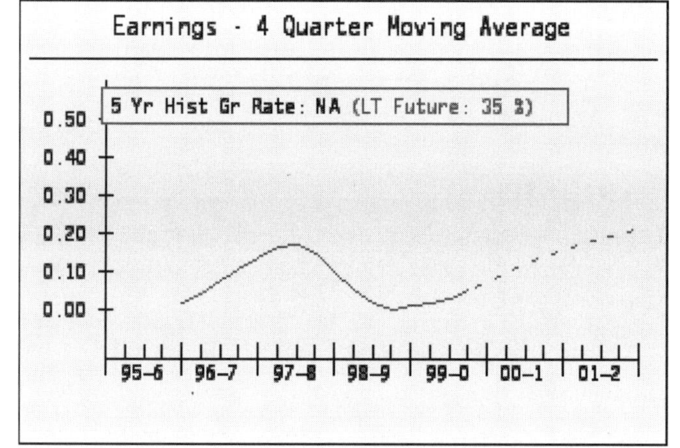

Revenue Growth Chart

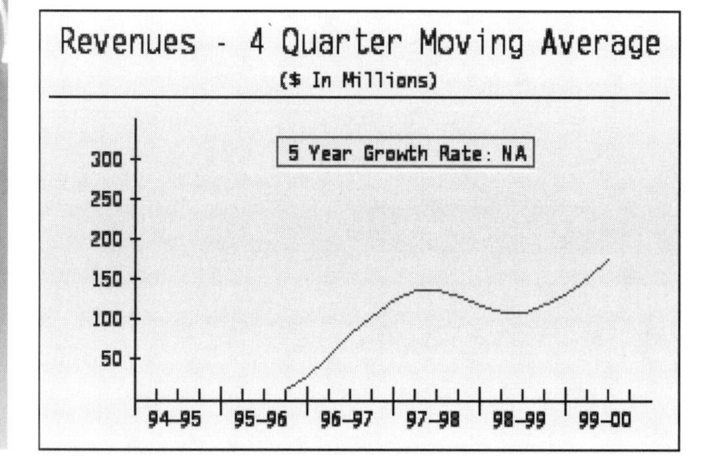

Charts provided by Baseline Financial Services.

42. CINTAS

Symbol: CTAS
Sector: Services (Personal Services)

COMPANY PROFILE

Cintas designs, manufactures, and implements corporate identity uniform programs throughout the United States for businesses of all types. Its customers range from small service and manufacturing companies to major corporations employing thousands of people. Cintas also offers uniform rental, cleaning, and upgrading services to each client. In addition, Cintas offers ancillary services, including the rental or sale of walk-off mats, fender covers, towels, mops, linen products, and first-aid products and services. Cintas owns and operates 13 manufacturing facilities in five U.S. states and three Latin American countries. These facilities meet a substantial part of its standard uniform needs. During the past year, Cintas acquired Unitog Company, which sells and rents industrial uniforms.

EARNINGS

During the past 12 months, Cintas earned $1.14 per share, up 19 percent from the previous year.

REVENUES

Revenues during the past 12 months totaled $1.9 billion, up 9 percent from a year earlier.

KEY RATIOS & MEASURES	5-YEAR RANGE	CURRENT
P/E	22–60	36.9
Price-to-Book	3.7–11.4	6.8
Price-to-Cash Flow	13.8–41.4	25.1
Price-to-Sales	2–4.9	3.7
Return on Equity	18.2–21.3%	21.3%
Beta		0.81

CONTACT INFORMATION

Cintas Corporation, 6800 Cintas Boulevard, Cincinnati, OH 45262-5737
(513) 459-1200
www.cintas-corp.com

Cintas (CTAS)

Price Action Chart

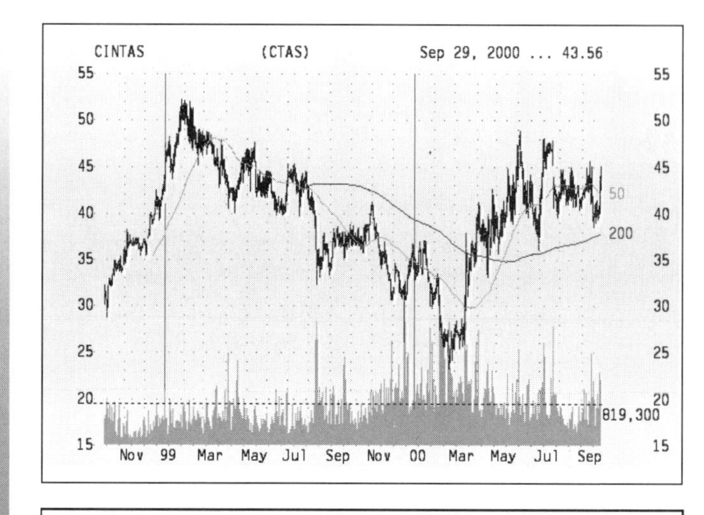

Earnings Growth Chart

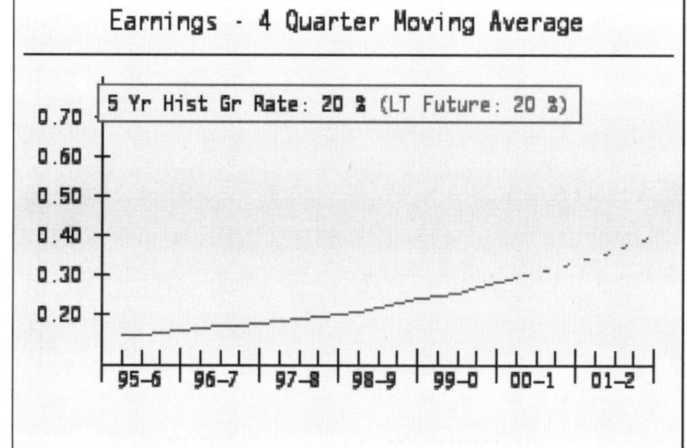

Revenue Growth Chart

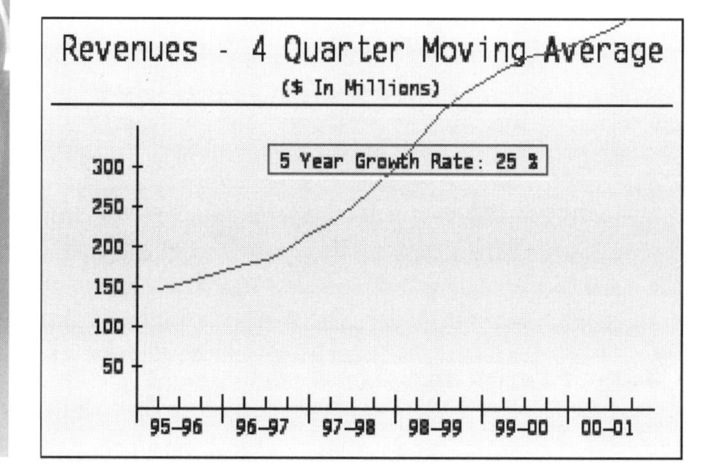

Charts provided by Baseline Financial Services.

43. CITRIX SYSTEMS

Symbol: CTXS
Sector: Technology (Software and Programming)

COMPANY PROFILE

Citrix Systems develops, markets, sells, and supports client and application server software designed to enable the efficient enterprise-wide deployment of Windows business applications. The company's MetaFrame and WinFrame product lines, developed under license agreements with Microsoft, allow organizations to execute Windows applications on a multiuser server. These products also provide end-users with access to the server from a variety of client platforms through the company's Independent Computing Architecture (ICA) protocol. This approach minimizes the communications, memory, and processing requirements of client systems, providing a scalable, bandwidth-independent solution for deployment of Windows applications across a range of platforms and network environments.

EARNINGS

During the past 12 months, Citrix Systems earned $0.68 per share, up 23 percent from the previous year.

REVENUES

Revenues during the past 12 months totaled $457 million, up 42 percent from a year earlier.

KEY RATIOS & MEASURES	5-YEAR RANGE	CURRENT
P/E	12–309	33.3
Price-to-Book	1.3–37.6	6.9
Price-to-Cash Flow	6.2–148.5	27.3
Price-to-Sales	2.1–49.5	9.11
Return on Equity	20.2–28.1%	22.9%
Beta		1.76

CONTACT INFORMATION

Citrix Systems, Inc., 6400 Northwest 6th Way, Fort Lauderdale, FL 33309
(954) 267-3000
www.citrix.com

Citrix Systems (CTXS)

Price Action Chart

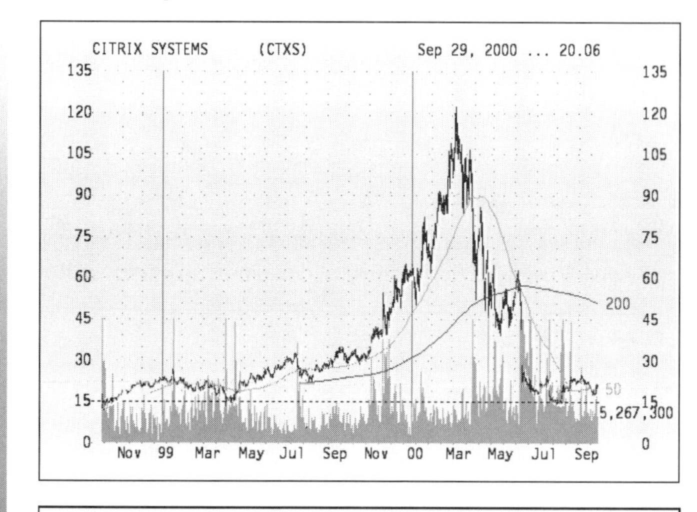

Earnings Growth Chart

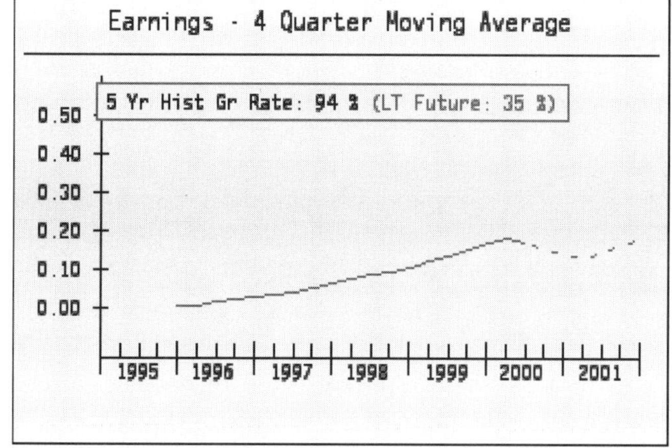

Revenue Growth Chart

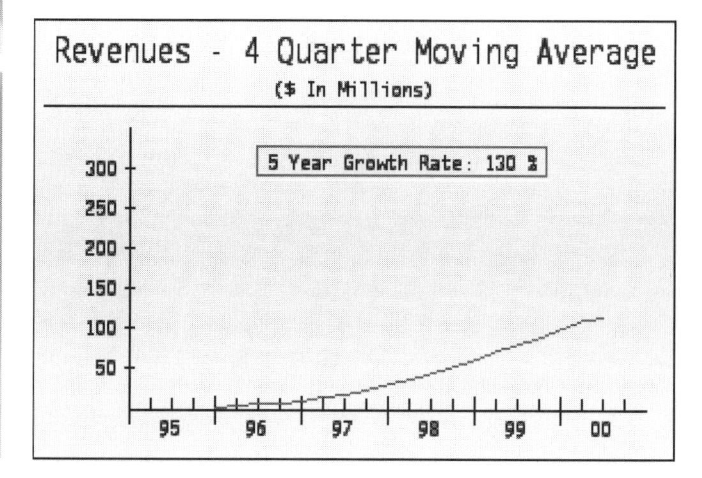

Charts provided by Baseline Financial Services.

44. CMGI

Symbol: CMGI
Sector: Financial (Miscellaneous Financial Services)

COMPANY PROFILE

CMGI develops, operates, and invests in a broad array of Internet companies. The company has 15 majority-owned subsidiaries, including Activerse, Adsmart, AltaVista Blaxxun, CMGI Solutions, Engage, iCAST, Magnitude Network, MyWay.com, Nascent, NaviNet, Navisite, Netwright, Signatures Network, and ZineZone. It develops and operates these companies, and promotes opportunities for synergistic relationships among them. CMGI also runs three Internet venture funds that hold equity investments in more than 30 online companies. The company provides fulfillment services through three wholly-owned subsidiaries, with product and literature fulfillment, turnkey outsourcing, telemarketing, and sales/lead inquiry management. CMGI continues to expand through acquisition. Its most recent conquests include AdForce, Yesmailcom, AdKnowledge, Flycast Communications, Tallan, and Ubid.com.

EARNINGS

During the past 12 months, CMGI lost $0.87 per share, down 422 percent from the previous year.

REVENUES

Revenues during the past 12 months totaled $557 million, up 276 percent from a year earlier.

KEY RATIOS & MEASURES	5-YEAR RANGE	CURRENT
P/E	4–306	NM
Price-to-Book	1.5–59.5	16.7
Price-to-Cash Flow	4.7–90.7	NM
Price-to-Sales	1.3–94.1	24.3
Return on Equity	NA	NM
Beta		2.55

NM, Not Meaningful; NA, Not Applicable

CONTACT INFORMATION

CMGI, Inc., 100 Brickstone Square, Andover, MA 01810
(978) 684-3600
www.cmgi.com

CMGI (CMGI)

Price Action Chart

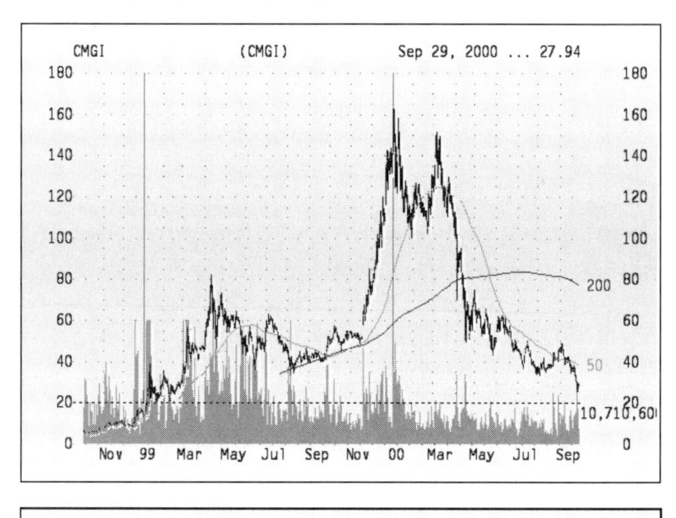

Earnings Growth Chart

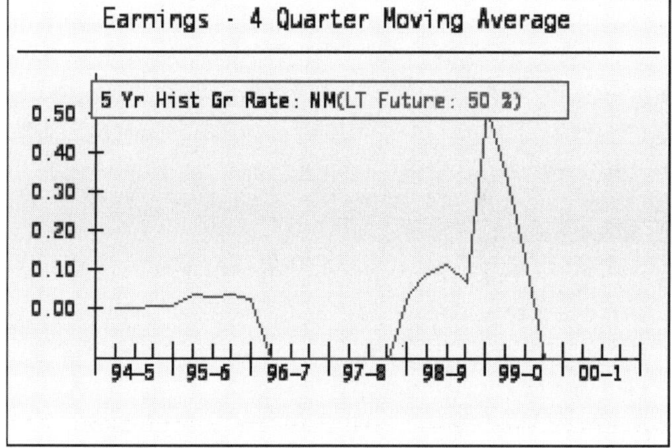

Revenue Growth Chart

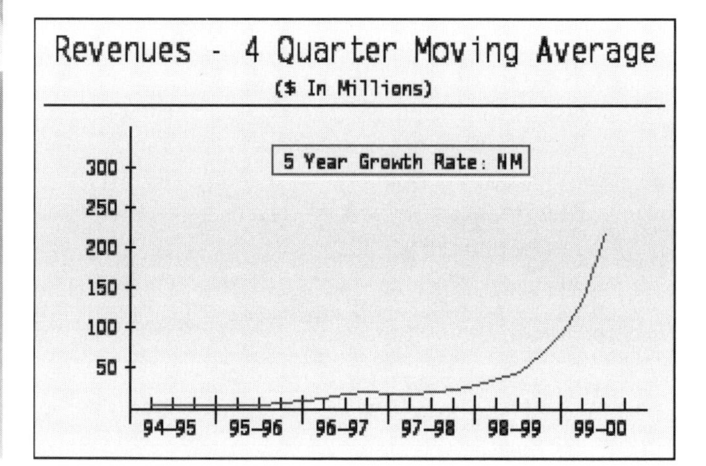

Charts provided by Baseline Financial Services.

45. CNET NETWORKS

Symbol: CNET
Sector: Technology (Computer Services)

COMPANY PROFILE

CNET Networks is a global media company. It operates a branded Internet network, and creates television and radio programming for both consumers and businesses. CNET's online division produces a network of information and services through its CNET.com gateway. This portal is for users interested in news and information about technology. CNET also provides shopping services, which are designed to link buyers and sellers of technology products and services. CNET Data Services offers online computer retailers, systems integrators, and others a multilingual database of computer product images, descriptions, and specifications. CNET's television division produces two television shows, CNET News.com and TV.com. CNET and AMFM Inc. jointly produce CNET Radio, an all-technology radio format. In an effort to expand its media presence, CNET agreed to buy ZDNet in the summer of 2000.

EARNINGS

During the past 12 months, CNET lost $0.67 per share, down 494 percent from the previous year.

REVENUES

Revenues during the past 12 months totaled $164 million, up 106 percent from a year earlier.

KEY RATIOS & MEASURES	5-YEAR RANGE	CURRENT
P/E	NM	NM
Price-to-Book	1.2–16.8	3.5
Price-to-Cash Flow	123.5–393.7	NM
Price-to-Sales	6.8–52.3	17.66
Return on Equity	NA	NM
Beta		1.28

NM, Not Meaningful; NA, Not Applicable

CONTACT INFORMATION

CNET Networks, Inc., 150 Chestnut Street, San Francisco, CA 94111
(415) 364-8000
www.cnet.com

CNET Networks (CNET)

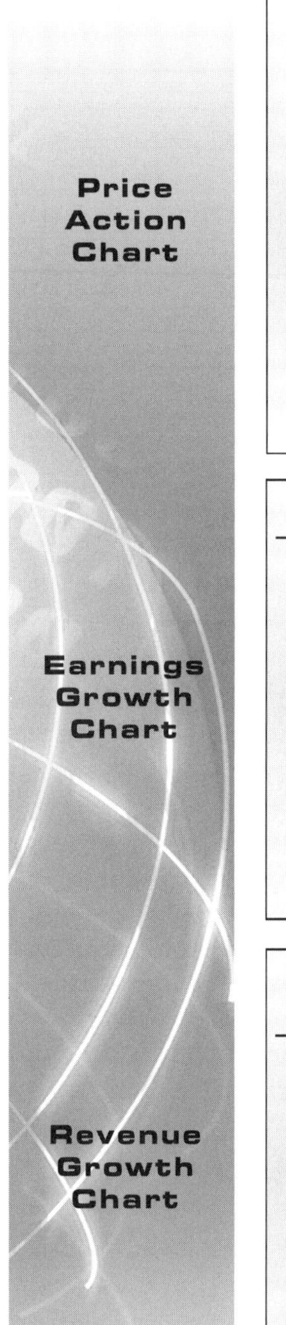

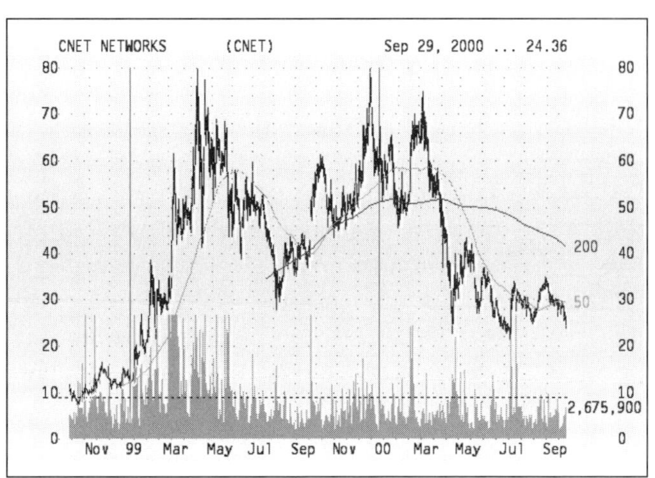

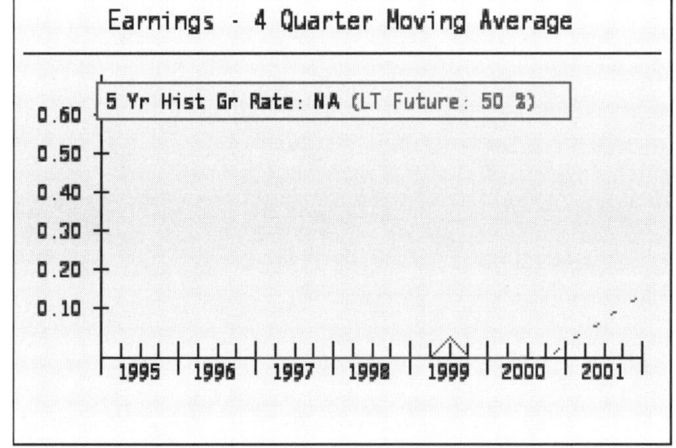

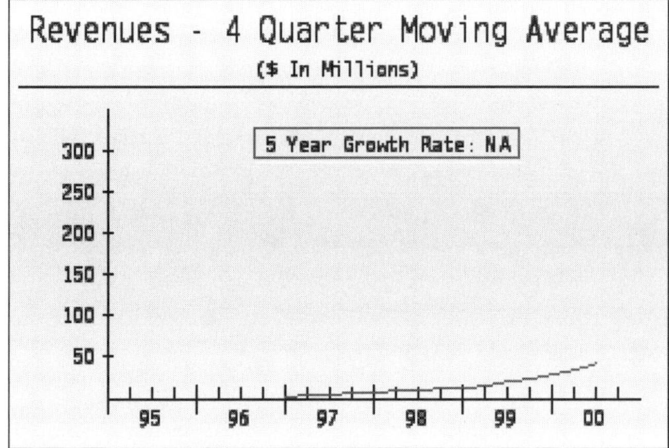

Charts provided by Baseline Financial Services.

46. COMCAST

Symbol: CMCSK
Sector: Service (Broadcasting and Cable Television)

COMPANY PROFILE

Comcast operates hybrid fiber-coaxial broadband cable communications networks. Comcast's consolidated cable operations, which serve some 5.7 million subscribers, provide access to national television networks, specialty television stations, satellite-delivered programming, locally-originated programs, and premium movie channels. Comcast also offers retailing services through its QVC subsidiary, and programming content through its Comcast-Spectacor, Comcast SportsNet, and E! Entertainment Television divisions. In addition, Comcast provides Internet access via cable modem in certain markets through Comcast@Home, its joint venture with Excite@Home. During 2000, Comcast acquired both Lenfest Communications and Jones Intercable.

EARNINGS

During the past 12 months, Comcast lost $0.19 per share, up 47 percent from the previous year.

REVENUES

Revenues during the past 12 months totaled $7.1 billion, up 29 percent from a year earlier.

KEY RATIOS & MEASURES	5-YEAR RANGE	CURRENT
P/E	NM	NM
Price-to-Book	2.1–11.9	2.9
Price-to-Cash Flow	7–47.9	32.5
Price-to-Sales	1.7–7.1	4.77
Return on Equity	11–36.9%	NM
Beta		1.08

NM, Not Meaningful

CONTACT INFORMATION

Comcast Corporation, 1500 Market Street, 35th Floor, Philadelphia, PA 19102-2148
(215) 665-1700
www.comcast.com

Comcast (CMCSK)

Price Action Chart

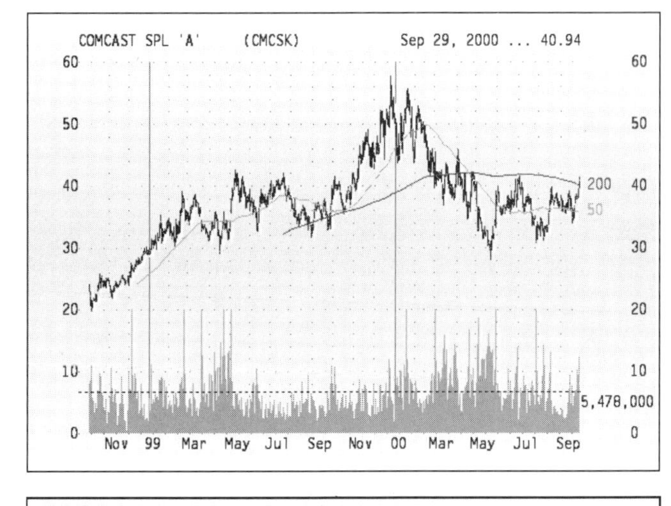

Earnings Growth Chart

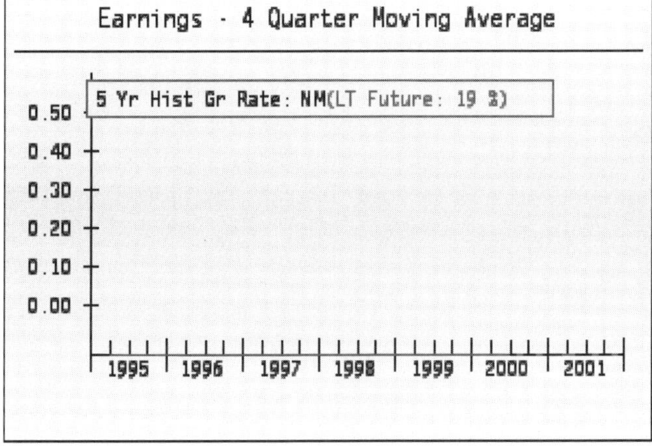

Revenue Growth Chart

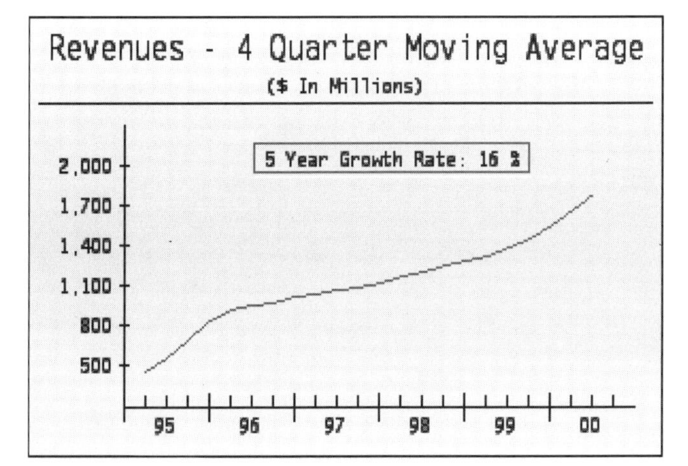

Charts provided by Baseline Financial Services.

47. COMPUWARE

Symbol: CPWR
Sector: Technology (Software and Programming)

COMPANY PROFILE

Compuware provides software products and professional services designed to increase the productivity of the information systems departments of various enterprises. The company provides mainframe testing tools, including file and data management tools, fault management tools, automated testing tools, and interactive analysis and debugging tools. It also offers mainframe application management tools, distributed systems application development tools, distributed and Web testing file and data management tools, Numega (which accelerates team development of multilanguage components), and application performance management tools. Compuware markets its products in North America, Europe, Asia, Brazil, and South Africa. The company also owns Nomex, Inc.

EARNINGS

During the past 12 months, Compuware earned $0.87 per share, up 32 percent from the previous year.

REVENUES

Revenues during the past 12 months totaled $2.3 billion, up 32 percent from a year earlier.

KEY RATIOS & MEASURES	5-YEAR RANGE	CURRENT
P/E	8–60	12
Price-to-Book	2–20.3	3.1
Price-to-Cash Flow	6.8–65.3	9.8
Price-to-Sales	0.8–9.9	1.63
Return on Equity	25.5–39.1%	30%
Beta		1.3

CONTACT INFORMATION

Compuware Corp., 31440 North Western Highway, Farmington Hills, MI 48334-2564
(248) 737-7300
www.compuware.com

Compuware (CPWR)

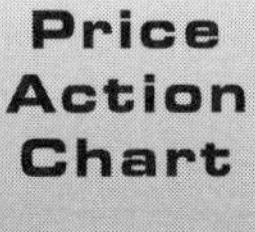

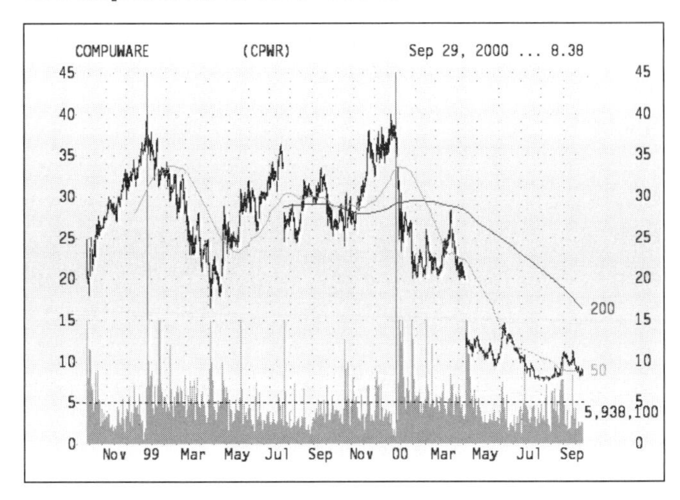

Earnings
Growth
Chart

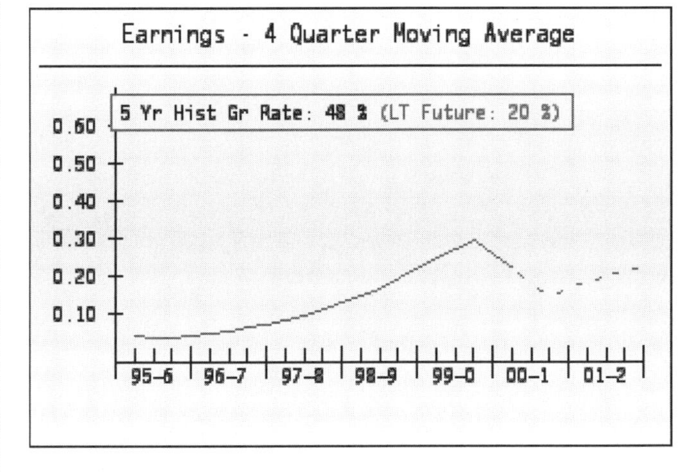

Revenue
Growth
Chart

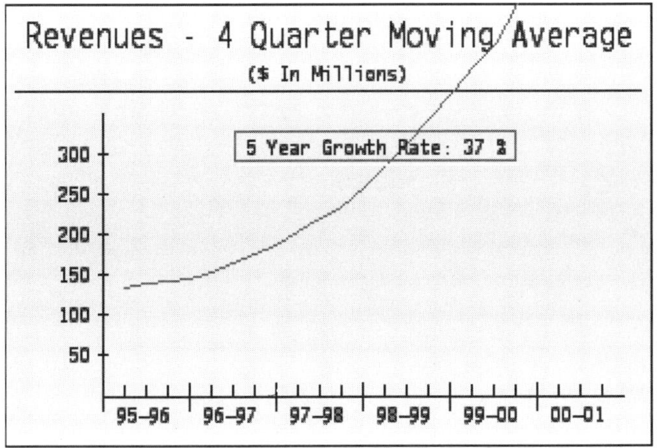

Charts provided by Baseline Financial Services.

48. CONCORD EFS

Symbol: CEFT
Sector: Financial (Consumer Financial Services)

COMPANY PROFILE

Concord EFS provides electronic transaction authorization, processing, settlement, and funds transfer services around the nation. The company offers services for credit card, debit card, and electronic benefits card transactions to supermarket chains, convenience stores, grocery stores, and other retailers. Concord EFS also offers check verification services to retail merchants, and electronic payment and banking facilities to truck-stop customers. The company provides fuel purchase cards, ATM bank cards, and general banking services to truck drivers, plus payroll deposit, cash forwarding, and other services to trucking companies. Most recently, the company acquired Electronic Payment Services and merged this business with its own.

EARNINGS

During the past 12 months, Concord EFS earned $0.75 per share, up 44 percent from the previous year.

REVENUES

Revenues during the past 12 months totaled $1 billion, up 43 percent from a year earlier.

KEY RATIOS & MEASURES	5-YEAR RANGE	CURRENT
P/E	24–77	41.5
Price-to-Book	3.3–12.4	8.2
Price-to-Cash Flow	14.4–52.6	29.5
Price-to-Sales	2–10.9	6.52
Return on Equity	17.6–22.5%	22.5%
Beta		1.25

CONTACT INFORMATION

Concord EFS, Inc., 2525 Horizon Lake Drive, #120, Memphis, TN 38133-8119
(901) 371-8000
www.ceft.com

Concord EFS (CEFT)

Price Action Chart

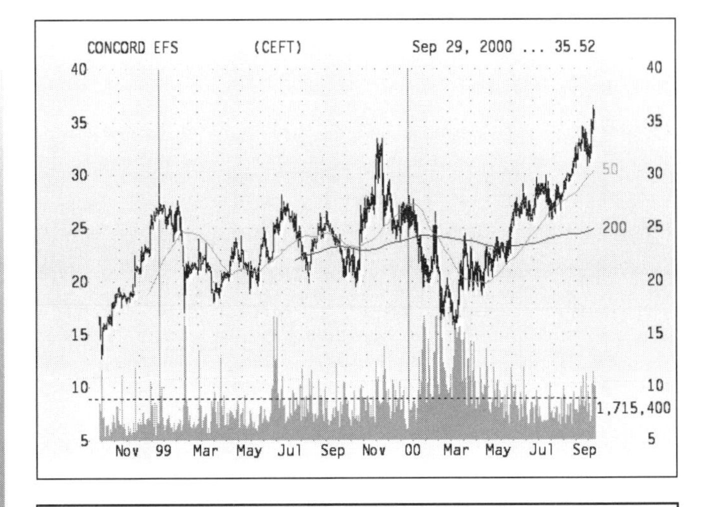

Earnings Growth Chart

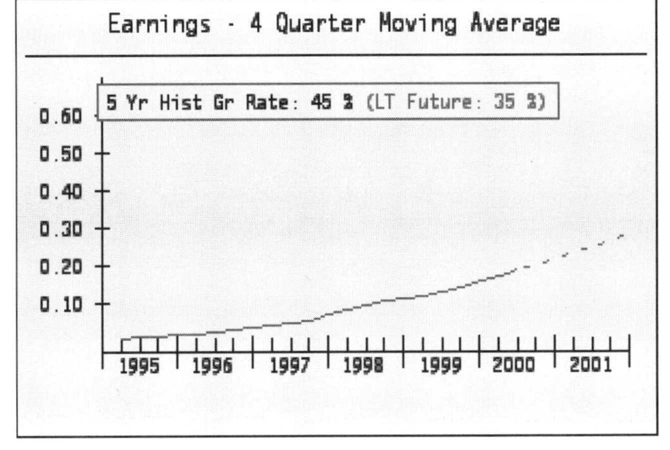

Revenue Growth Chart

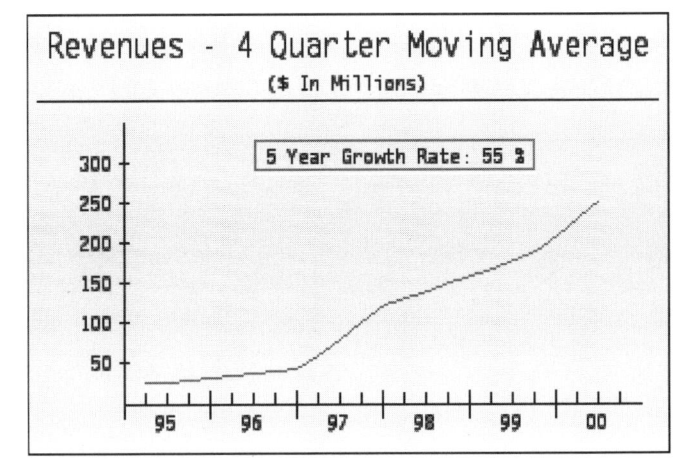

Charts provided by Baseline Financial Services.

49. CONEXANT SYSTEMS

Symbol: CNXT
Sector: Technology (Semiconductors)

COMPANY PROFILE

Conexant Systems provides semiconductor products for electronic communications. Its products facilitate communications worldwide through wireline voice and data communications networks, cordless and cellular wireless telephony systems, personal imaging devices and equipment, and cable and wireless broadband communications networks. Conexant's products span applications in personal computing, digital infotainment, wireless communications, plus personal imaging and network access infrastructure. The company has marketing, design, engineering, sales, and service offices in North America, the Asia-Pacific region, Europe, Japan, and Israel, along with manufacturing facilities in Texas, California, and Mexico. In 2000, Conexant agreed to acquire both Maker Communications and HotRail.

EARNINGS

During the past 12 months, Conexant earned $0.85 per share.

REVENUES

Revenues during the past 12 months totaled $2 billion.

KEY RATIOS & MEASURES	5-YEAR RANGE	CURRENT
P/E	31–229	44.9
Price-to-Book	1.2–22.4	6.4
Price-to-Cash Flow	4.5–69.1	19.9
Price-to-Sales	0.8–14.5	4.16
Return on Equity	1.2–9.8%	9.8%
Beta		2.14

CONTACT INFORMATION

Conexant Systems, Inc., 4311 Jamboree Road, P.O. Box C, Newport Beach, CA 92660
(949) 483-4600
www.conexant.com

Conexant (CNXT) Systems

Price Action Chart

CONEXANT SYSTEMS (CNXT) Sep 29, 2000 ... 41.88

135 120 105 90 75 60 45 30 15 0

200 50 4,709,200

Mar May Jul Sep Nov 00 Mar May Jul Sep

Earnings Growth Chart

Earnings - 4 Quarter Moving Average

5 Yr Hist Gr Rate: NA (LT Future: 25 %)

0.60 0.50 0.40 0.30 0.20 0.10

95-6 96-7 97-8 98-9 99-0 00-1 01-2

Revenue Growth Chart

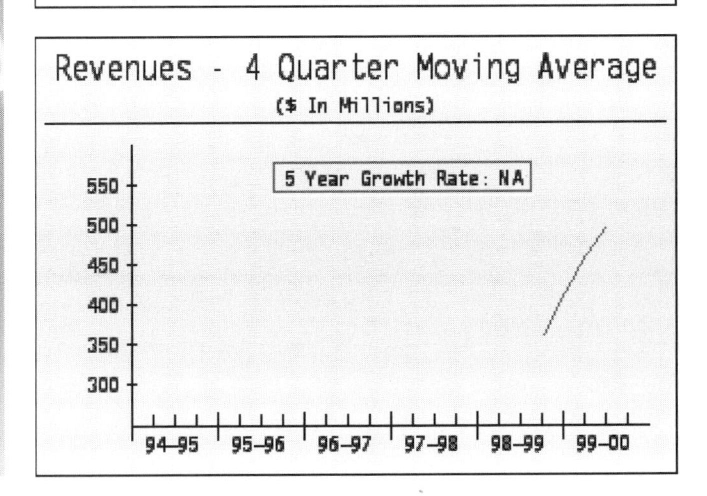

Charts provided by Baseline Financial Services.

50. COSTCO WHOLESALE

Symbol: COST
Sector: Services (Specialty Retail)

COMPANY PROFILE

Costco Wholesale operates 292 membership warehouses in the United States, Canada, the United Kingdom, Korea, Taiwan, and Japan, primarily under the Costco Wholesale name. The warehouses, which average about 132,000 square feet of floor space, offer members a variety of brand-name and private-label products at discount prices. Unlike other discount retailers, which normally stock 40,000 to 60,000 product items, Costco limits specific items in each product line to fast-selling models, sizes, and colors, carrying only 3,600 to 4,400 product items per warehouse. The company believes that operating efficiencies, high sales volume, and rapid inventory turnover enable it to operate profitably at much lower gross margins than traditional wholesalers and discount retailers.

EARNINGS

During the past 12 months, Costco Wholesale earned $1.33 per share, up 18 percent from the previous year.

REVENUES

Revenues during the past 12 months totaled $30.4 billion, up 15 percent from a year earlier.

KEY RATIOS & MEASURES	5-YEAR RANGE	CURRENT
P/E	12–47	26.7
Price-to-Book	1.6–6.8	4
Price-to-Cash Flow	7.1–33.1	19.3
Price-to-Sales	0.1–0.9	0.52
Return on Equity	14.7–16.9%	15.8%
Beta		1.13

CONTACT INFORMATION

Costco Wholesale Corporation, 999 Lake Drive, Issaquah, WA 98027
(425) 313-8100
www.costco.com

Costco Wholesale (COST)

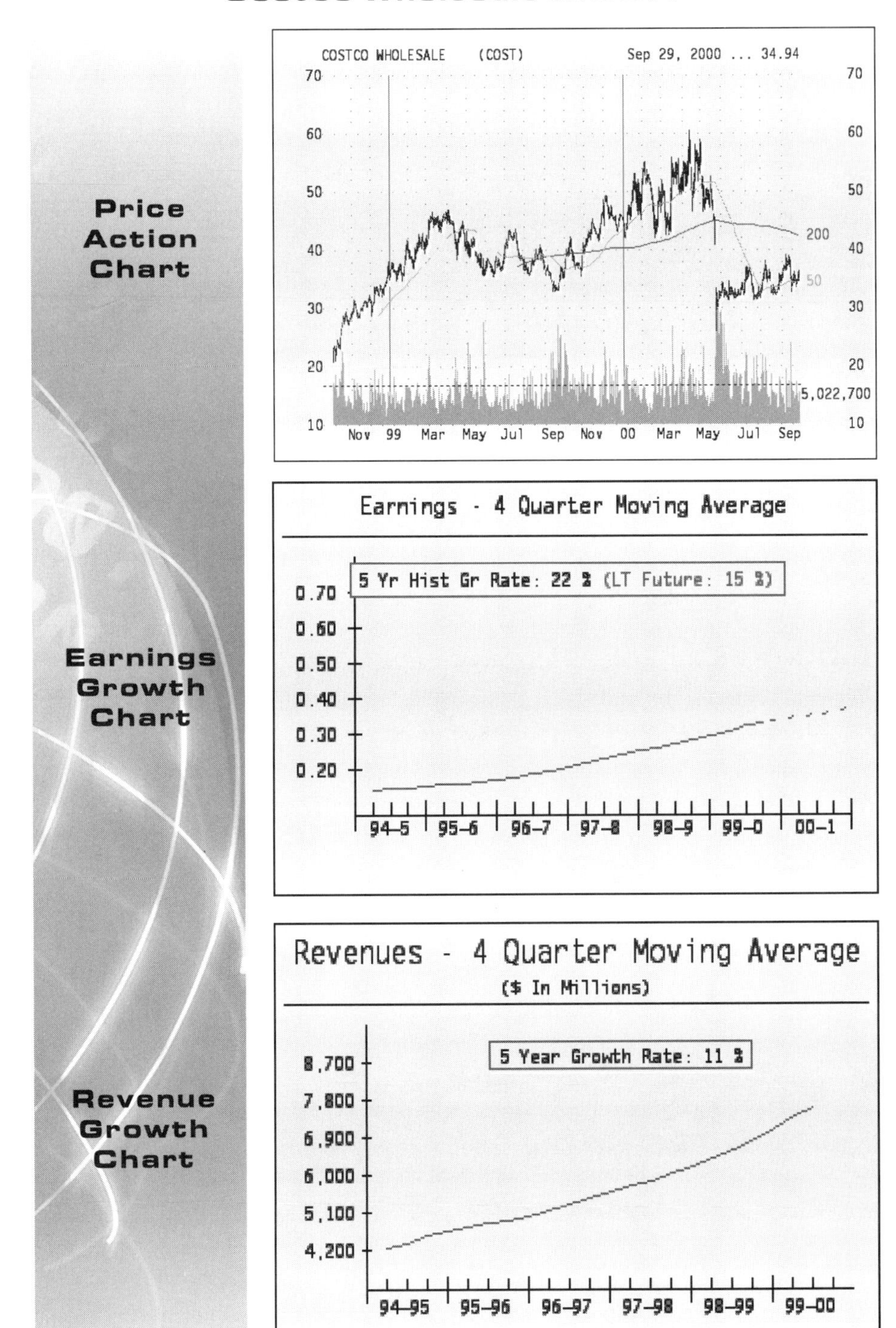

Charts provided by Baseline Financial Services.

51. DELL COMPUTER

Symbol: DELL
Sector: Technology (Computer Hardware)

COMPANY PROFILE

Dell Computer is the world's largest direct marketer of computer systems. The company offers a full range of computer systems, including desktop computers, notebook computers, workstations, network servers, and storage products. It also provides a complete selection of peripheral hardware, computing software, and related services. Dell's direct model offers in-person relationships with corporate and institutional customers, as well as telephone and Internet purchasing, built-to-order computer systems, telephone and online technical support, and onsite product service. Customers include large corporations, government entities, healthcare and educational institutions, small businesses, and individuals. Dell's www.dell.com Web site receives more than 2.6 million visits per week.

EARNINGS

During the past 12 months, Dell Computer earned $0.75 per share, up 15 percent from the previous year.

REVENUES

Revenues during the past 12 months totaled $28.5 billion, up 32 percent from a year earlier.

KEY RATIOS & MEASURES	5-YEAR RANGE	CURRENT
P/E	8–103	57.4
Price-to-Book	2.4–41.6	17.4
Price-to-Cash Flow	3.7–73.7	53.1
Price-to-Sales	0.2–5.7	3.89
Return on Equity	43.7–89.9%	45.8%
Beta		1.45

CONTACT INFORMATION

Dell Computer Corporation, 1 Dell Way, Round Rock, TX 78682-2244
(512) 338-4400
www.dell.com

Dell Computer (DELL)

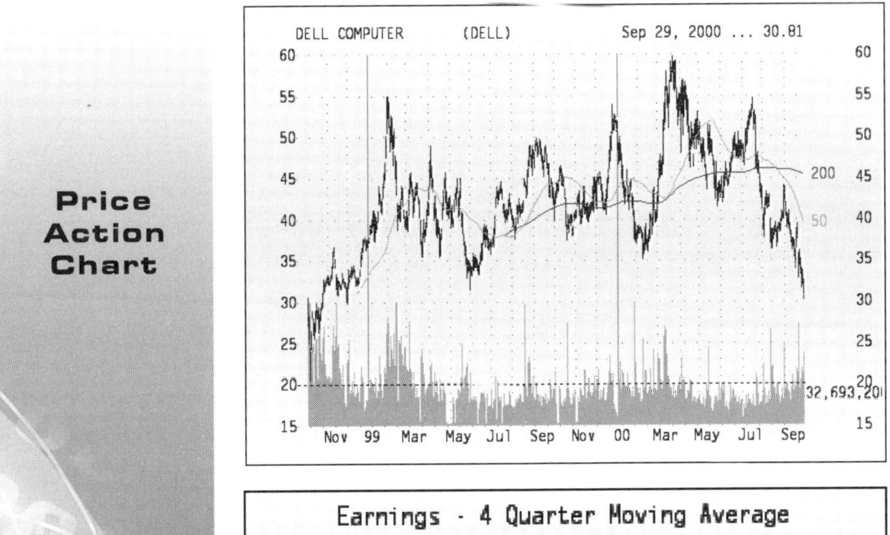

Earnings Growth Chart

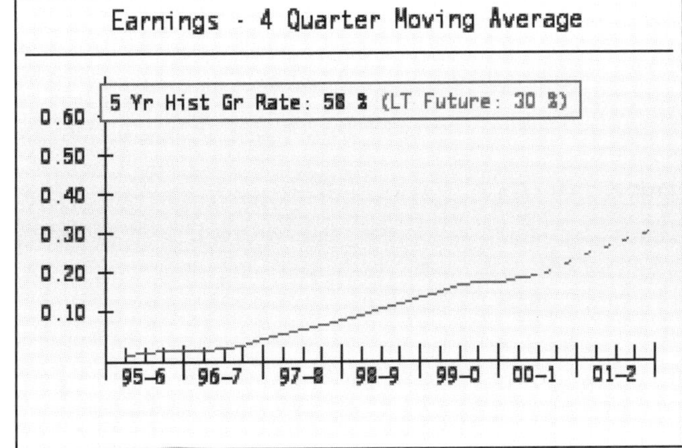

Revenue Growth Chart

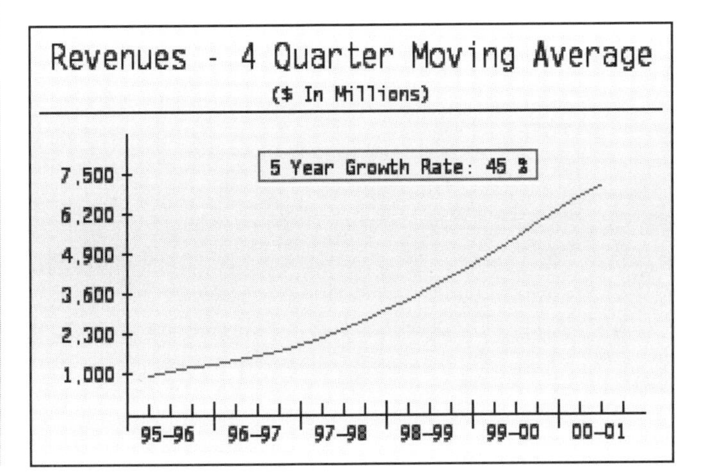

Charts provided by Baseline Financial Services.

52. eBAY

Symbol: EBAY
Sector: Services (Business Services)

COMPANY PROFILE

eBay is a person-to-person Internet trading community. The company's ten-million-plus registered users are brought together in an auction format to buy and sell items such as antiques, coins, collectibles, computers, stamps, memorabilia, and toys. The eBay service allows sellers to list items for sale, buyers to bid on items of interest, and all users to browse through the listed inventory. The company's 24-hour-a-day, seven-day-a-week, fully automated, and topically arranged service lists more than three million auctions in some 3,000 categories. Browsers and buyers can search for items by category, keyword, seller name, recently commenced auctions, or auctions about to end. The company also owns Half.com.

EARNINGS

During the past 12 months, eBay earned $0.11 per share, up 73 percent from the previous year.

REVENUES

Revenues during the past 12 months totaled $316 million, up 118 percent from a year earlier.

KEY RATIOS & MEASURES	5-YEAR RANGE	CURRENT
P/E	NM	571.6
Price-to-Book	8.4–148.7	18.7
Price-to-Cash Flow	82.7–1020	304.1
Price-to-Sales	11.8–145.5	52.29
Return on Equity	2.9–3.3%	3.3%
Beta		2.7

NM, Not Meaningful

CONTACT INFORMATION

eBay, Inc., 2145 Hamilton Avenue, San Jose, CA 95125
(408) 558-7400
www.ebay.com

eBay (EBAY)

Price Action Chart

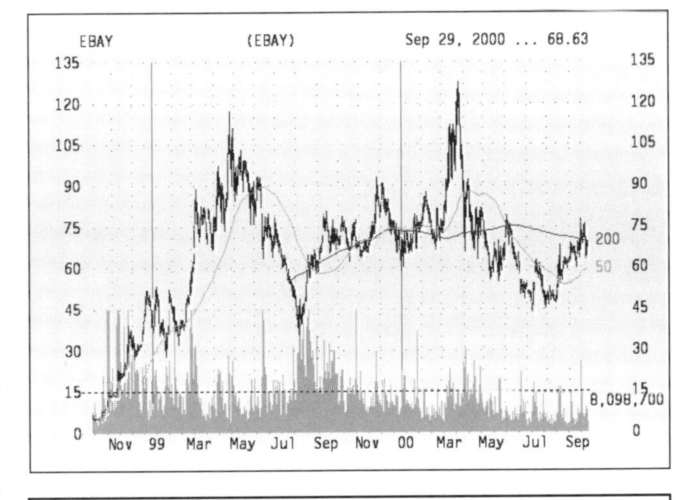

Earnings Growth Chart

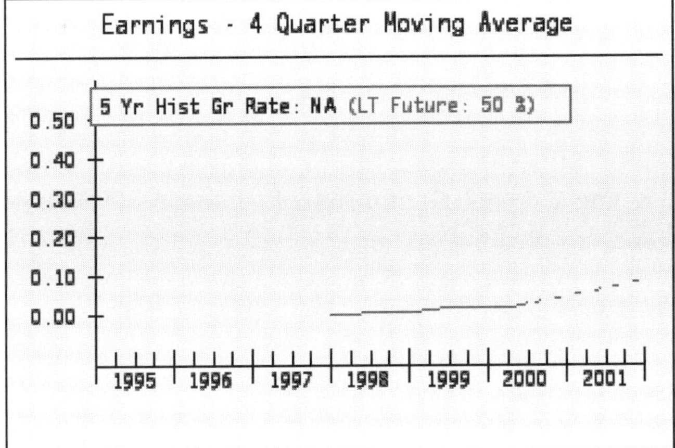

Revenue Growth Chart

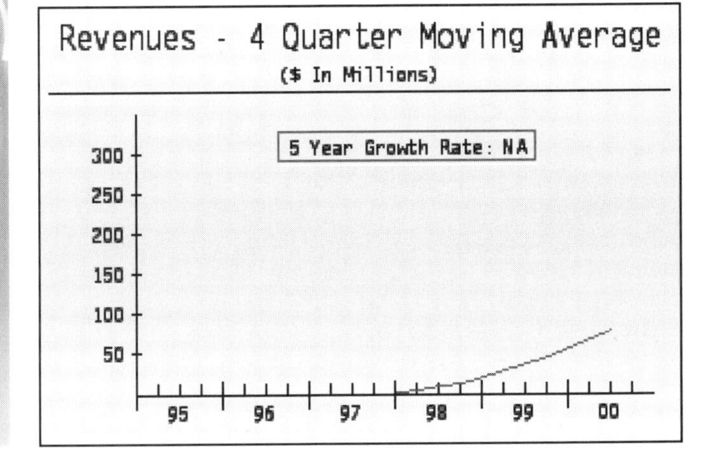

Charts provided by Baseline Financial Services.

53. ECHOSTAR COMMUNICATIONS

Symbol: DISH
Sector: Services (Broadcasting and Cable Television)

COMPANY PROFILE

EchoStar Communications operates the DISH Network, a direct broadcast satellite (DBS) subscription television service. EchoStar's five operational DBS satellites are in geostationary orbit at 22,500 miles above the equator. They provide 3.4 million DISH Network subscribers in the continental United States with more than 200 channels of digital television programming and CD-quality audio programming. EchoStar Technologies Corporation, the company's engineering division, creates the digital set-top boxes required for reception of DISH Network programming. This division also designs and supervises the construction of uplink centers for international direct-to-home ventures. EchoStar's Satellite Services division provides video, audio, and data services to business television customers and other users.

EARNINGS

During the past 12 months, EchoStar Communications lost $1.44 per share, down 44 percent from the previous year.

REVENUES

Revenues during the past 12 months totaled $2.2 billion, up 82 percent from a year earlier.

KEY RATIOS & MEASURES	5-YEAR RANGE	CURRENT
P/E	NM	NM
Price-to-Book	19–38.7	NM
Price-to-Cash Flow	412.9–836.4	NM
Price-to-Sales	0.7–17.9	11.65
Return on Equity	NA	NM
Beta		1.67

NM, Not Meaningful; NA, Not Applicable

CONTACT INFORMATION

EchoStar Communications Corporation, 5701 S. Santa Fe Drive, Littleton, CO 80120
(303) 723-1000
www.echostar.com

EchoStar Communications (DISH)

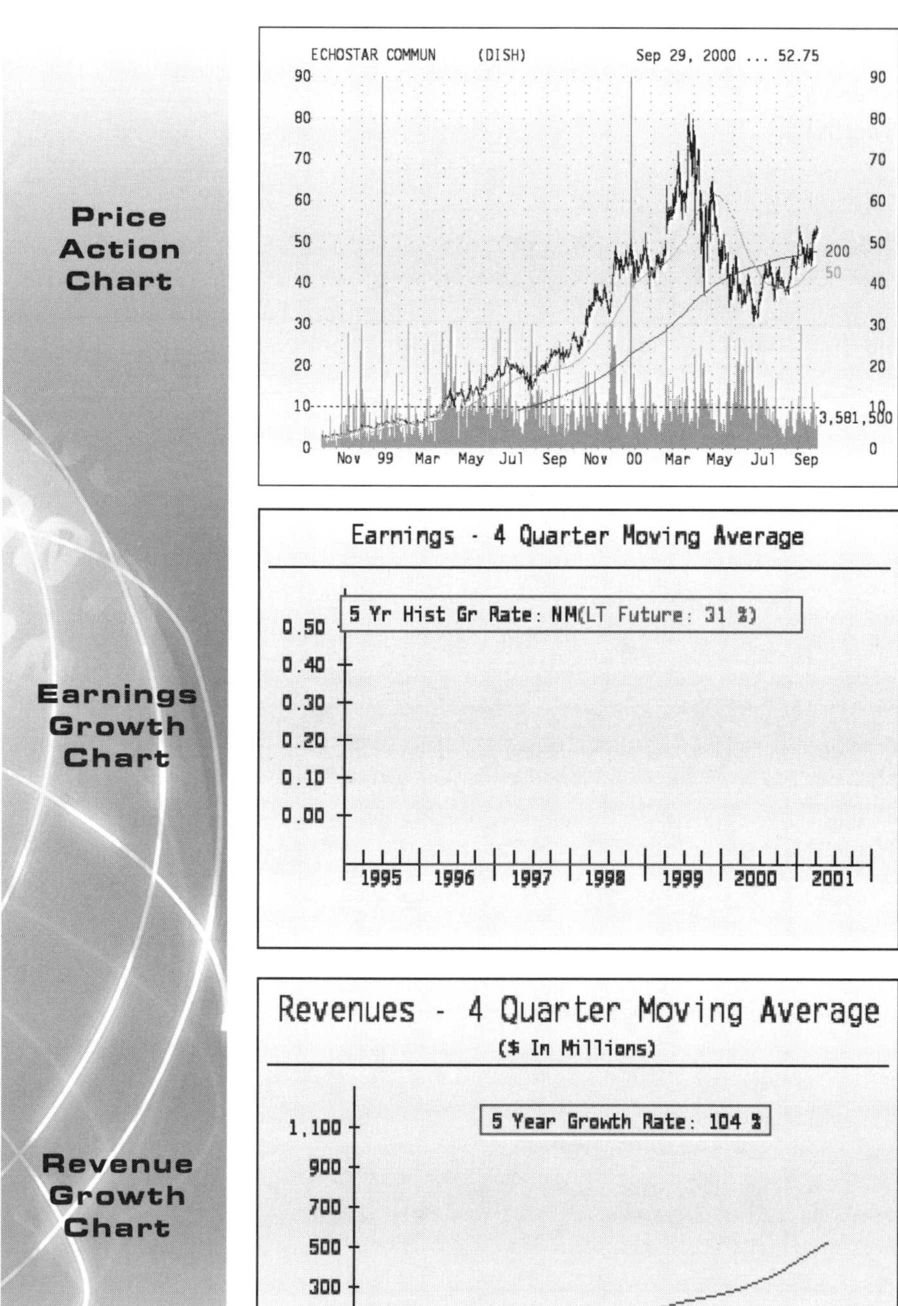

Charts provided by Baseline Financial Services.

54. ELECTRONIC ARTS

Symbol: ERTS
Sector: Technology (Software and Programming)

COMPANY PROFILE

Electronic Arts creates and distributes interactive entertainment software for a variety of hardware platforms. The company distributes some 110 of its own titles and about 20 titles developed by others in North America. Its most popular products include FIFA: Road to World Cup, NBA Live, NASCAR, Madden NFL, and NHL. The company also distributes more than 1,000 additional titles abroad. Electronic Arts has developed products for 38 different computer hardware platforms, including IBM-compatible personal computers, the 16-bit Sega Genesis video game system, the 16-bit Super Nintendo Entertainment System, the Sony PlayStation and PlayStation II, and Nintendo 64. In 2000, Electronic Arts acquired Kesmai from News America.

EARNINGS

During the past 12 months, Electronic Arts earned $122 per share, down 29 percent from the previous year.

REVENUES

Revenues during the past 12 months totaled $1.4 billion, up 13 percent from a year earlier.

KEY RATIOS & MEASURES	5-YEAR RANGE	CURRENT
P/E	16–91	89.3
Price-to-Book	2.6–11.5	8.7
Price-to-Cash Flow	15.5–59.2	56
Price-to-Sales	1.3–5.7	5.04
Return on Equity	10–15.2%	10%
Beta		1.11

CONTACT INFORMATION

Electronic Arts, Inc., 209 Redwood Shores Parkway, Redwood City, CA 94065
(650) 628-1500
www.ea.com

Electronic Arts (ERTS)

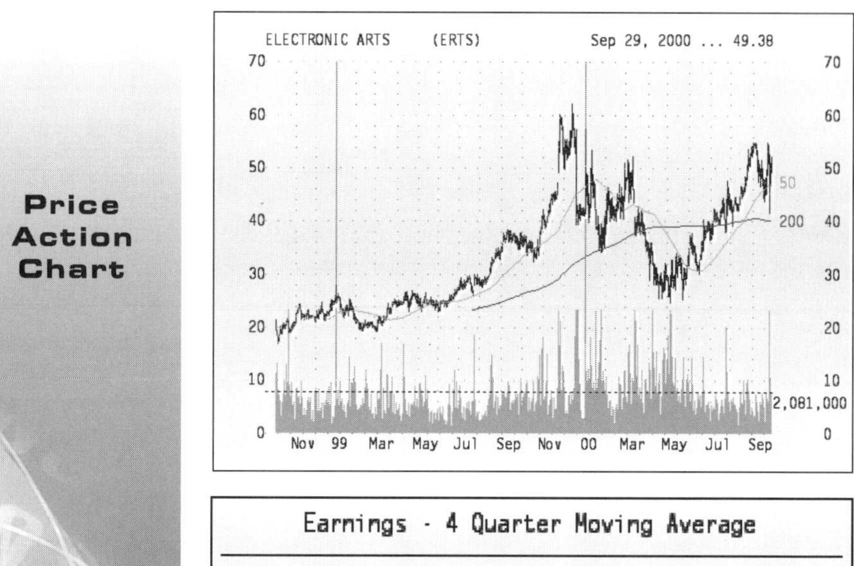

Earnings Growth Chart

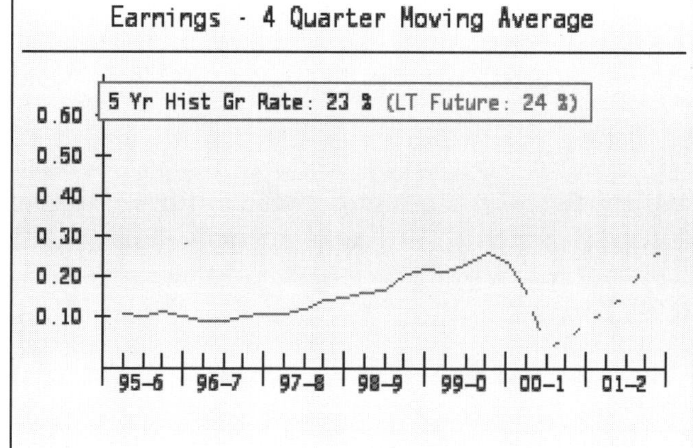

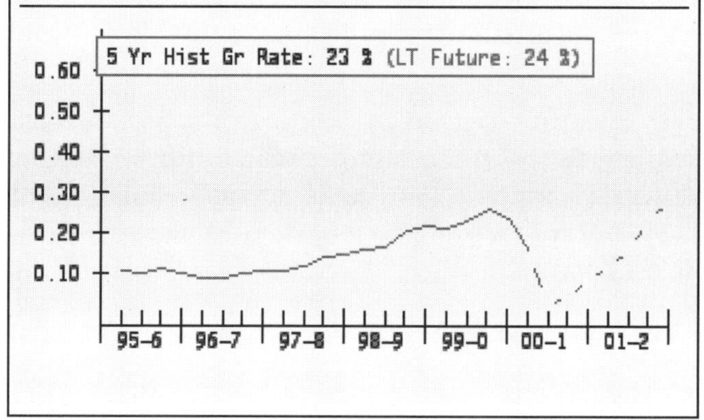

Revenue Growth Chart

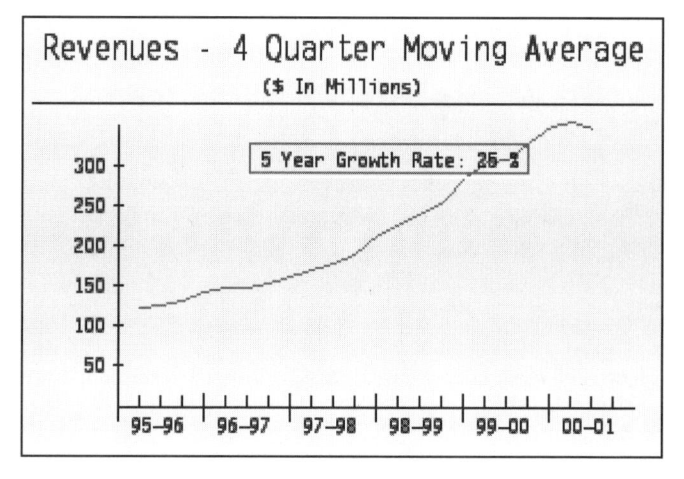

Charts provided by Baseline Financial Services.

55. EXCITE@HOME

Symbol: ATHM
Sector: Technology (Computer Services)

COMPANY PROFILE

Excite@Home provides Internet services over cable TV and leased digital telecommunications lines to both consumers and businesses. The company's @Home service enables residential subscribers to connect their personal computers via cable modems to a company-developed and -managed high-speed Internet backbone network. Its @Work division provides businesses with managed connectivity for Internet and Intranet solutions over existing cable infrastructure and leased digital telecommunications lines. Excite@Home has distribution arrangements for its @Home service with Tele-Communications, Cablevision Systems, Comcast, Cox Enterprises, Shaw Cablesystems, InterMedia Partners IV, and others. The company acquired Excite and IMall in 1999. In 2000, it added to its growing list of businesses with the purchase of Rucker Design Group.

EARNINGS

During the past 12 months, Excite@Home lost $0.13 per share, down 4 percent from the previous year.

REVENUES

Revenues during the past 12 months totaled $537 million, up 239 percent from a year earlier.

KEY RATIOS & MEASURES	5-YEAR RANGE	CURRENT
P/E	NM	NM
Price-to-Book	0.6–30.6	0.7
Price-to-Cash Flow	4.1–30	4.7
Price-to-Sales	9.2–488.4	10.39
Return on Equity	NA	NM
Beta		1.85

NM, Not Meaningful; NA, Not Applicable

CONTACT INFORMATION

At Home Corporation (Excite@Home), 450 Broadway Street, Redwood City, CA 94063
(650) 556-5000
www.home.net

Excite@Home (ATHM)

Price Action Chart

Earnings Growth Chart

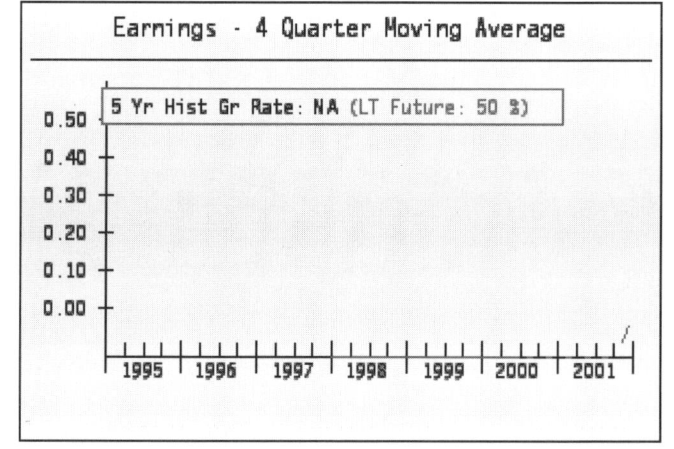

Revenue Growth Chart

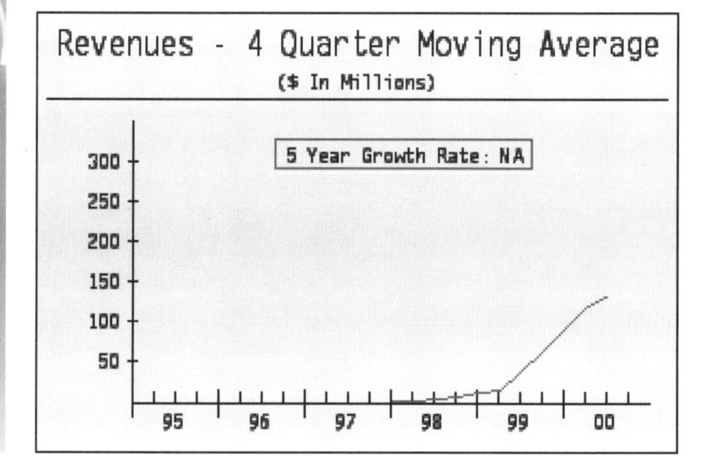

Charts provided by Baseline Financial Services.

56. EXODUS COMMUNICATIONS

Symbol: EXDS
Sector: Technology (Computer Services)

COMPANY PROFILE

Exodus Communications provides Internet system and network management solutions for enterprises with mission-critical Internet operations. The company's solutions are designed to integrate seamlessly with existing enterprise systems and to enable customers to outsource the administration and optimization of their equipment, applications, and overall Internet operations. Exodus delivers its services from eight Internet Data Centers in Boston, Los Angeles, New York, Seattle, San Francisco, and Washington, D.C. The company's more than 800 customers include Lycos, eBay, Yahoo!, MSNBC, SportsLine USA, Applied Materials, Hewlett-Packard, and National Semiconductor Corporation.

EARNINGS

During the past 12 months, Exodus Communications lost $0.41 per share, down 63 percent from the previous year.

REVENUES

Revenues during the past 12 months totaled $483 million, up 346 percent from a year earlier.

KEY RATIOS & MEASURES	5-YEAR RANGE	CURRENT
P/E	NM	NM
Price-to-Book	16.4–953.5	NM
Price-to-Cash Flow	NA	NM
Price-to-Sales	4.8–77.6	42.63
Return on Equity	NA	NM
Beta		2.81

NM, Not Meaningful; NA, Not Applicable

CONTACT INFORMATION

Exodus Communications, Inc., 2831 Mission College Boulevard, Santa Clara, CA 95054
(408) 346-2200
www.exodus.com

Exodus (EXDS)

Price Action Chart

Earnings Growth Chart

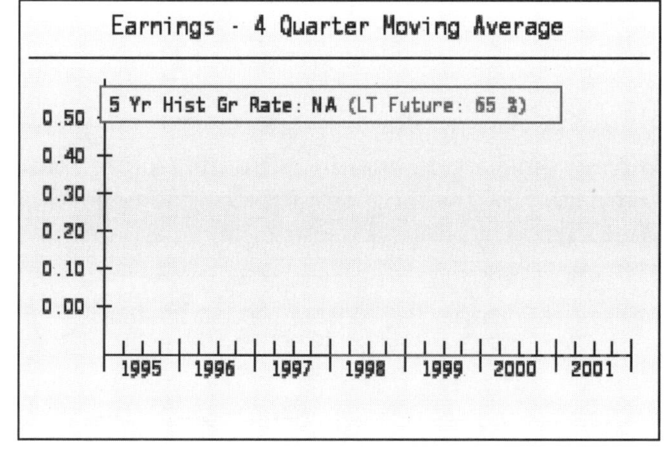

Revenue Growth Chart

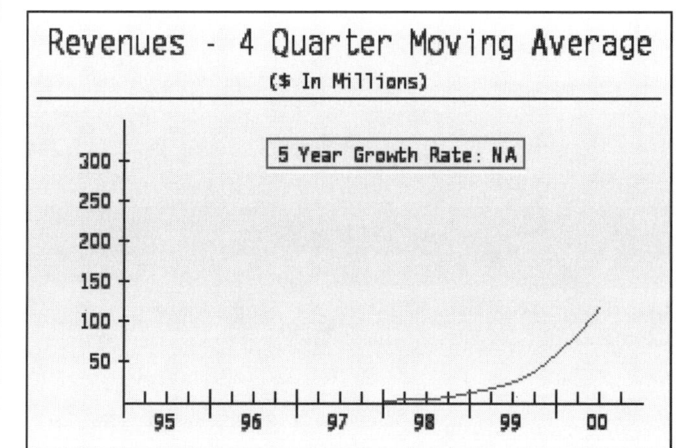

Charts provided by Baseline Financial Services.

57. FISERV

Symbol: FISV
Sector: Technology (Computer Services)

COMPANY PROFILE

Fiserv is a technology resource for information management systems used by the financial industry. The company's core business is serving the needs of banking, lending, insurance, financial planners, and securities providers. Fiserv offers account and transaction processing solutions and services, securities processing solutions, and retirement plan administration services. It also provides plastic card services and document solutions. The company further offers client training sessions in its technology centers, plus local and on-site training services. Apart from its operations in the United States, Fiserv has business support centers in Australia, Canada, Indonesia, the Philippines, Poland, Singapore, and the United Kingdom.

EARNINGS

During the past 12 months, Fiserv earned $1.24 per share, up 25 percent from the previous year.

REVENUES

Revenues during the past 12 months totaled $1.5 billion, up 16 percent from a year earlier.

KEY RATIOS & MEASURES	5-YEAR RANGE	CURRENT
P/E	20–46	43.2
Price-to-Book	2.2–6	5.6
Price-to-Cash Flow	8.3–25.8	24.2
Price-to-Sales	1.2–4.6	4.28
Return on Equity	13.1–14.2%	13.6%
Beta		0.95

CONTACT INFORMATION

Fiserv, Inc., 255 Fiserv Drive, Brookfield, WI 53045-5817
(262) 879-5000
www.fiserv.com

Fiserv (FISV)

Price Action Chart

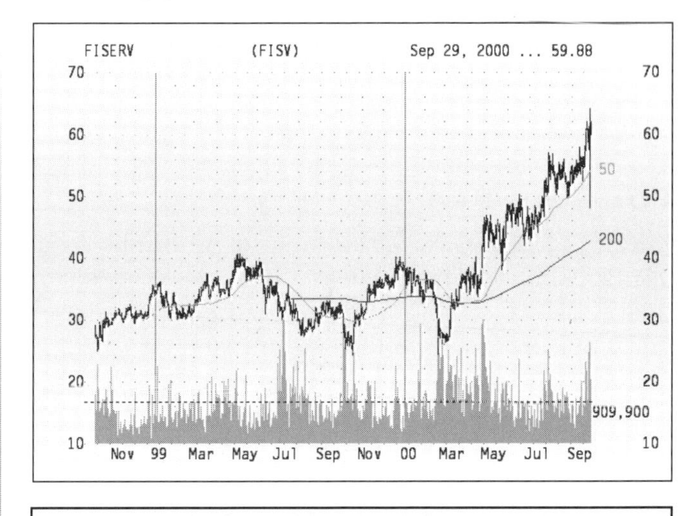

Earnings Growth Chart

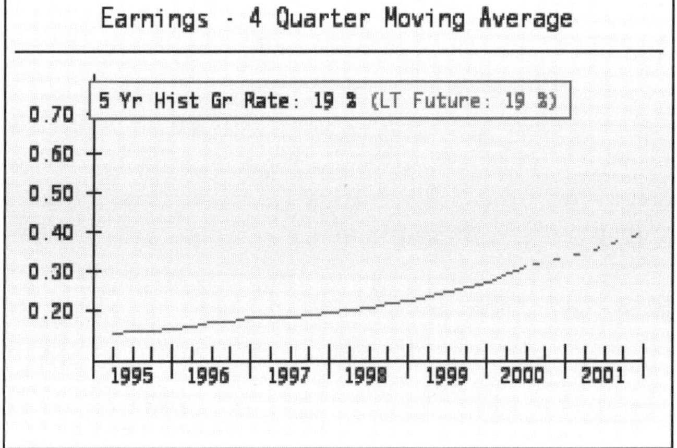

Revenue Growth Chart

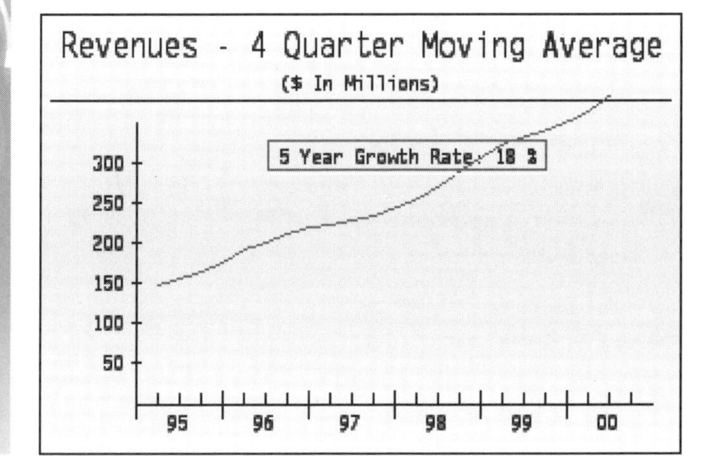

Charts provided by Baseline Financial Services.

58. FLEXTRONICS INTERNATIONAL

Symbol: FLEX
Sector: Technology (Semiconductors)

COMPANY PROFILE

Flextronics International provides advanced electronics manufacturing services to original equipment manufacturers (OEMs) in the telecommunications, networking, computer, consumer electronics, and medical device industries. The company's services include product design, printed-circuit board fabrication and assembly, materials procurement, inventory management, final assembly, test, packaging, and distribution. The manufactured components, sub-assemblies, and finished products incorporate advanced interconnect, miniaturization, and packaging technologies. Flextronics serves customers around the globe through facilities in North America, South America, Asia, and Central and Western Europe. Customers include Bay Networks, Microsoft, Cisco Systems, and Philips Electronics.

EARNINGS

During the past 12 months, Flextronics International earned $1.20 per share, up 82 percent from the previous year.

REVENUES

Revenues during the past 12 months totaled $6.2 billion, up 218 percent from a year earlier.

KEY RATIOS & MEASURES	5-YEAR RANGE	CURRENT
P/E	11–93	68.7
Price-to-Book	2.1–10.3	6.1
Price-to-Cash Flow	6.5–48.1	44
Price-to-Sales	0.2–3	2.66
Return on Equity	9.7–16.4%	16.4%
Beta		1.92

CONTACT INFORMATION

Flextronics International Ltd., 11 Ubi Road 1, #07-01/02, 408723, Singapore
011-65-844-3366
www.flextronics.com

Flextronics (FLEX)

Price Action Chart

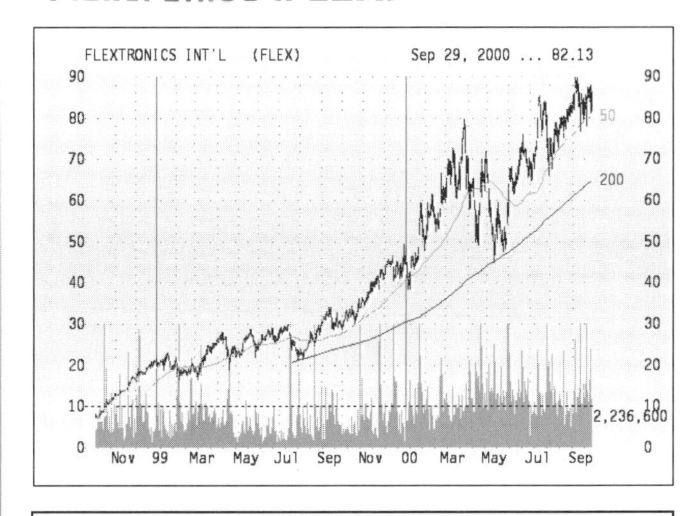

Earnings Growth Chart

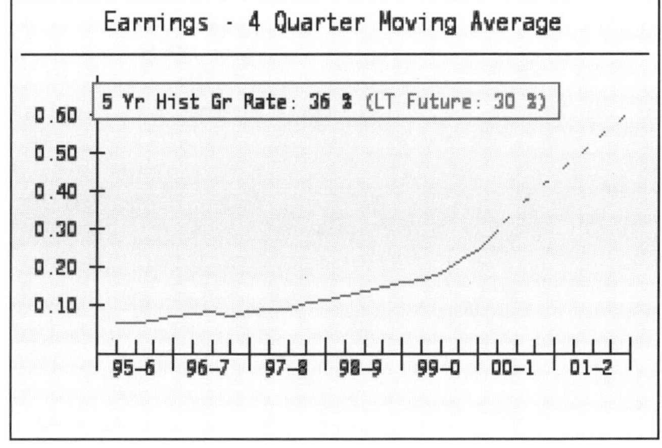

Revenue Growth Chart

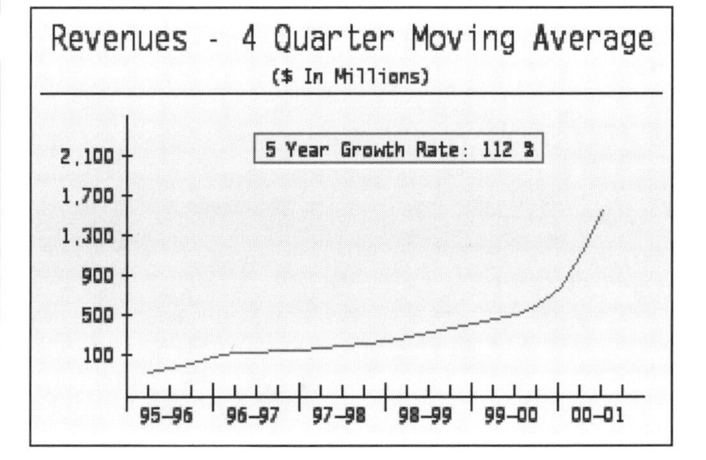

Charts provided by Baseline Financial Services.

59. GEMSTAR-TV GUIDE INTL.

Symbol: GMST
Sector: Consumer Cyclical (Audio and Video Equipment)

COMPANY PROFILE

Gemstar-TV Guide International develops, sells, and licenses proprietary technologies and systems. The company's products simplify consumer interactions with electronics products and other platforms that deliver video, programming information, and other data. Gemstar's VCR Plus+, the de facto industry standard for programming VCRs, enables consumers to record a television program by simply entering a PlusCode number of one to eight digits into a VCR or TV equipped with the VCR Plus+ technology. PlusCode numbers are printed next to TV program listings in more than 1,800 publications in approximately 40 countries worldwide. Licensees of Gemstar's VCR Plus+ technology include Sony Corporation and Thomson Consumer Electronics. Gemstar acquired TV Guide in 2000.

EARNINGS

During the past 12 months, Gemstar-TV Guide International earned $0.52 per share, up 45 percent from the previous year.

REVENUES

Revenues during the past 12 months totaled $256 million, up 46 percent from a year earlier.

KEY RATIOS & MEASURES	5-YEAR RANGE	CURRENT
P/E	14–253	169.3
Price-to-Book	5.7–85.5	44.1
Price-to-Cash Flow	12.7–226.4	160.2
Price-to-Sales	2.7–84.4	68.48
Return on Equity	28.5–51.4%	36.4%
Beta		1.41

CONTACT INFORMATION

Gemstar-TV Guide International, Inc., 135 N. Los Robles Avenue, #800, Pasadena, CA 91101-4501
(626) 792-5700

Gemstar-TV Guide Intl. (GMST)

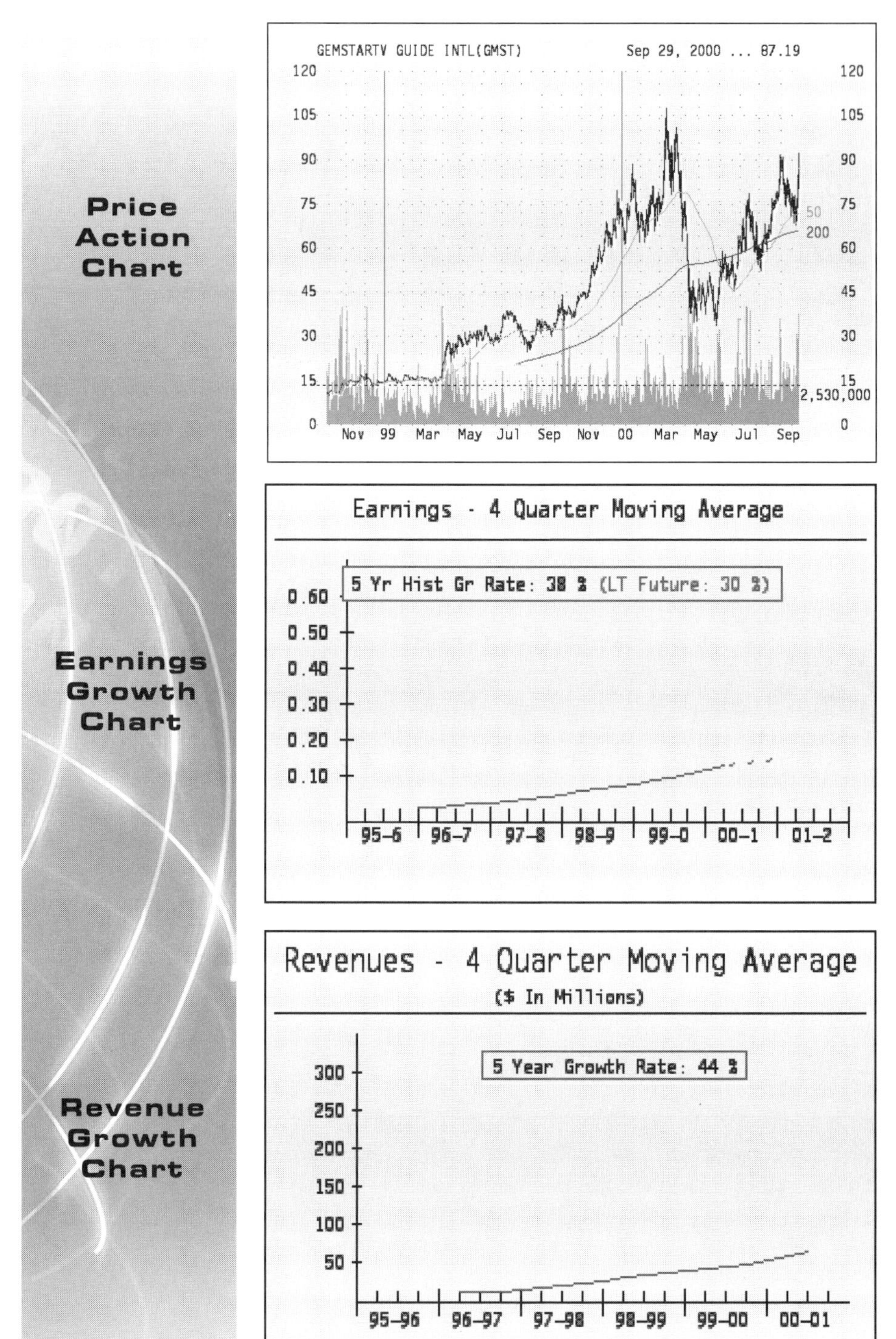

Charts provided by Baseline Financial Services.

60. GENZYME GENERAL

Symbol: GENZ
Sector: Healthcare (Biotechnology and Drugs)

COMPANY PROFILE

Genzyme General, one of four separately traded divisions of Genzyme Corporation, develops and markets therapeutic and diagnostic products and services. Genzyme General's therapeutics business unit focuses on developing and marketing specialty products for genetic diseases, including a family of diseases known as lysosomal storage diseases. Genzyme General also sells synthetic phospholipids, synthetic peptides, and amino acid derivatives that are used as raw materials in pharmaceutical research. Its diagnostics business unit develops, markets, and distributes in vitro diagnostic products (including devices and reagents for measuring LDL and HDL cholesterol and blood sugar levels). It also provides biochemical, DNA, and cytogenetic testing services.

EARNINGS

During the past 12 months, Genzyme General earned $2.10 per share, up 31 percent from the previous year.

REVENUES

Revenues during the past 12 months totaled $688 million, up 1 percent from a year earlier.

KEY RATIOS & MEASURES	5-YEAR RANGE	CURRENT
P/E	17–41	35.4
Price-to-Book	1.5–5.9	5.7
Price-to-Cash Flow	11.1–28.5	27.6
Price-to-Sales	2.6–9.5	9.17
Return on Equity	1.4–15.3%	15.3%
Beta		0.87

CONTACT INFORMATION
Genzyme General Division, 1 Kendall Square, Cambridge, MA 02139-1562
(617) 252-7500
www.genzyme.com

Genzyme General (GENZ)

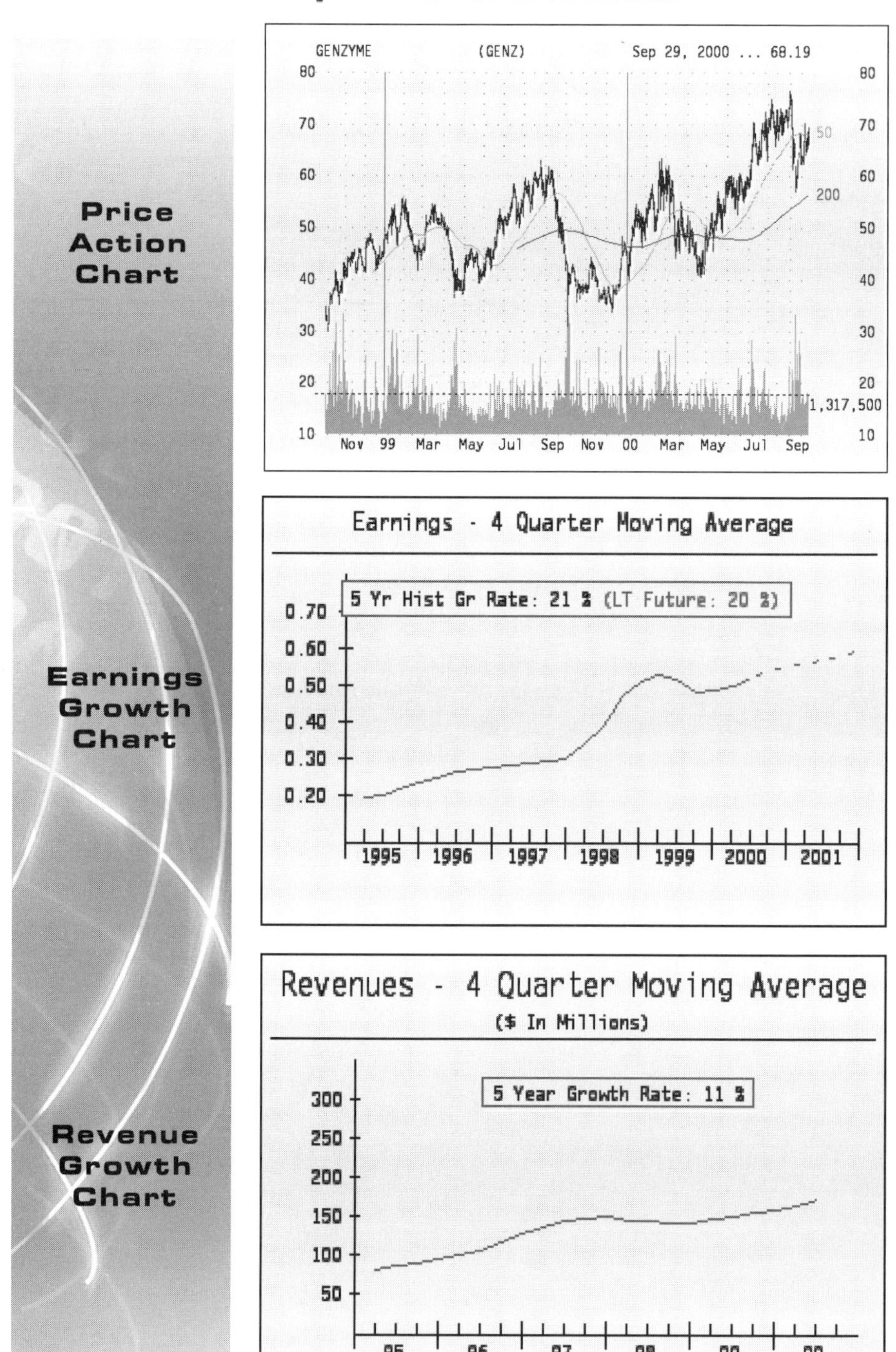

Charts provided by Baseline Financial Services.

61. HUMAN GENOME SCIENCES

Symbol: HGSI
Sector: Healthcare (Biotechnology and Drugs)

COMPANY PROFILE

Human Genome Sciences develops pharmaceutical and diagnostic products using automated high-throughput gene sequencing technology. It has generated a large collection of partial human gene sequences corresponding to most of the expressed genes in the human body. The company possesses a proprietary database of several thousand full-length human and microbial genes. With this genomic database, the company is developing therapeutic product candidates, including two proteins in phase II clinical studies. Human Genome Sciences is also evaluating several additional therapeutic protein products. It has collaborative agreements with SmithKline Beecham, Shering-Plough, Roche, Pharmacia, MedImmune, Vascular Genetics, Transgene, and others.

EARNINGS

During the past 12 months, Human Genome Sciences lost $2.10 per share, down 228 percent from the previous year.

REVENUES

Revenues during the past 12 months totaled $21.6 million, down 28 percent from a year earlier.

KEY RATIOS & MEASURES	5-YEAR RANGE	CURRENT
P/E	NM	NM
Price-to-Book	2.4–109.6	81.5
Price-to-Cash Flow	NA	NM
Price-to-Sales	12.3–587.1	436.68
Return on Equity	NA	NM
Beta		1.13

NM, Not Meaningful; NA, Not Applicable

CONTACT INFORMATION

Human Genome Sciences, Inc., 9410 Key West Avenue, Rockville, MD 20850-3331
(301) 309-8504
www.hgsi.com

Human Genome Sciences (HGSI)

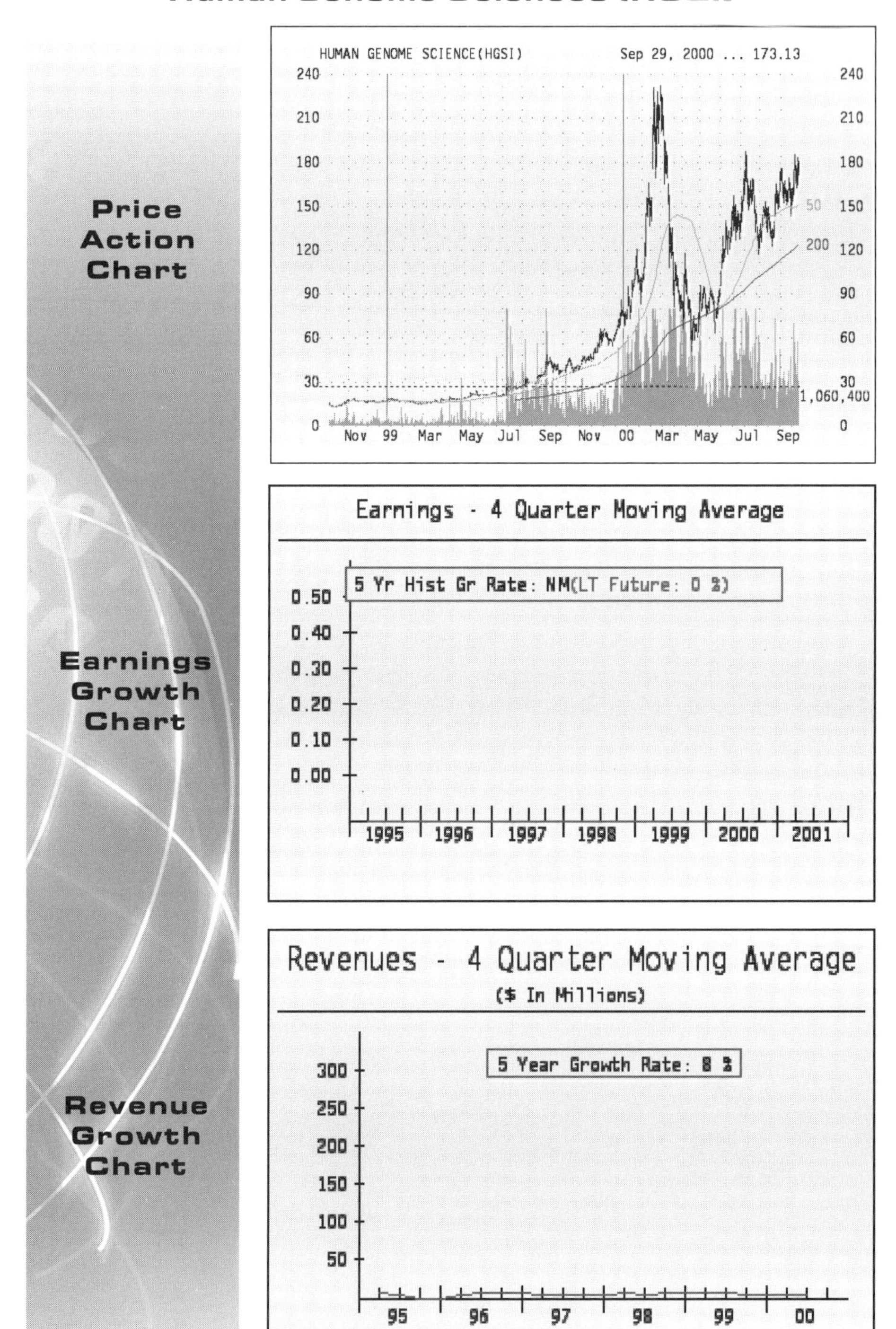

Charts provided by Baseline Financial Services.

62. IDEC PHARMACEUTICALS

Symbol: IDPH
Sector: Healthcare (Biotechnology and Drugs)

COMPANY PROFILE

IDEC Pharmaceuticals develops and commercializes therapies for the treatment of cancer and autoimmune and inflammatory diseases. IDEC's only FDA-approved product, Rituxan, is used for the treatment of B-cell non-Hodgkin's lymphomas. Delivered intravenously as an alternative to chemotherapy, Rituxan offers increased quality of life during treatment and a favorable response rate. Rituxan is marketed in partnership with Genetech. The company's most advanced product candidate, Zevalin, is in phase III trials for the treatment of non-Hodgkin's lymphomas in partnership with Schering AG. Other drug candidates are being developed to treat various autoimmune, inflammatory, and allergic conditions such as rheumatoid arthritis, psoriasis, and allergic asthma.

EARNINGS

During the past 12 months, IDEC Pharmaceuticals earned $0.69 per share, up 5 percent from the previous year.

REVENUES

Revenues during the past 12 months totaled $125 million, up 24 percent from a year earlier.

KEY RATIOS & MEASURES	5-YEAR RANGE	CURRENT
P/E	43–262	254.1
Price-to-Book	2.7–44.2	43
Price-to-Cash Flow	15.1–228.6	222.5
Price-to-Sales	3.9–64.7	62.93
Return on Equity	18.5–32.4%	18.5%
Beta		1.52

CONTACT INFORMATION

IDEC Pharmaceuticals Corp., 3030 Callan Road, San Diego, CA 92121-1104
(858) 431-8500
www.idecpharm.com

IDEC Pharmaceuticals (IDPH)

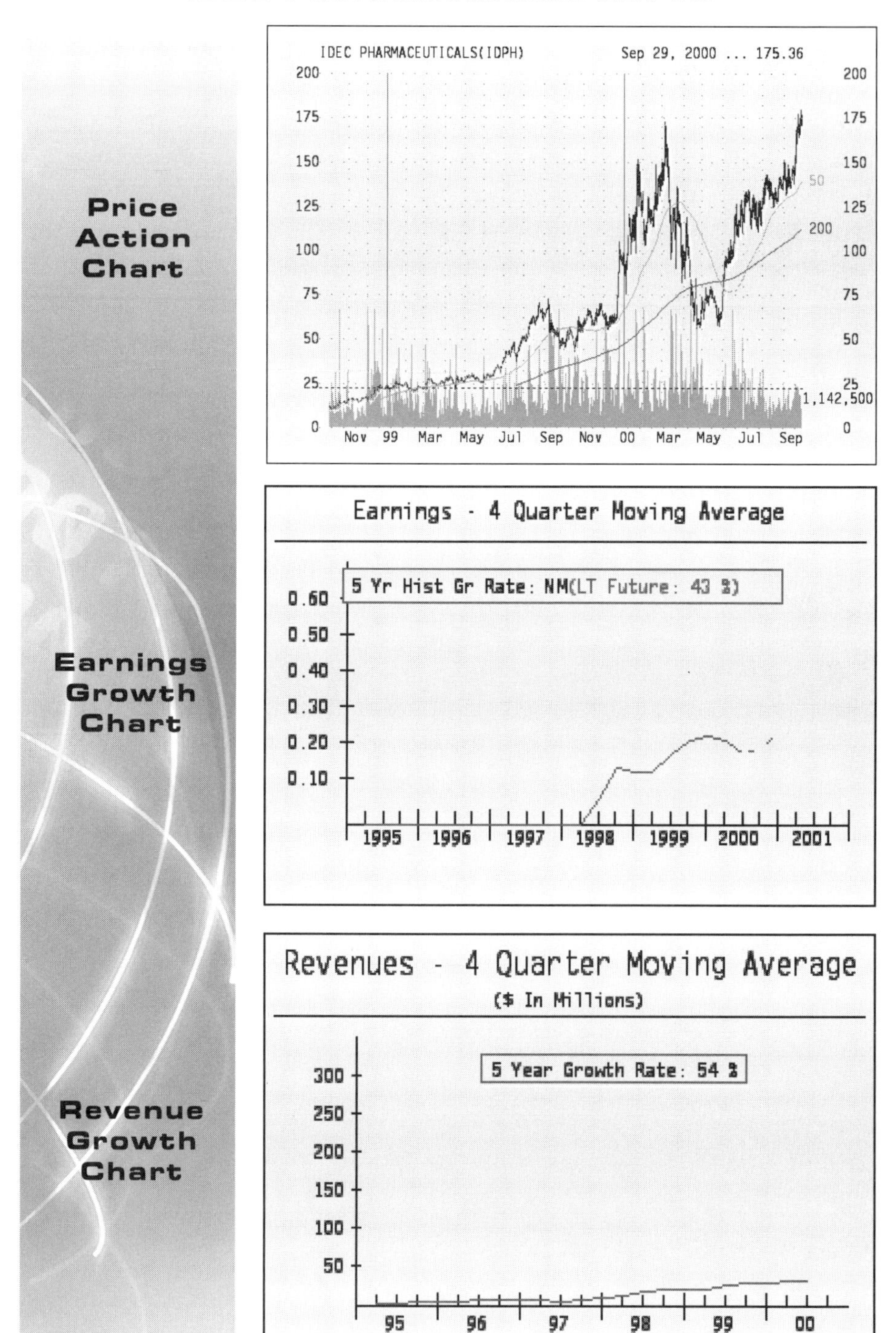

Charts provided by Baseline Financial Services.

63. IMMUNEX

Symbol: IMNX
Sector: Healthcare (Biotechnology and Drugs)

COMPANY PROFILE

Immunex is a biopharmaceutical company that discovers, develops, manufactures, and markets therapeutic products for the treatment of cancer, infectious diseases, and immunological disorders, such as rheumatoid arthritis. The company's principal FDA-approved products include Enbrel, used for the treatment of rheumatoid arthritis, and Leukine, Novantrone, Thioplex, Methotrexate sodium injectable, Leucovorin Calcium, and Amicar, used in the treatment of various cancers. Immunex also has several products in clinical trials for the treatment of cancer and immune disorders. American Home Products Corporation owns some 54 percent of the company's outstanding common stock.

EARNINGS

During the past 12 months, Immunex earned $0.21 per share, up 734 percent from the previous year.

REVENUES

Revenues during the past 12 months totaled $707 million, up 94 percent from a year earlier.

KEY RATIOS & MEASURES	5-YEAR RANGE	CURRENT
P/E	NM	235.7
Price-to-Book	3.2–97.5	57.7
Price-to-Cash Flow	77.1–5185.6	197.9
Price-to-Sales	2.9–59.2	35.03
Return on Equity	0.5–25.7%	25.7%
Beta		1.61

NM, Not Meaningful

CONTACT INFORMATION

Immunex Corporation, 51 University Street, Seattle, WA 98101-2918
(206) 587-0430
www.immunex.com

Immunex (IMNX)

Price Action Chart

Earnings Growth Chart

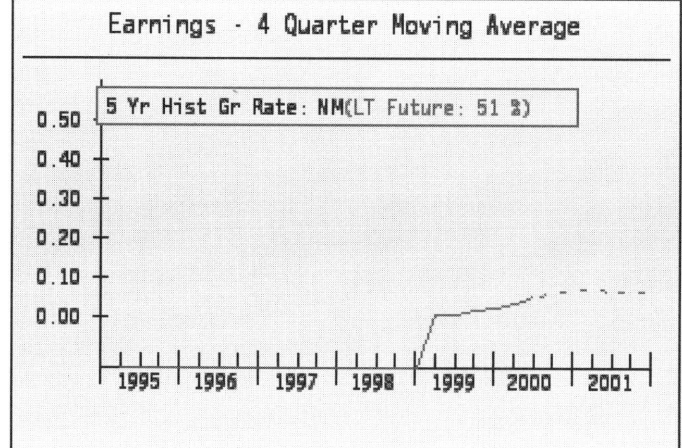

Revenue Growth Chart

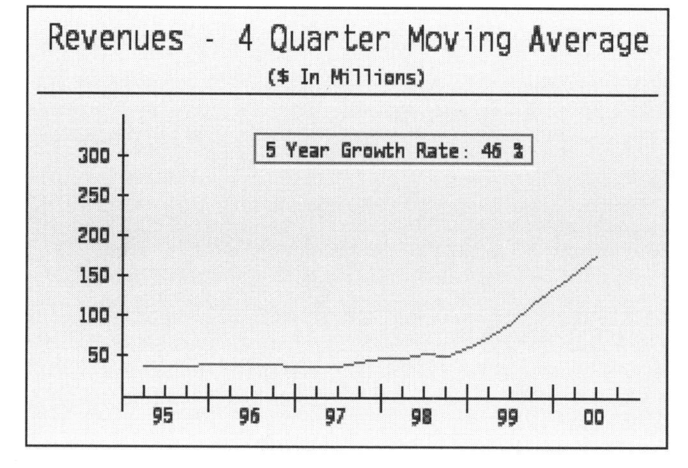

Charts provided by Baseline Financial Services.

64. INKTOMI

Symbol: INKT
Sector: Technology (Software and Programming)

COMPANY PROFILE

Inktomi develops, markets, and supports various software applications which enhance performance, intelligence, and manageability of large-scale networks. Its applications offer scalability without limit or significant deterioration in performance as additional workstations are added. If one station fails, work is automatically redistributed, preventing the whole cluster from failing. One workstation can handle thousands of operations. Current applications include a large-scale network cache called Traffic Server, which addresses capacity constraints in high traffic network routes. The company also has a network search engine and shopping engine.

EARNINGS

During the past 12 months, Inktomi lost $0.02 per share, up 93 percent from the previous year.

REVENUES

Revenues during the past 12 months totaled $171 million, up 222 percent from a year earlier.

KEY RATIOS & MEASURES	5-YEAR RANGE	CURRENT
P/E	NM	NM
Price-to-Book	8.1–85.6	35.2
Price-to-Cash Flow	998.8–3063.3	1446
Price-to-Sales	25–161	75.96
Return on Equity	NA	NM
Beta		2.76

NM, Not Meaningful; NA, Not Applicable

CONTACT INFORMATION

Inktomi, Inc., 4100 East 3rd Avenue, Foster City, CA 94404
(650) 653-2800
www.inktomi.com

Inktomi (INKT)

Price Action Chart

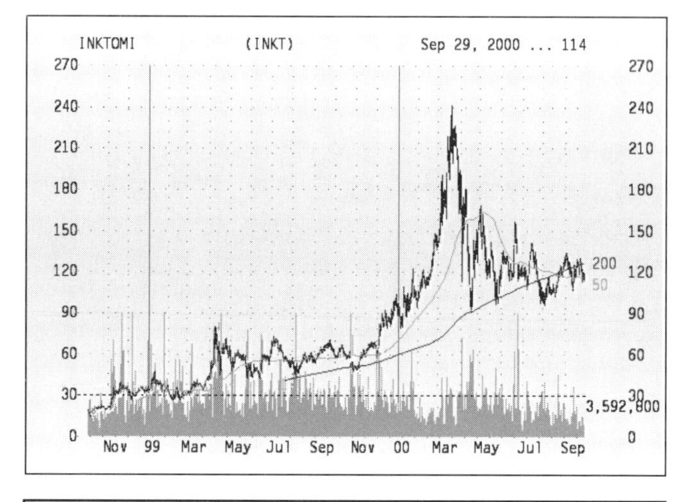

Earnings Growth Chart

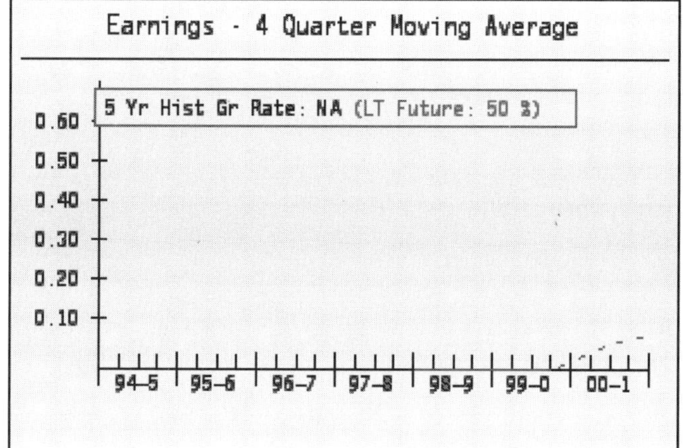

Revenue Growth Chart

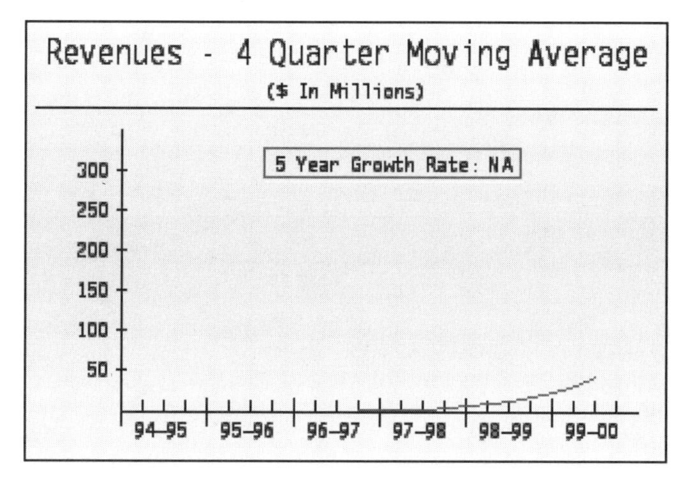

Charts provided by Baseline Financial Services.

65. INTUIT

Symbol: INTU
Sector: Technology (Software and Programming)

COMPANY PROFILE

Intuit provides a range of small-business accounting, tax preparation, and consumer finance software and online services. The company's offerings include QuickBooks, a small-business accounting program; QuickBooks Online Payroll, an online payroll-processing service; TurboTax, a personal tax-preparation program; WebTurboTax, an online version of TurboTax; ProSeries and Lacerte, professional tax software; Quicken, a personal finance application; Quicken.com, a financial Web site; Quicken InsureMarket, which enables consumers to shop for insurance online; and QuickenMortgage, which allows users to shop for mortgages online. In 2000, the company agreed to form a new interactive media services company with Excalibur Technologies Corporation.

EARNINGS

During the past 12 months, Intuit earned $0.64 per share, up 41 percent from the previous year.

REVENUES

Revenues during the past 12 months totaled $1.1 billion, up 27 percent from a year earlier.

KEY RATIOS & MEASURES	5-YEAR RANGE	CURRENT
P/E	26–245	92.1
Price-to-Book	1.4–12	6.8
Price-to-Cash Flow	10.2–67.2	44
Price-to-Sales	1.7–16.9	11.01
Return on Equity	6.9–29%	6.9%
Beta		1.63

CONTACT INFORMATION

Intuit, Inc., 2535 Garcia Avenue, Mountain View, CA 94043
(650) 944-6000
www.intuit.com

Intuit (INTU)

Price Action Chart

Earnings Growth Chart

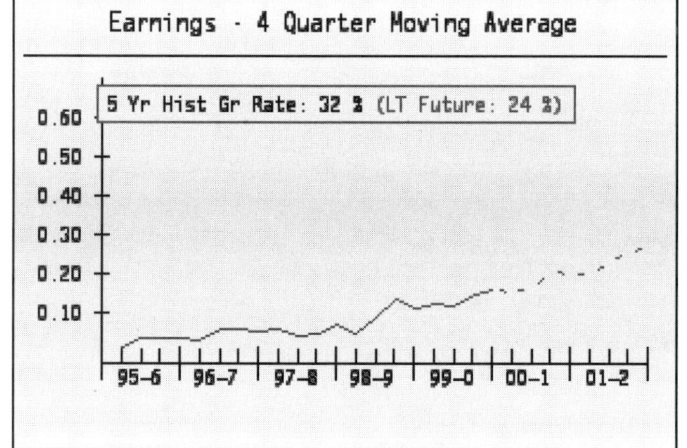

Revenue Growth Chart

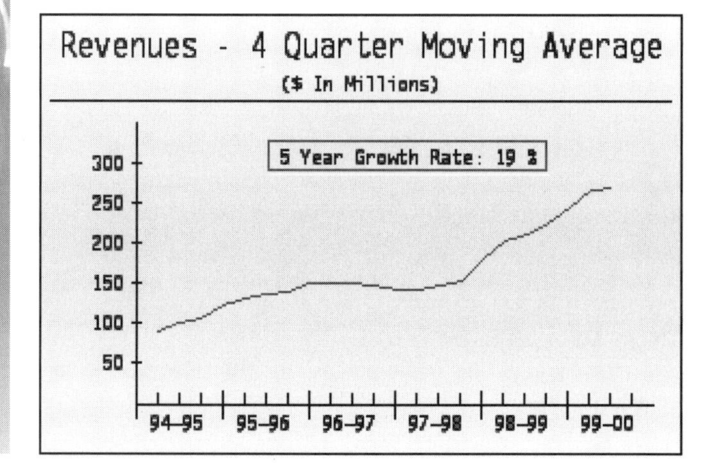

Charts provided by Baseline Financial Services.

66. i2 TECHNOLOGIES

Symbol: ITWO
Sector: Technology (Software and Programming)

COMPANY PROFILE

i2 Technologies produces client–server-based supply-chain management and business-process optimization software. i2's Rhythm software products help businesses forecast demand, procure raw materials, allocate resources, optimize work processes, and plan collaboration within and between businesses. The software enables businesses to reengineer their supply chains to increase revenues and reduce expenses by improving their ability to determine when, where, what, and how much to buy, make, move, store, and sell. The company is extending its supply-chain management products to enable customers to optimize a broader range of business functions, including customer management, product life-cycle management, interprocess planning, and strategic planning.

EARNINGS

During the past 12 months, i2 Technologies earned $0.33 per share, up 71 percent from the previous year.

REVENUES

Revenues during the past 12 months totaled $750 million, up 65 percent from a year earlier.

KEY RATIOS & MEASURES	5-YEAR RANGE	CURRENT
P/E	29–952	551.5
Price-to-Book	2.8–96.9	77.7
Price-to-Cash Flow	17.8–542.8	435.3
Price-to-Sales	1.8–57.7	46.22
Return on Equity	1.3–17.7%	1.3%
Beta		2.29

CONTACT INFORMATION

i2 Technologies, Inc., One i2 Place, 11701 Luna Road, Dallas, TX 75234
(469) 357-1000
www.i2.com

i2 Technologies (ITWO)

Price Action Chart

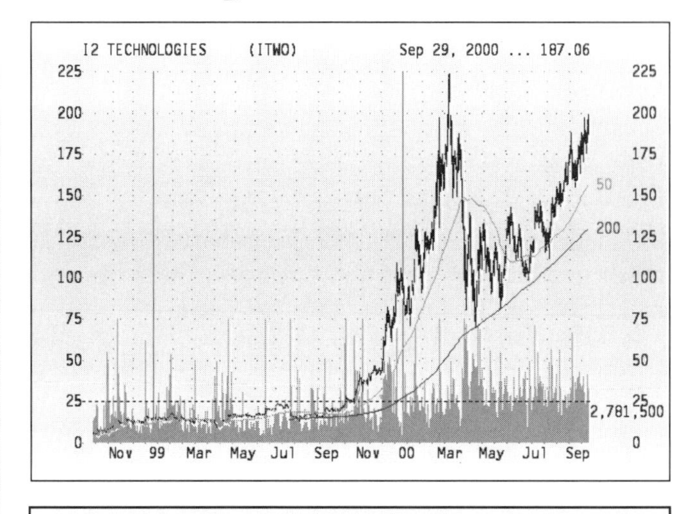

Earnings Growth Chart

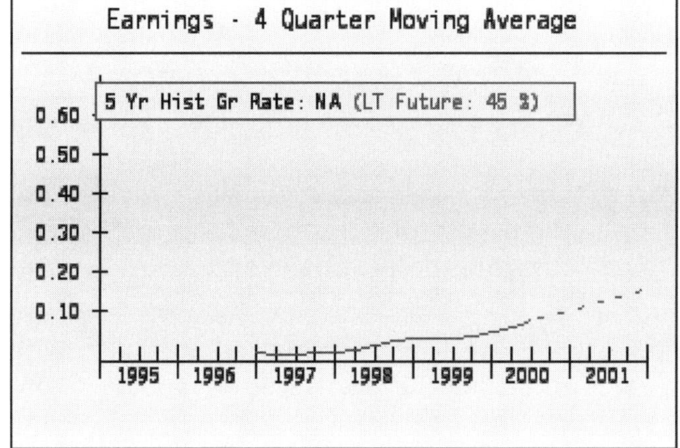

Revenue Growth Chart

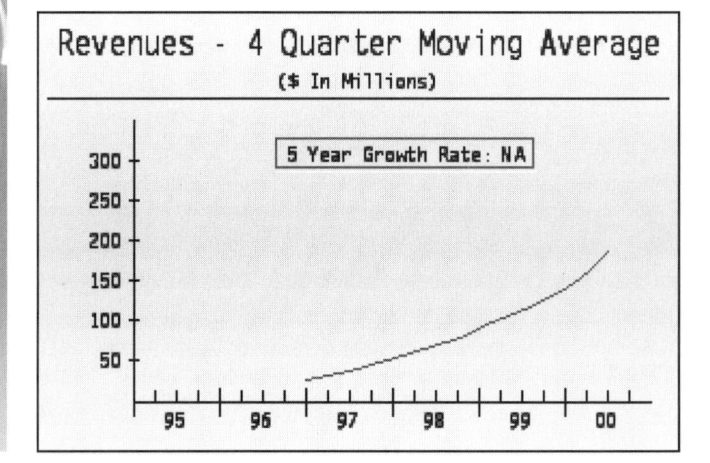

Charts provided by Baseline Financial Services.

67. JUNIPER NETWORKS

Symbol: JNPR
Sector: Technology (Communications Equipment)

COMPANY PROFILE

Juniper Networks provides next-generation Internet backbone routers designed specifically for service-provider networks. The company's routers offer increased reliability, interoperability, performance, scalability, and flexibility, along with reduced complexity and cost. Juniper's flagship product, the M40 Internet backbone router, is manufactured by Solectron. It combines the features of Juniper's JUNOS Internet Software, high-performance application-specific integrated circuit-based packet forwarding technology, and Internet-optimized architecture into a purpose-built solution for service providers. Its M40 Internet backbone router is used by several leading service providers, including Cable & Wireless USA, and is sold largely through the company's direct sales force.

EARNINGS

During the past 12 months, JNPR earned $.12 per share.

REVENUES

Revenues during the past 12 months totaled $252 million.

KEY RATIOS & MEASURES	5-YEAR RANGE	CURRENT
P/E	NM	NM
Price-to-Book	152.1–324	138.7
Price-to-Cash Flow	1592.9–47.4	1453
Price-to-Sales	300.5	274.07
Return on Equity	NA	11.6%
Beta		2.4

NM, Not Meaningful; NA, Not Applicable

CONTACT INFORMATION

Juniper Networks, 385 Ravendale Drive, Mountain View, CA 94043
(650) 318-3384
www.juniper.com

Juniper Networks (JNPR)

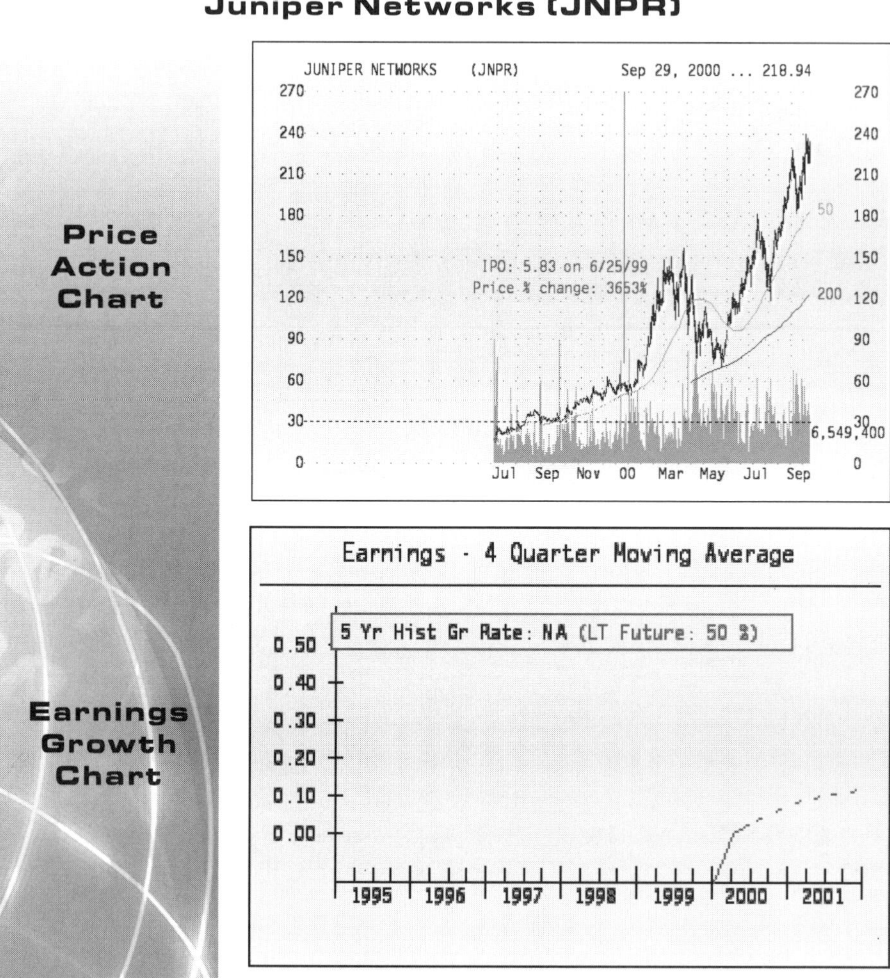

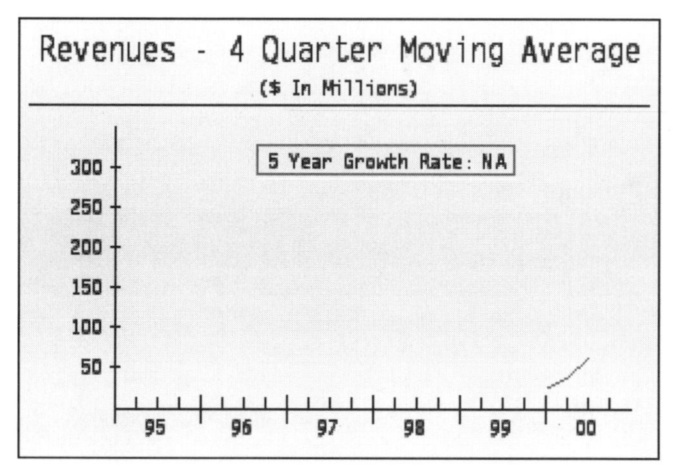

Charts provided by Baseline Financial Services.

68. KLA-Tencor

Symbol: KLAC
Sector: Technology (Scientific and Technical Instruments)

Company Profile

KLA-Tencor designs, manufactures, and markets yield-management and process-monitoring systems for the semiconductor industry. The company's wafer inspection, thin-film measurement, electron-beam inspection, metrology, and reticle-inspection systems are used to analyze product and process quality at critical points in the integrated-circuit (IC) manufacturing process. This provides important feedback to customers and enables them to identify, address, and contain fabrication problems. The ability to locate and contain defects in turn allows customers to increase yields, lowering semiconductor manufacturing costs. KLA-Tencor's direct sales force sells its products worldwide to all major IC and semiconductor wafer manufacturers.

Earnings

During the past 12 months, KLA-Tencor earned $1.30 per share, up 261 percent from the previous year.

Revenues

Revenues during the past 12 months totaled $1.5 billion, up 78 percent from a year earlier.

Key Ratios & Measures	5-Year Range	Current
P/E	7–131	51.4
Price-to-Book	1.4–11.9	8.1
Price-to-Cash Flow	6.5–90.1	42.9
Price-to-Sales	0.8–12.2	8.29
Return on Equity	3.2–25.7%	18.1%
Beta		1.87

CONTACT INFORMATION

KLA-Tencor Corporation, 160 Rio Robles, San Jose, CA 95134
(408) 875-3000
www.kla-tencor.com

KLA-Tencor (KLAC)

Price Action Chart

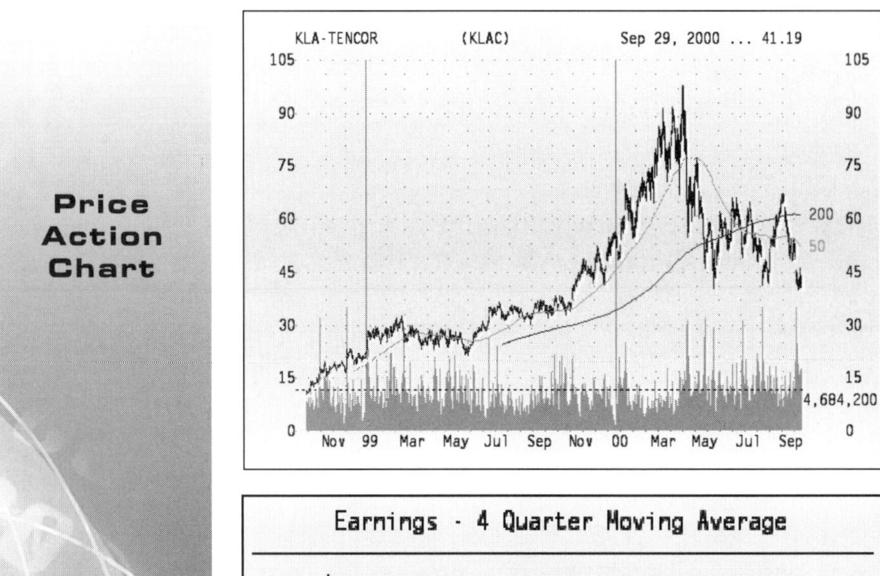

Earnings Growth Chart

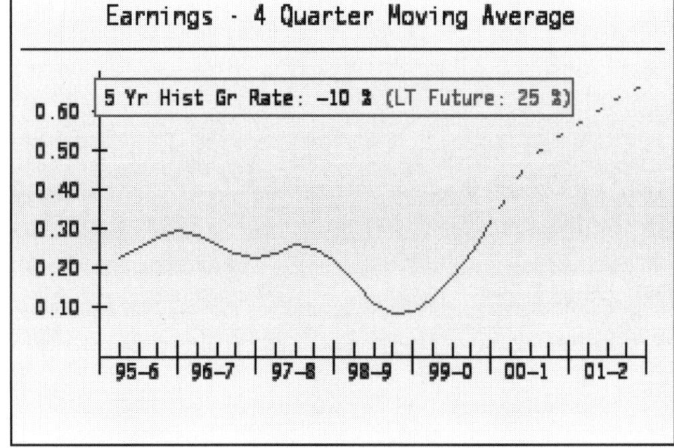

Revenue Growth Chart

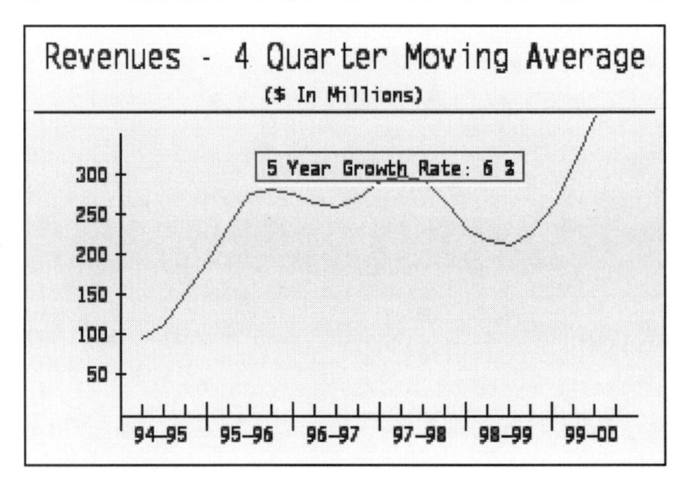

Charts provided by Baseline Financial Services.

69. LM ERICSSON TELEPHONE ADR

Symbol: ERICY
Sector: Technology (Communications Equipment)

COMPANY PROFILE

LM Ericsson Telephone is a Swedish telecommunications equipment manufacturer that operates in three business segments. Its network operators and service providers segment develops mobile telephone systems, large wireline exchanges, and data and telecommunications networks for public telecommunications service providers. Its consumer-products segment manufactures and sells mobile telephones and other end-user equipment to private customers through distributors. Its enterprise-solutions segment provides complete data communications and telecommunications services to private business customers. Ericsson has subsidiaries and offices in more than 140 countries throughout Europe, North America, Latin America, Africa, the Middle East, and the Asia-Pacific region.

EARNINGS

During the past 12 months, LM Ericsson Telephone earned $0.22 per share, up 37 percent from the previous year.

REVENUES

Revenues during the past 12 months totaled $29 billion, up 22 percent from a year earlier.

KEY RATIOS & MEASURES	5-YEAR RANGE	CURRENT
P/E	15–153	94.4
Price-to-Book	2.8–23.8	19
Price-to-Cash Flow	9.2–82.6	65.9
Price-to-Sales	0.9–7.1	5.66
Return on Equity	18.8–24.1%	NA
Beta		1.5
NM, Not Meaningful		

CONTACT INFORMATION

LM Ericsson Telephone Company, Telefonvagen 30, Stockholm, SE-126-25, SWEDEN
011-46-8-719-5340; U.S. Investor Contact: Lars Jonsteg (212) 685-4030
www.ericsson.com

LM Ericsson Telephone (ERICY)

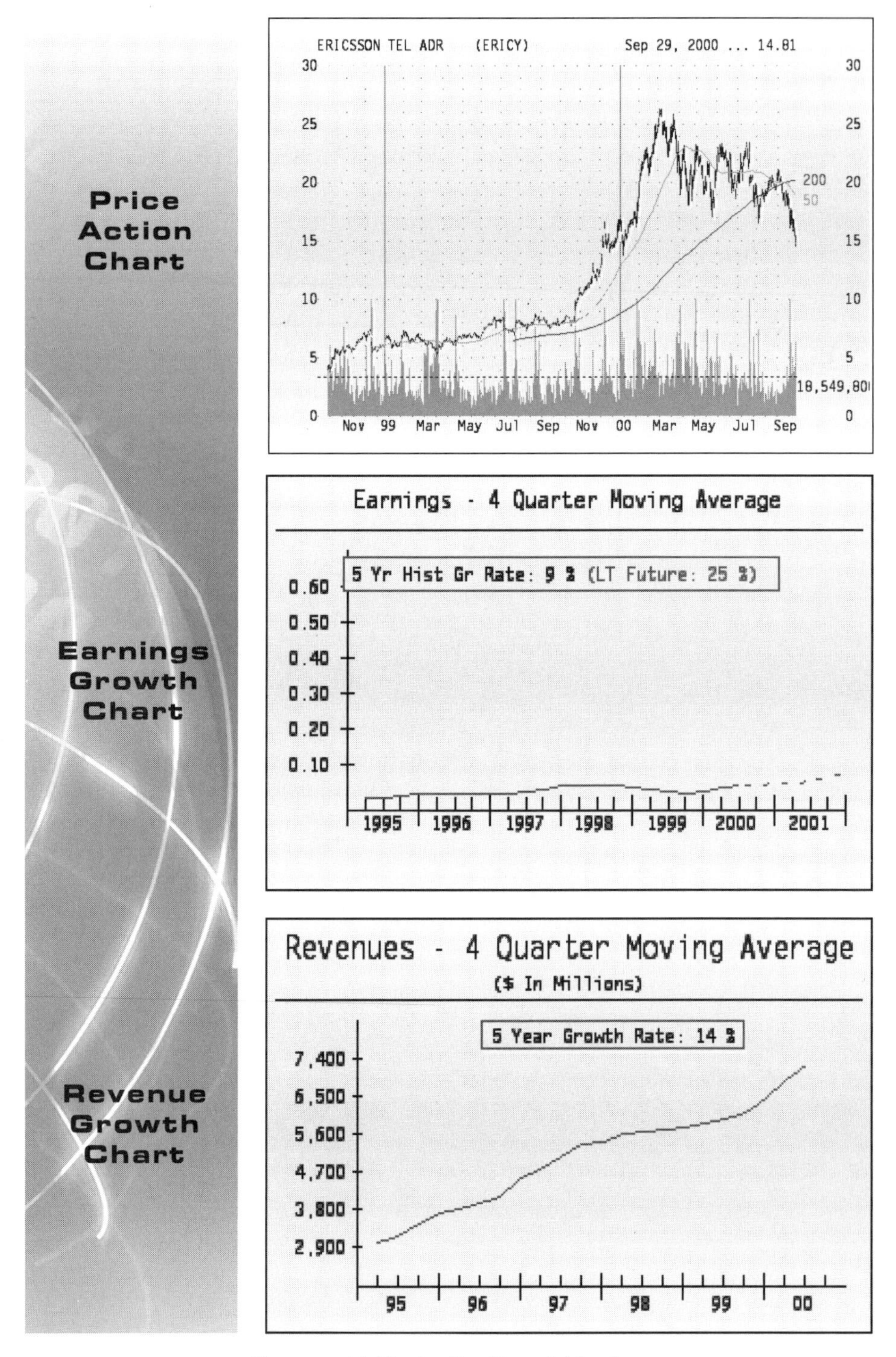

Charts provided by Baseline Financial Services.

70. Lycos

Symbol: LCOS
Sector: Technology (Computer Services)

Company Profile

Lycos provides Web search and directory services, aggregated third-party content, personal Web publishing services, and an online shopping experience. The company draws viewers to its Web sites by providing a means for identifying, selecting, and accessing resources, services, and information on the Web. Internet users can also create personal home pages through its main site. The company generates revenues primarily in three different ways: by selling advertising to companies (including Coca-Cola, Disney, Dell, The Gap, and others); by enabling electronic commerce (for companies such as Barnes & Noble, First USA Bank, Fleet Bank, and WebMD); and by licensing its products and technology (to companies such as Fidelity Investments, IBM, Microsoft, and others). In 2000, the company agreed to be acquired by Terra Networks.

Earnings

During the past 12 months, Lycos earned $0.23 per share, up 611 percent from the previous year.

Revenues

Revenues during the past 12 months totaled $291 million, up 120 percent from a year earlier.

Key Ratios & Measures	5-Year Range	Current
P/E	NM	324.5
Price-to-Book	1.7–15.9	9.6
Price-to-Cash Flow	46.2–174.7	101.2
Price-to-Sales	4–44.1	28.3
Return on Equity	NA	2.7%
Beta		1.70

NM, Not Meaningful; NA, Not Applicable

CONTACT INFORMATION

Lycos, Inc., 400-2 Totten Pond Road, Waltham, MA 02451-2000
(781) 370-2700
www.lycos.com

Lycos (LCOS)

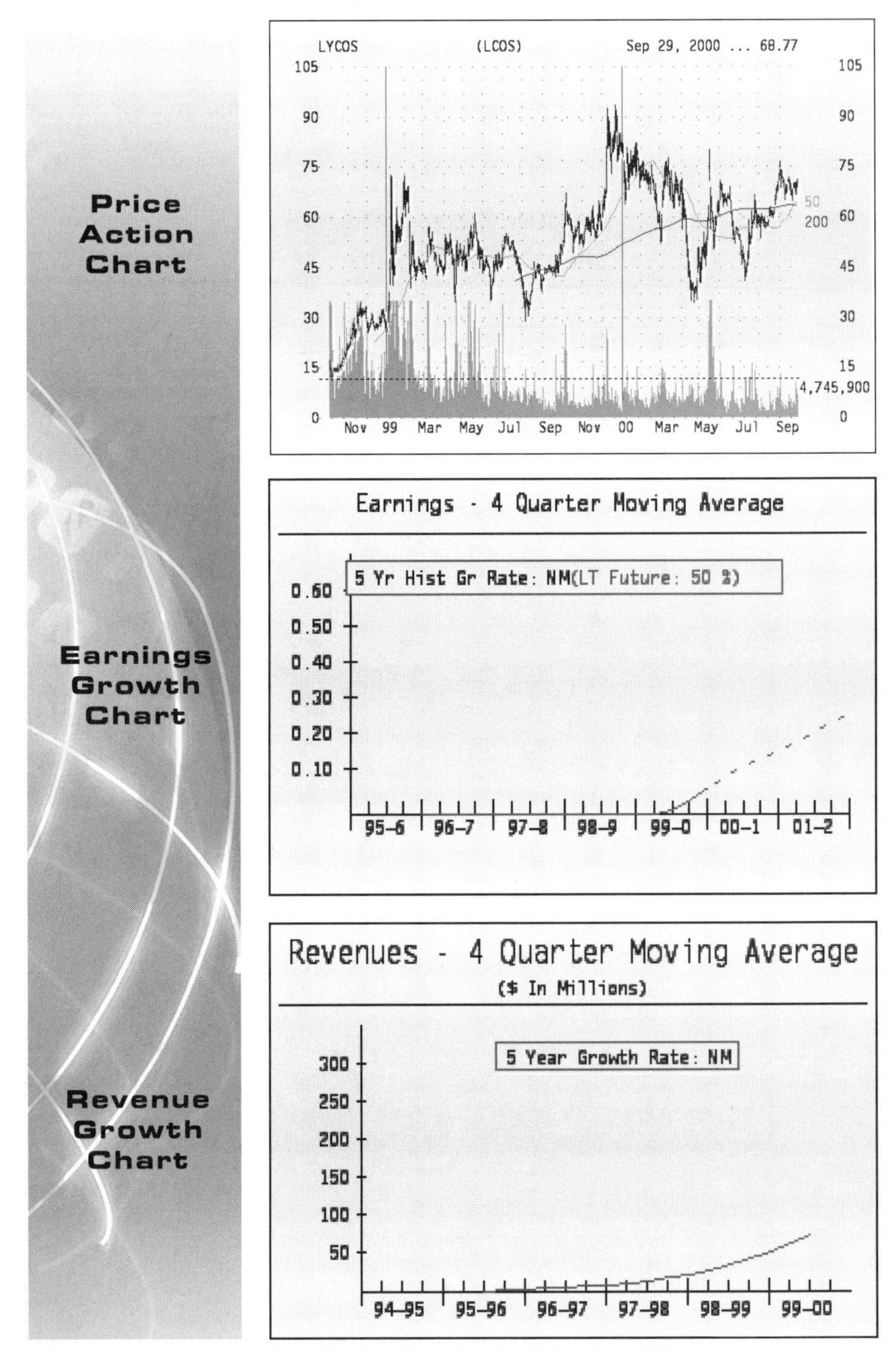

Charts provided by Baseline Financial Services.

71. MAXIM INTEGRATED PRODUCTS

Symbol: MXIM
Sector: Technology (Semiconductors)

COMPANY PROFILE

Maxim Integrated Products designs, develops, manufactures, and markets a broad range of linear (analog) and mixed-signal (analog and digital) integrated circuits. The company's integrated circuits are used in communications networks and devices, industrial-control and robotics systems, and in a variety of measuring instruments, data-processing systems, military systems, and medical equipment. The company also provides an array of custom-built high-frequency design processes and capabilities. Maxim operates wafer-manufacturing facilities in Beaverton, Oregon and San Jose, California, and subcontracts the fabrication of a portion of its silicon wafers to outside silicon foundries.

EARNINGS

During the past 12 months, Maxim Integrated Products earned $0.88 per share, up 36 percent from the previous year.

REVENUES

Revenues during the past 12 months totaled $865 million, up 42 percent from a year earlier.

KEY RATIOS & MEASURES	5-YEAR RANGE	CURRENT
P/E	11–105	99.5
Price-to-Book	3.8–22	21.2
Price-to-Cash Flow	10.5–96.2	92.9
Price-to-Sales	2.9–29.5	28.45
Return on Equity	25.7–48.9%	25.7%
Beta		1.53

CONTACT INFORMATION

Maxim Integrated Products, Inc., 120 San Gabriel Drive, Sunnyvale, CA 94086-5150
(408) 737-7600
www.maxim-ic.com

Maxim Integrated Products (MXIM)

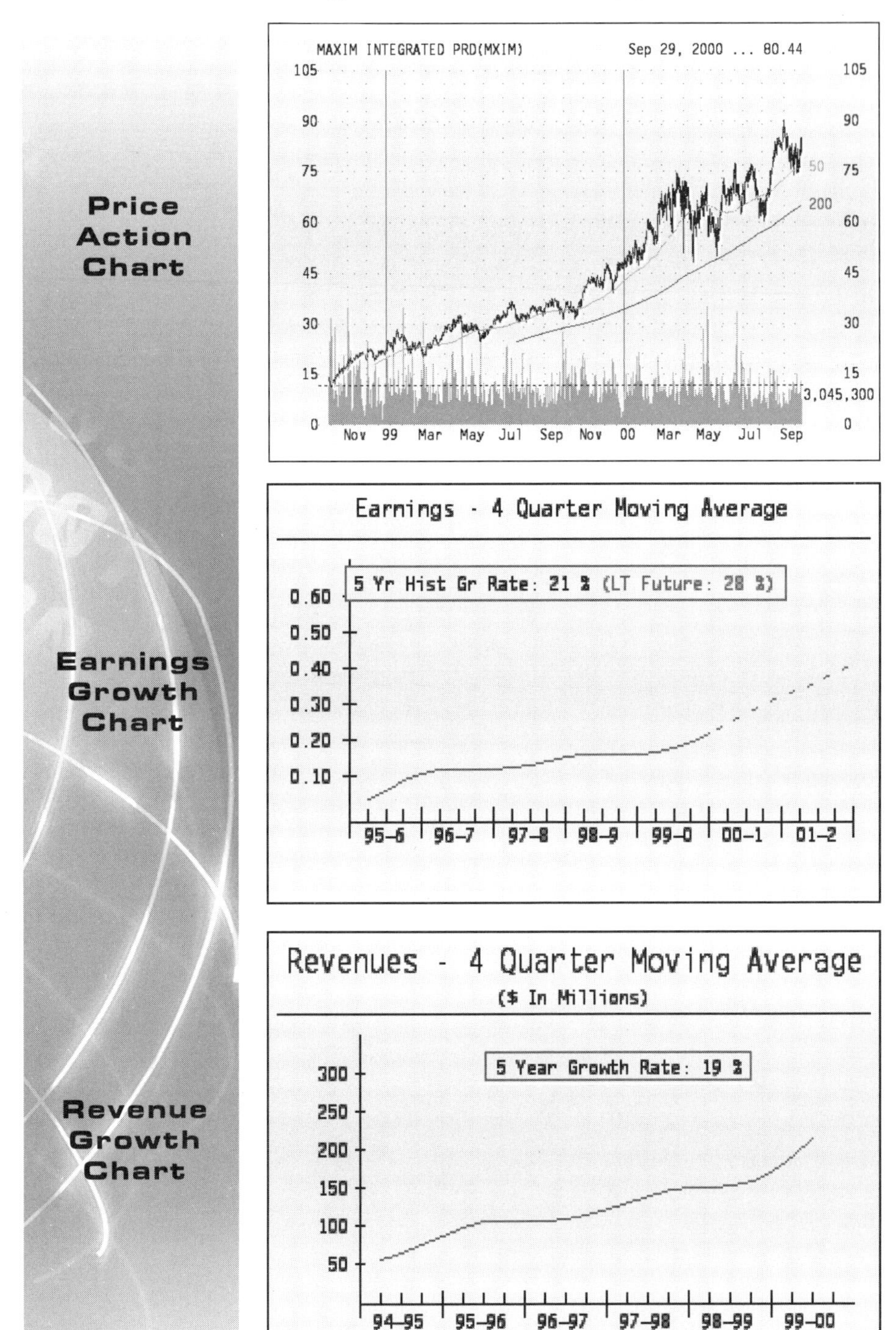

Charts provided by Baseline Financial Services.

72. MERCURY INTERACTIVE

Symbol: MERQ
Sector: Technology (Software and Programming)

COMPANY PROFILE

Mercury Interactive provides integrated performance management solutions. The company's products include load testing, functional testing, and test management products that automate the testing of Internet and other applications. The suite also includes Web performance monitoring products that monitor and measure Web site performance from the end-user's perspective and alert Mercury's customers to performance problems. The company's customers include Amazon.com, E*Trade, Apple, Cisco Systems, Oracle, and Ariba.

EARNINGS

During the past 12 months, Mercury Interactive earned $0.53 per share, up 54 percent from the previous year.

REVENUES

Revenues during the past 12 months totaled $238 million, up 57 percent from a year earlier.

KEY RATIOS & MEASURES	5-YEAR RANGE	CURRENT
P/E	20–306	295.8
Price-to-Book	1.4–57	55.9
Price-to-Cash Flow	10.4–263.5	258.5
Price-to-Sales	2–53.8	52.69
Return on Equity	4.8–21.1%	21.1%
Beta		1.8

CONTACT INFORMATION

Mercury Interactive Corp., 1325 Borregas Avenue, Sunnyvale, CA 94089
(408) 822-5200
www.mercuryinteractive.com

Mercury Interaction (MERQ)

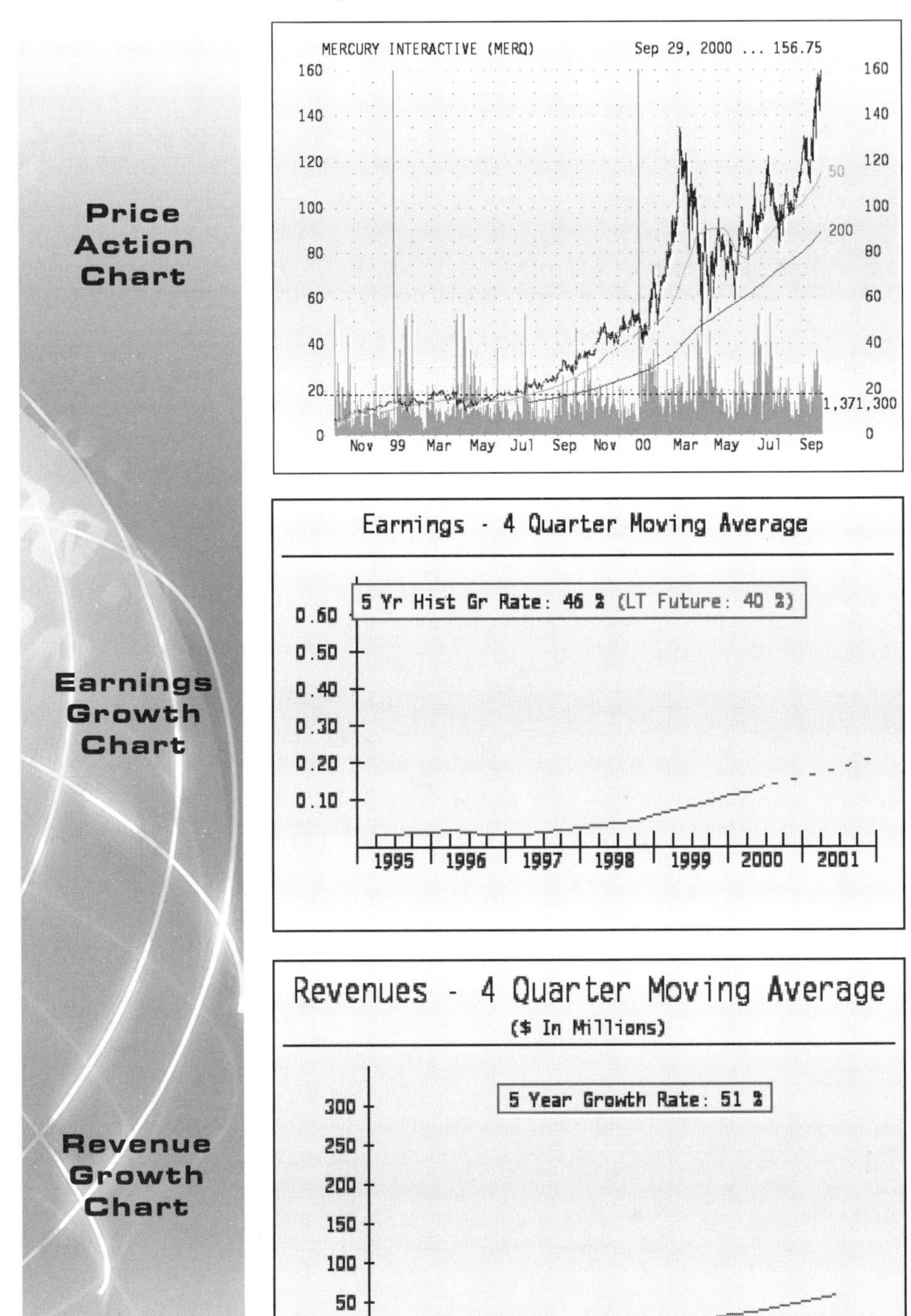

Charts provided by Baseline Financial Services.

73. MICROCHIP TECHNOLOGY

Symbol: MCHP
Sector: Technology (Semiconductors)

COMPANY PROFILE

Microchip Technology develops, makes, and markets field-programmable eight-bit microcontrollers under the PIC brand name. These products are used for embedded control applications in the auto markets for many items, including airbags and automatic door locks. They are also used for the consumer, office automation, communications, and industrial markets. The company sells memory products for data storage in devices where data must be modified frequently, such as in portable computers, and cellular and cordless phones. Microchip also manufactures application-specific standard products, including KEELOQ security devices, including automotive remote keyless entry products and immobilizers, automatic garage and gate openers, and smart cards. The company has two wafer-fabrication plants in Arizona, and final-testing facilities in Taiwan and Thailand.

EARNINGS

During the past 12 months, Microchip Technology earned $1.43 per share, up 52 percent from the previous year.

REVENUES

Revenues during the past 12 months totaled $546 million, up 32 percent from a year earlier.

KEY RATIOS & MEASURES	5-YEAR RANGE	CURRENT
P/E	13–70	50
Price-to-Book	2.4–11.6	8.5
Price-to-Cash Flow	7.4–33.6	31
Price-to-Sales	2.1–11.1	10.22
Return on Equity	13.8–21.1%	21.1%
Beta		1.53

CONTACT INFORMATION

Microchip Technology, Inc., 2355 West Chandler Boulevard, Chandler, AZ 85224-6199
(480) 786-7200
www.microchip.com

Microchip Technology (MCHP)

Price Action Chart

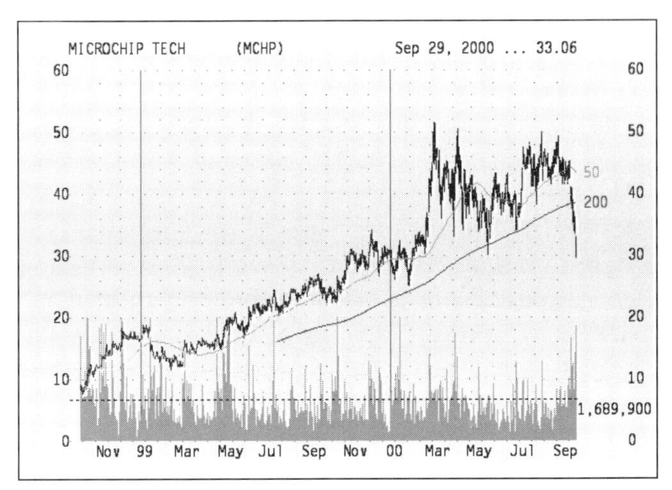

Earnings Growth Chart

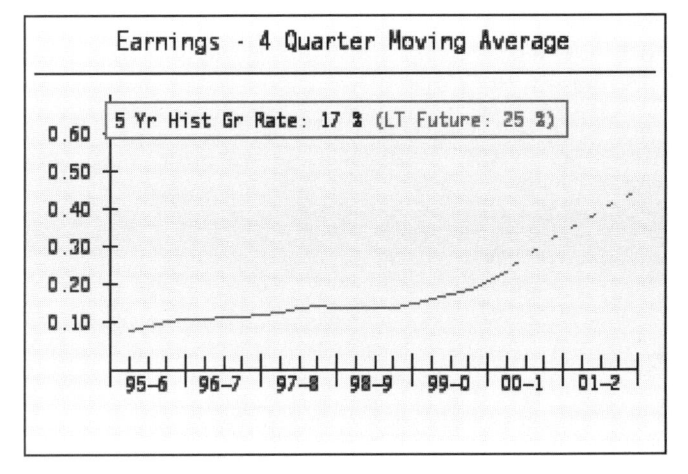

Revenue Growth Chart

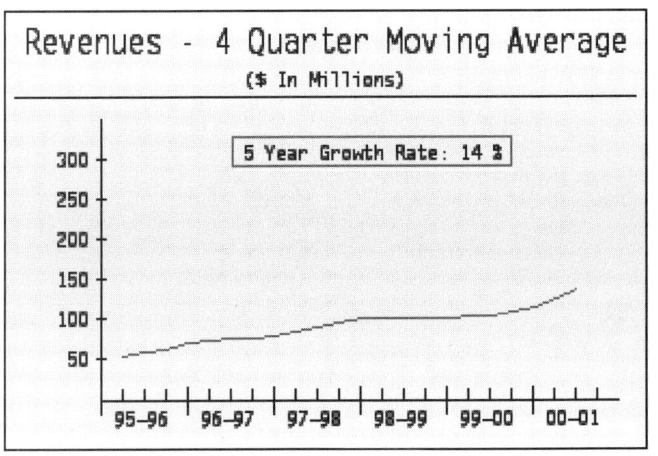

Charts provided by Baseline Financial Services.

74. MILLENNIUM PHARMACEUTICALS

Symbol: MLNM
Sector: Healthcare (Biotechnology and Drugs)

COMPANY PROFILE

Millennium Pharmaceuticals discovers and develops proprietary therapeutic and diagnostic human healthcare products. The company's technology platform includes advanced capabilities in genetics, genomics, cell biology, molecular biology, biochemistry, analytical instrumentation, and chemistry. Subsidiary Millennium Bio-Therapeutics develops vaccines and gene therapy, antisense products, and therapeutic proteins and antibodies. Subsidiary Millennium Predictive Medicine focuses on genomics-based diagnostics (Diagnomics) and pharmacogenomics, or the correlation of patient genotypes to drug responses. Millennium has alliances with pharmaceutical firms such as Bayer AG, Eli Lilly, and Becton Dickinson.

EARNINGS

During the past 12 months, Millennium Pharmaceuticals lost $0.53 per share, down 291 percent from the previous year.

REVENUES

Revenues during the past 12 months totaled $189 million, up 9 percent from a year earlier.

KEY RATIOS & MEASURES	5-YEAR RANGE	CURRENT
P/E	65–225	NM
Price-to-Book	1.6–36.7	33
Price-to-Cash Flow	13.4–298.1	NM
Price-to-Sales	2.5–80.6	72.48
Return on Equity	NA	NM
Beta		1.19

NM, Not Meaningful; NA, Not Applicable

CONTACT INFORMATION

Millennium Pharmaceuticals, Inc., 75 Sidney Street, Cambridge, MA 02139
(617) 679-7000
www.mlnm.com

Millennium Pharmaceuticals (MLNM)

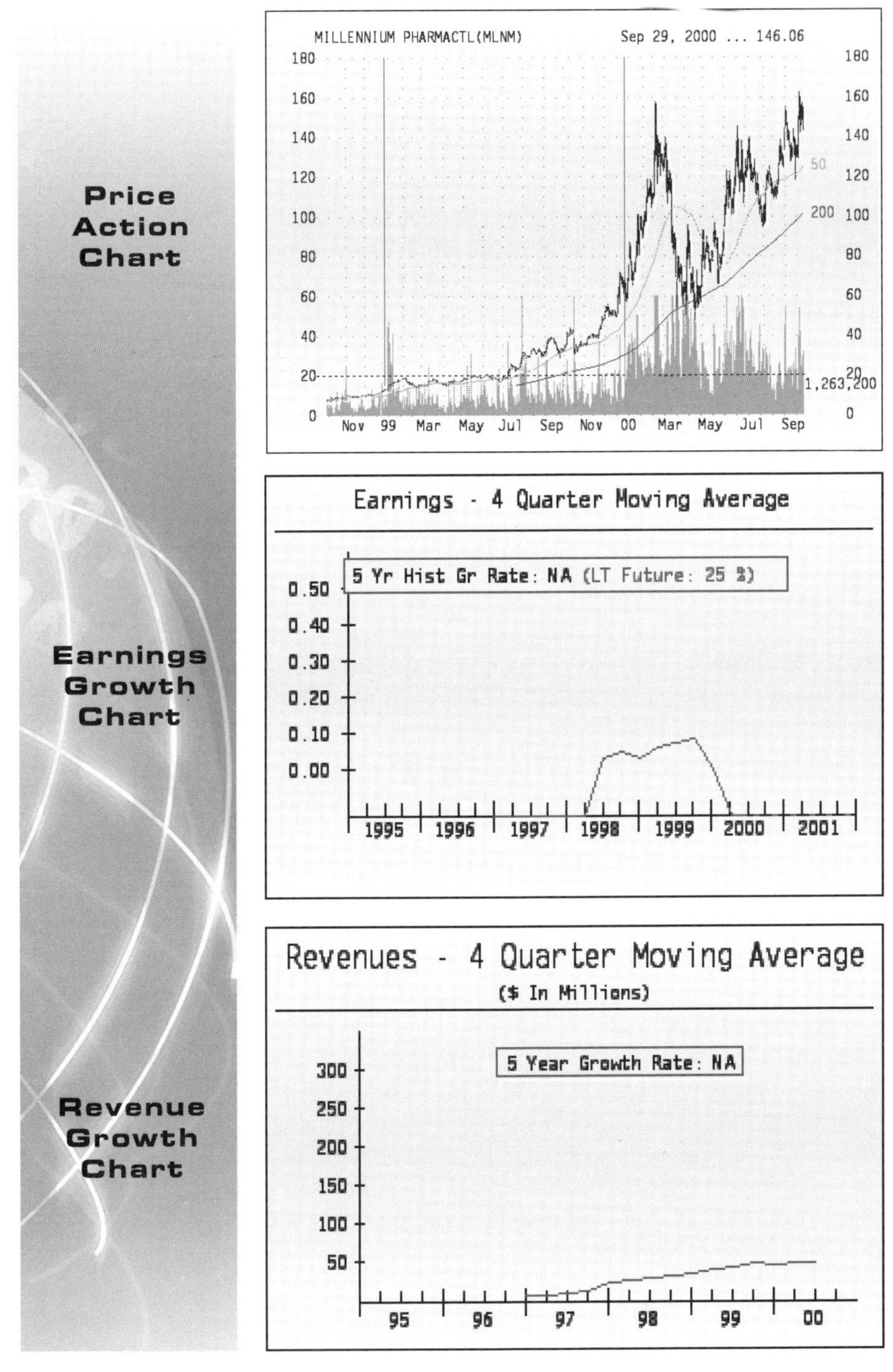

Charts provided by Baseline Financial Services.

75. MOLEX

Symbol: MOLX
Sector: Technology (Electronic Instruments and Controls)

COMPANY PROFILE

Molex makes and sells electrical and electronic components. The company designs, manufactures, and distributes electrical and electronic devices, such as terminals, connectors, planer cables, cable assemblies, interconnection systems, fiber-optic interconnection systems, backplanes, and mechanical and electronic switches. Molex also leases or sells crimping machines and terminal-inserting equipment (also known as application tooling) to its customers for the purpose of applying components to various products. Molex sells more than 100,000 devices to automobile, computer, computer peripheral, business equipment, telecommunications equipment, and consumer products manufacturers. The company operates nearly 50 plants in 21 countries.

EARNINGS

During the past 12 months, Molex earned $1.12 per share, up 23 percent from the previous year.

REVENUES

Revenues during the past 12 months totaled $2.2 billion, up 30 percent from a year earlier.

KEY RATIOS & MEASURES	5-YEAR RANGE	CURRENT
P/E	18–65	46.9
Price-to-Book	3–9	7.4
Price-to-Cash Flow	10.1–31.6	26.1
Price-to-Sales	1.9–5.7	4.66
Return on Equity	12.9–14.6%	13.8%
Beta		0.97

CONTACT INFORMATION

Molex, Inc., 2222 Wellington Court, Lisle, IL 60532-3820
(630) 969-4550
www.molex.com

Molex (MOLX)

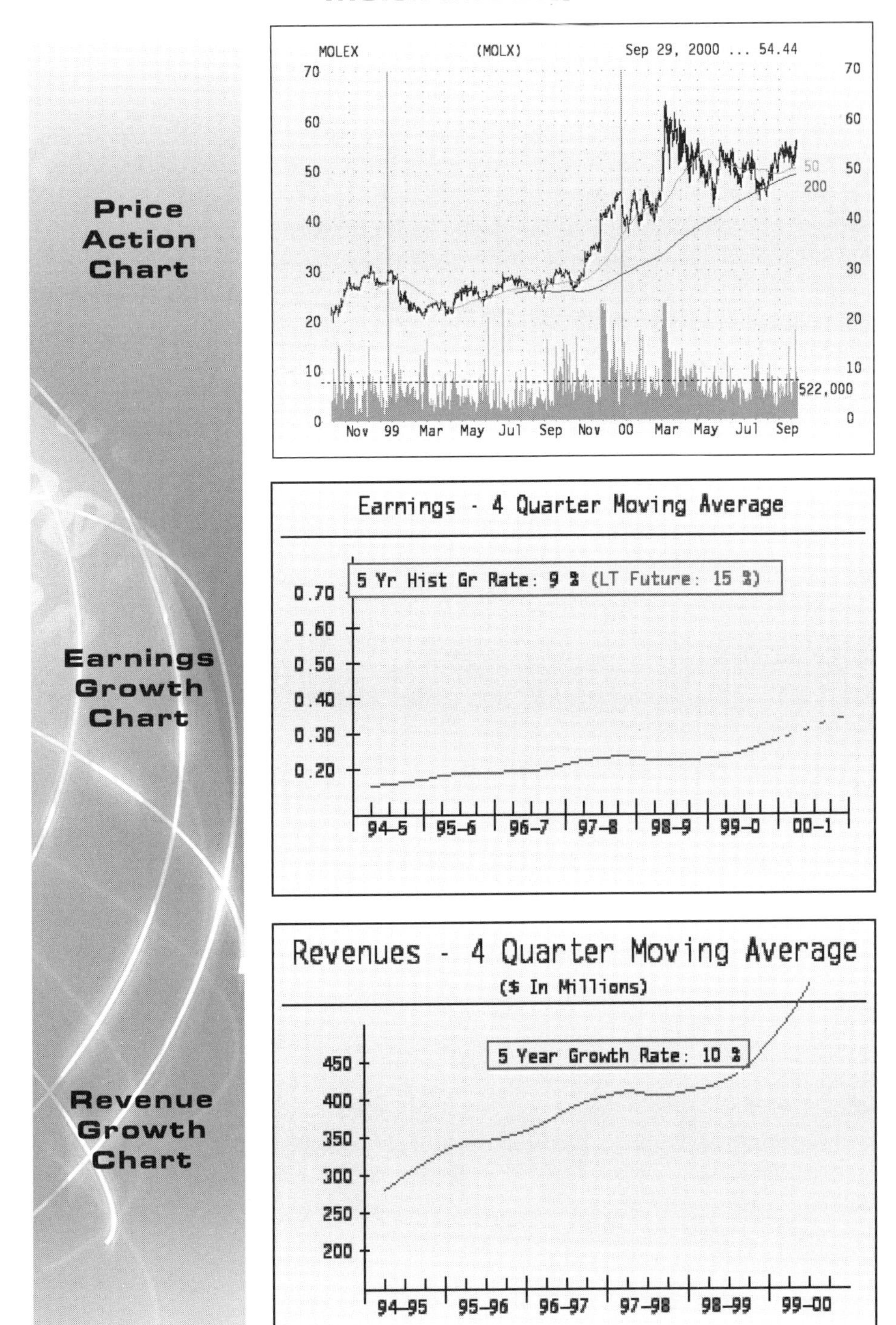

Charts provided by Baseline Financial Services.

76. NOVELL

Symbol: NOVL
Sector: Technology (Computer Networks)

COMPANY PROFILE

Novell is one of the world's top providers of network software. The company's Novell Directory Services product family is designed to enable a business to manage its entire heterogeneous network as a single, unified entity from a central location. Novell's NetWare line of server operating systems includes Netware 5, which supports Java server-side execution. Novell's GroupWise and related products provide network end-users with electronic mail, scheduling, calendaring, and task and document management capabilities. The company's network security and connectivity products include BorderManager, NetScape Servers for NetWare, and IntranetWare HostPublisher. Novell's network management products include ManageWise, ZENworks, and ConsoleOne.

EARNINGS

During the past 12 months, Novell earned $0.35 per share, down 22 percent from the previous year.

REVENUES

Revenues during the past 12 months totaled $1.2 billion, up 1 percent from a year earlier.

KEY RATIOS & MEASURES	5-YEAR RANGE	CURRENT
P/E	13–88	34.8
Price-to-Book	1.4–9.4	2.6
Price-to-Cash Flow	13.7–92.5	21.6
Price-to-Sales	2.1–12	3.26
Return on Equity	6.7–12.8%	7.9%
Beta		1.63

CONTACT INFORMATION
Novell, Inc., 1800 South Novell Place, Provo, UT 84606
(801) 861-7000
www.novell.com

Novell (NOVL)

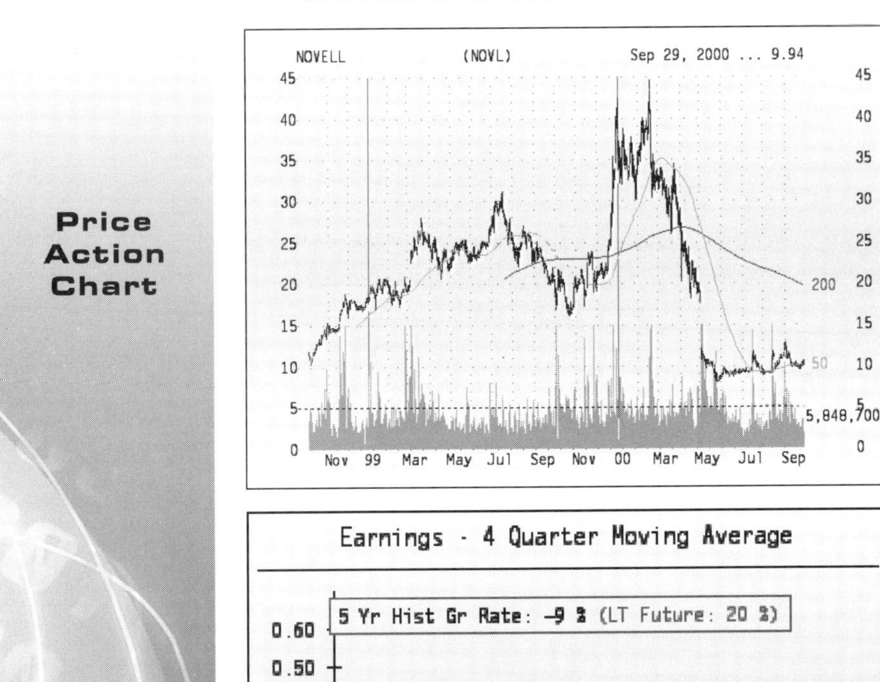

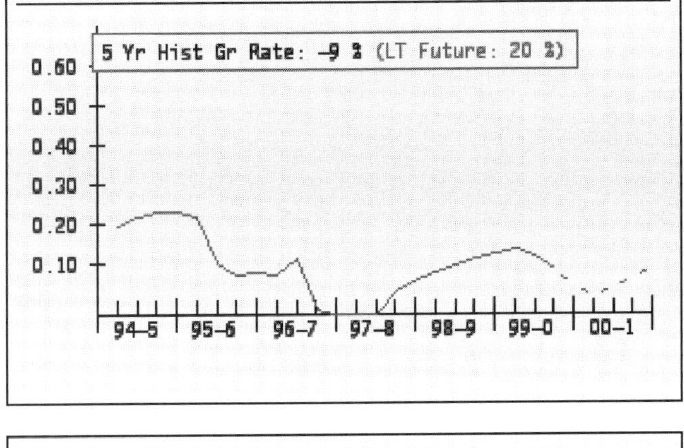

Revenue Growth Chart

Revenues - 4 Quarter Moving Average

($ In Millions)

5 Year Growth Rate: -9 %

450
400
350
300
250
200

94-95 95-96 96-97 97-98 98-99 99-00

Charts provided by Baseline Financial Services.

77. NTL

Symbol: NTLI
Sector: Services (Broadcasting and Cable Television)

COMPANY PROFILE

NTL Communications offers broadband communications services in the United Kingdom and Ireland. The company provides residential customers with telephony, cable TV, PC- and television-based Internet access, and interactive services. NTL provides business and wholesale customers with both national and international carrier telecom services, Internet services, and satellite communications services. NTL also provides wholesale customers with broadcast transmission and tower time, including digital and analog television and radio broadcast transmission, wireless network management, and tower site rental services. NTL's business and carrier customers include AT&T, Cisco Systems, WorldCom, and Microsoft.

EARNINGS

During the past 12 months, NTL Communications lost $11.20 per share, down 13 percent from the previous year.

REVENUES

Revenues during the past 12 months totaled $2.1 billion, up 85 percent from a year earlier.

KEY RATIOS & MEASURES	5-YEAR RANGE	CURRENT
P/E	NM	NM
Price-to-Book	2–11.5	5
Price-to-Cash Flow	NA	NM
Price-to-Sales	1.1–8.6	3.33
Return on Equity	NA	NM
Beta		1.34

NM, Not Meaningful; NA, Not Applicable

CONTACT INFORMATION

NTL, Inc., 110 East 59th Street, New York, NY 10022
(212) 906-8440
www.ntl.com

NTL (NTLI)

Price Action Chart

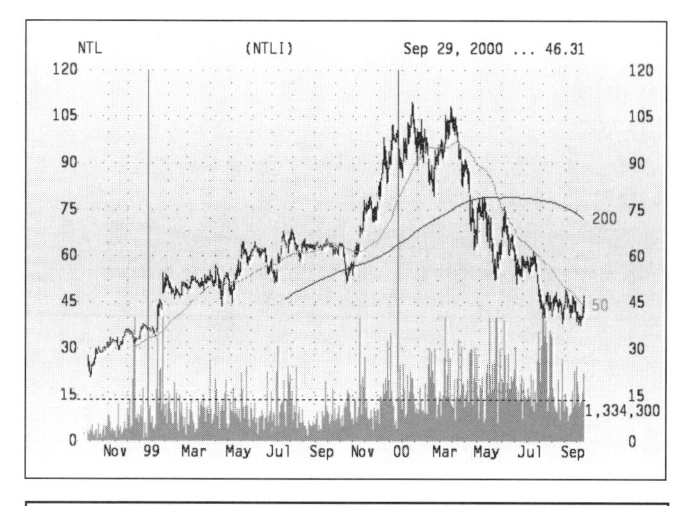

Earnings Growth Chart

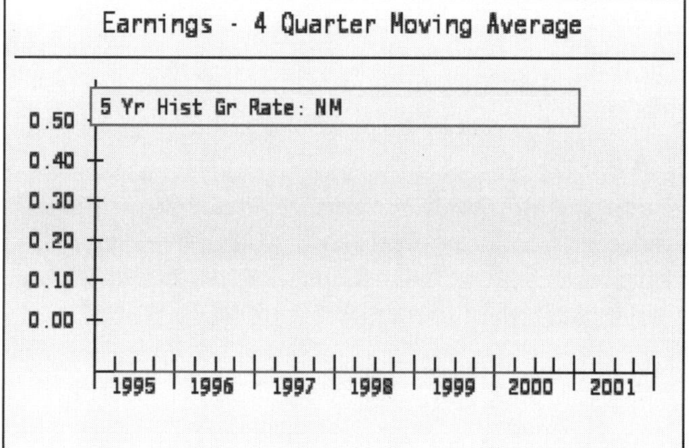

Revenue Growth Chart

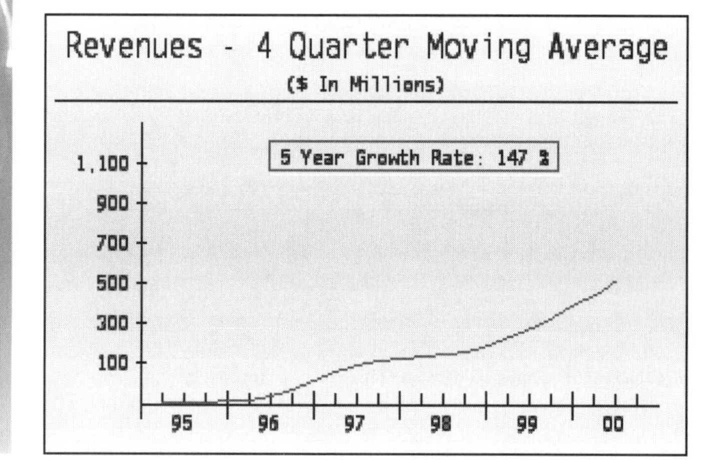

Charts provided by Baseline Financial Services.

78. PACCAR

Symbol: PCAR
Sector: Consumer Cyclical (Auto and Truck Manufacturers)

Company Profile

PACCAR manufactures light-, medium-, and heavy-duty trucks and related aftermarket parts. It also provides financial and leasing services. PACCAR's trucks are marketed under the DAF, Peterbilt, Kenworth, and Foden names. They are used worldwide for over-the-road and off-highway heavy-duty hauling of freight, wood products, petroleum, construction, and other materials. PACCAR also sells automotive parts and accessories under the names of Grand Auto and Al's Auto Supply, along with industrial winches under the Branden, Carco, and Gearmatics nameplates. Products are made and sold outside the United States in Australia, the United Kingdom, Mexico, and the Netherlands. PACCAR provides financing for its trucks in North America, Australia, and the United Kingdom, and also offers full-service truck leasing under the PacLease trade name.

Earnings

During the past 12 months, PACCAR earned $7.58 per share, up 27 percent from the previous year.

Revenues

Revenues during the past 12 months totaled $8.6 billion, up 5 percent from a year earlier.

Key Ratios & Measures	5-Year Range	Current
P/E	5–20	5.5
Price-to-Book	1.1–3.1	1.4
Price-to-Cash Flow	4.1–11	4.4
Price-to-Sales	0.3–0.8	0.37
Return on Equity	15.4–30.1%	27.75
Beta		0.96

CONTACT INFORMATION
PACCAR, Inc., 777 106th Avenue NE, Bellevue, WA 98004
(425) 468-7400
www.paccar.com

PACCAR (PCAR)

Price Action Chart

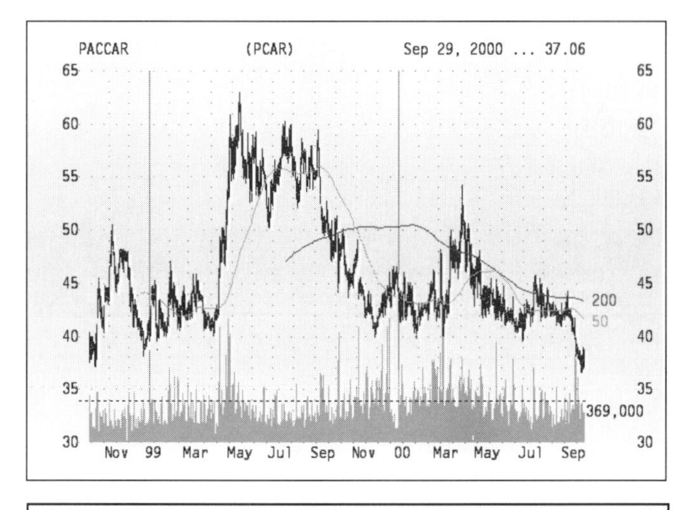

Earnings Growth Chart

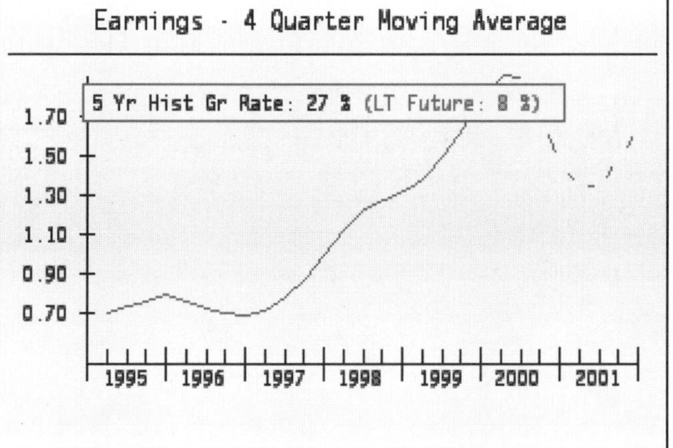

Revenue Growth Chart

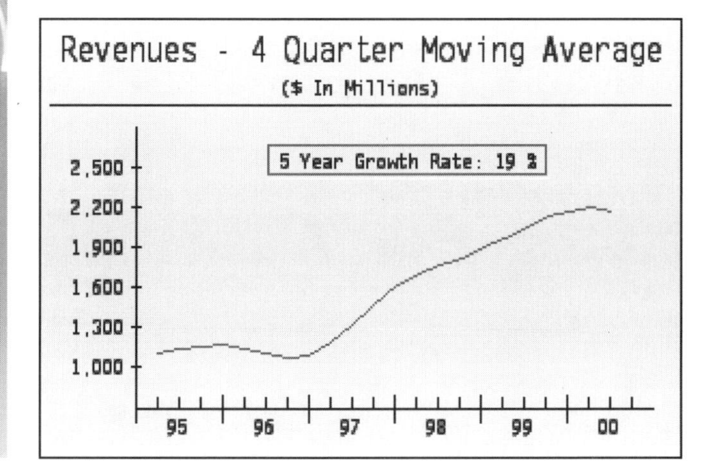

Charts provided by Baseline Financial Services.

79. PALM

Symbol: PALM
Sector: Technology (Computer Hardware)

COMPANY PROFILE

Palm is a late addition to the Nasdaq-100, replacing Global Crossing, which has decided to delist from the Nasdaq and now trades on the New York Stock Exchange. Palm provides handheld computing devices. The company develops, designs, and markets the Palm-III, Palm V, and Internet-enabled Palm VII product families, along with the new m100 entry-level device. The Palm platform combines the Palm OS system with HoySync technology enabling users to synchronize information between a Palm device and a personal computer. Palm also includes a pen-based input technology, and offers various personal information management applications such as a datebook and address book. Products are sold through distributors, retailers, resellers, and the Palm.com Web site.

EARNINGS

During the past 12 months, Palm earned $0.12 per share, up 100 percent from the previous year.

REVENUES

Revenues during the past 12 months totaled $1.3 billion, up 105 percent from a year earlier.

KEY RATIOS & MEASURES	5-YEAR RANGE	CURRENT
P/E	NM	441.1
Price-to-Book	10.9 - 90.6	28.4
Price-to-Cash Flow	148.1 - 1229.9	394.6
Price-to-Sales	8.7 - 72.8	23.3
Return on Equity	6.6 - 87.1%	6.6%
Beta		1.96

CONTACT INFORMATION

Palm, Inc., 5400 Bayfront Plaza, Santa Clara, CA 95052-8145
(408) 326-5000
www.palm.com

Palm (PALM)

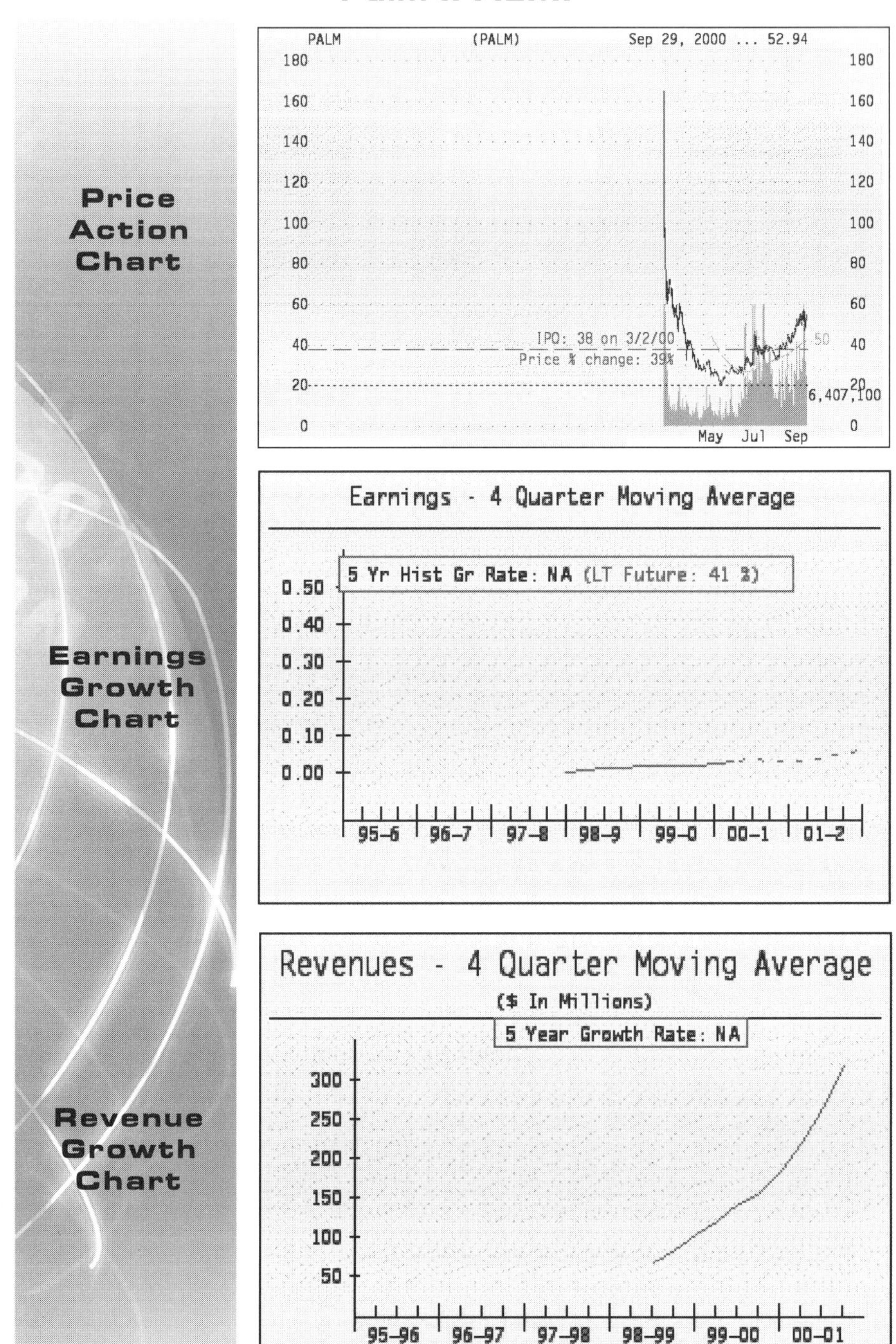

Charts provided by Baseline Financial Services.

80. PANAMSAT

Symbol: SPOT
Sector: Services (Communications Services)

COMPANY PROFILE

PanAmSat offers global satellite-based communication services. The company provides satellite capacity for television program distribution to network, cable, and other redistribution sources in the United States, Latin America, Africa, South Asia, the Asia-Pacific region, the Middle East, the Caribbean, and Europe. PanAmSat's global network of about 20 geostationary Earth-orbit satellites provides state-of-the-art video distribution and telecom services for customers worldwide. The company's satellites also serve as transmission platforms for about six direct-to-home services worldwide. Furthermore, PanAmSat offers satellite services to about 50 Internet service providers outside the U.S.

EARNINGS

During the past 12 months, PanAmSat earned $1.18 per share, up 46 percent from the previous year.

REVENUES

Revenues during the past 12 months totaled $1 billion, up 34 percent from a year earlier.

KEY RATIOS & MEASURES	5-YEAR RANGE	CURRENT
P/E	23–114	29.2
Price-to-Book	1.3–6.9	1.8
Price-to-Cash Flow	9.3–38.8	11.4
Price-to-Sales	4–12.9	4.96
Return on Equity	4.4–7.9%	6.2%
Beta		1.14

CONTACT INFORMATION
PanAmSat Corp., 1 Pickwick Plaza, Greenwich, CT 06830-5531
(203) 622-6664
www.panamsat.com

PanAmSat (SPOT)

Price Action Chart

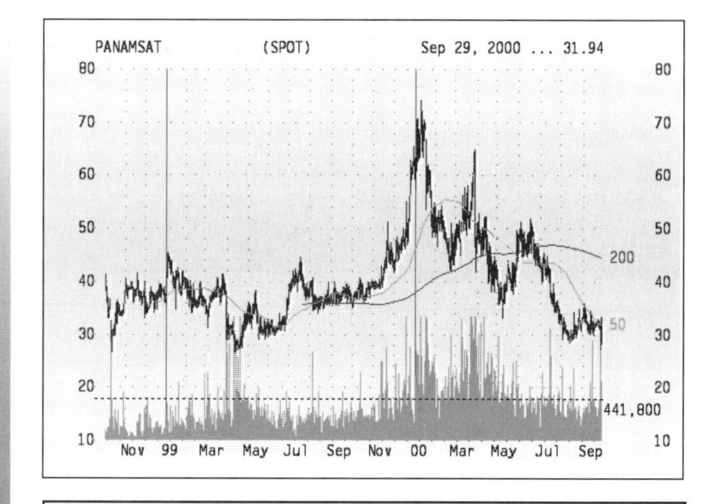

Earnings Growth Chart

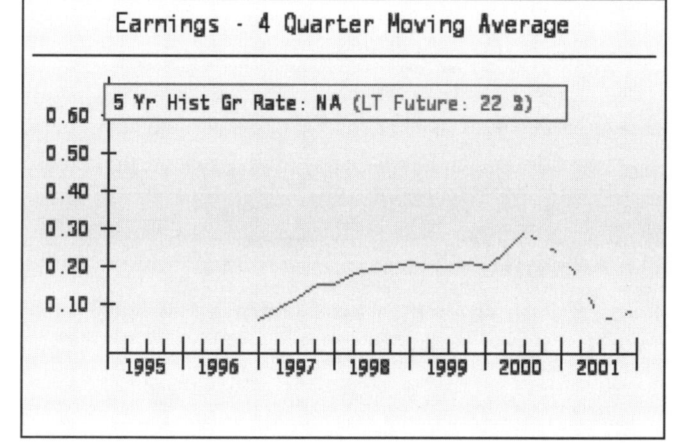

Revenue Growth Chart

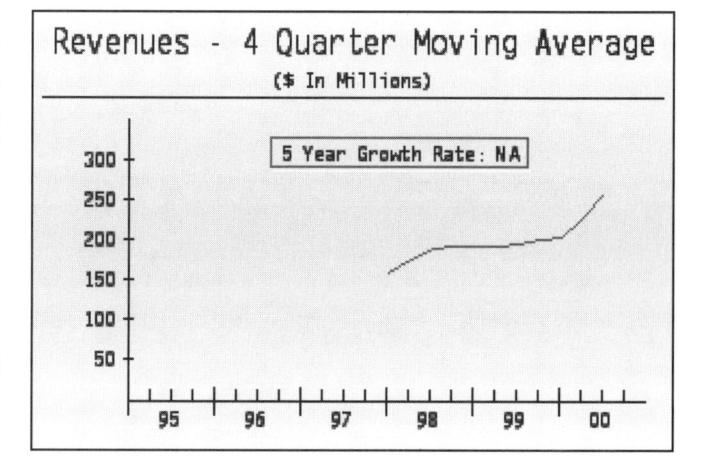

Charts provided by Baseline Financial Services.

81. PARAMETRIC TECHNOLOGY

Symbol: PMTC
Sector: Technology (Software and Programming)

COMPANY PROFILE

Parametric Technology develops, markets, and supports collaborative product commerce and flexible engineering solutions. The company provides software that streamlines engineering processes, improves product quality, optimizes product information management, and reduces cost and time-to-market cycles. Parametric's core business focus is to provide computer-aided design, manufacturing, and engineering solutions to customers through its Pro/Engineer design software. The company has also expanded its focus to include solutions offered by its Web-based Windchill information-management software. Parametric provides training, consulting, support, and implementation to its customers around the world. The company has more than 210 offices worldwide.

EARNINGS

During the past 12 months, Parametric Technology earned $0.18 per share, down 71 percent from the previous year.

REVENUES

Revenues during the past 12 months totaled $974 million, down 5 percent from a year earlier.

KEY RATIOS & MEASURES	5-YEAR RANGE	CURRENT
P/E	11–80	76.7
Price-to-Book	3.7–29.8	7.1
Price-to-Cash Flow	10.2–81.1	34
Price-to-Sales	2–10.4	3.91
Return on Equity	10–37.9%	10%
Beta		1.27

CONTACT INFORMATION

Parametric Technology Corp., 128 Technology Drive, Waltham, MA 02453
(781) 398-5000
www.ptc.com

Parametric Technology (PMTC)

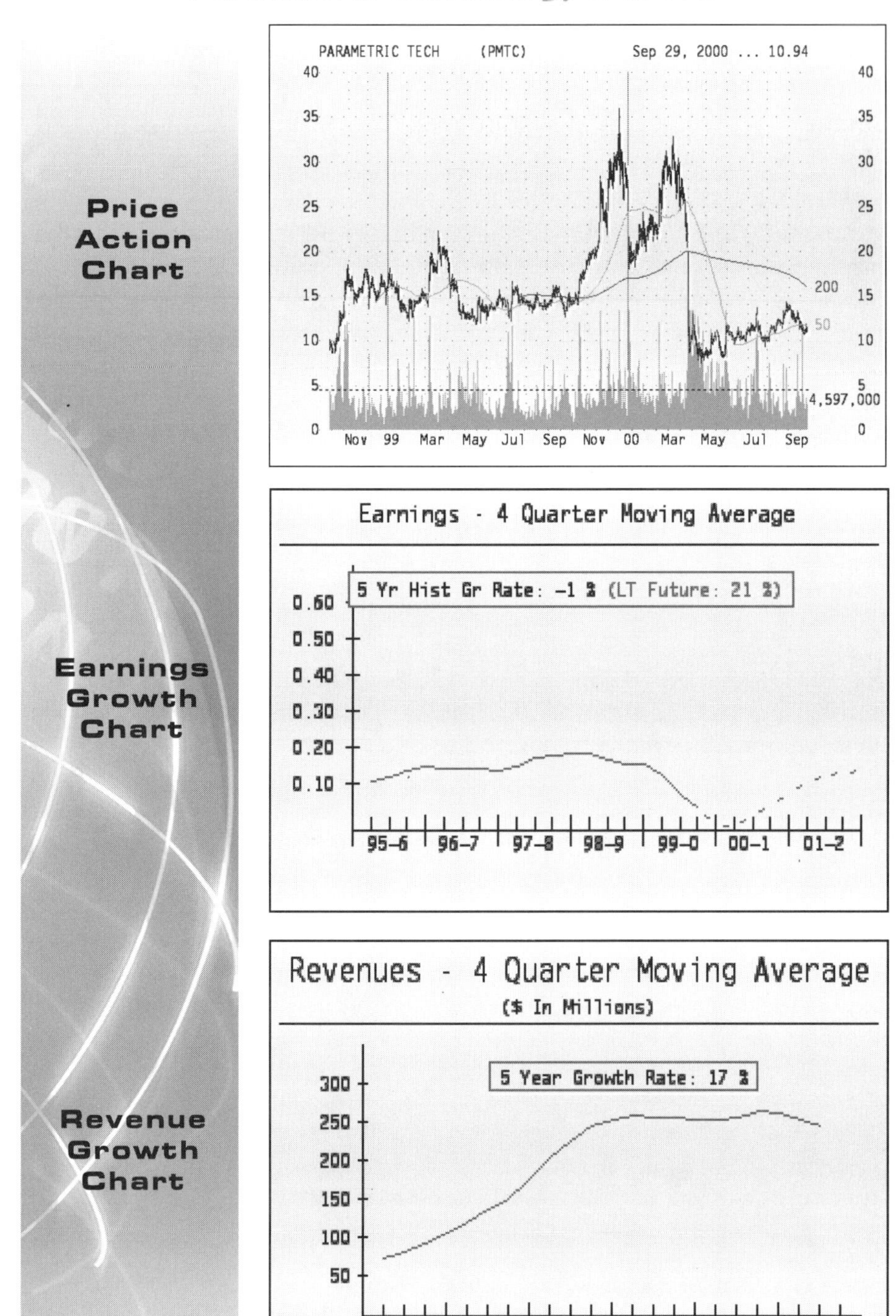

Charts provided by Baseline Financial Services.

82. PEOPLESOFT

Symbol: PSFT
Sector: Technology (Software and Programming)

COMPANY PROFILE

PeopleSoft develops, markets, and supports a family of enterprise Internet-based application software products designed for use in large- and medium-sized organizations. The company provides enterprise application software for customer-relationship management, human resource management, financial accounting, distribution, and supply-chain management, along with a range of industry-specific solutions. PeopleSoft's applications are designed to be flexible, rapidly implemented, scalable, and inexpensive to maintain and operate. PeopleSoft's more than 4,000 customers include corporations; higher education institutions; and federal, state, provincial, and local government agencies worldwide. The Vantive Corporation is also part of the PeopleSoft family.

EARNINGS

During the past 12 months, PeopleSoft earned $0.16 per share, down 57 percent from the previous year.

REVENUES

Revenues during the past 12 months totaled $1.5 billion, up 10 percent from a year earlier.

KEY RATIOS & MEASURES	5-YEAR RANGE	CURRENT
P/E	22–278	201.2
Price-to-Book	4–21.8	11
Price-to-Cash Flow	18.8–72.4	62.8
Price-to-Sales	2.2–12.3	6.04
Return on Equity	7–32.3%	7%
Beta		1.36

CONTACT INFORMATION

PeopleSoft, Inc., 4460 Hacienda Drive, Pleasanton, CA 94588-2738
(925) 694-3000
www.peoplesoft.com

PeopleSoft (PSFT)

Price Action Chart

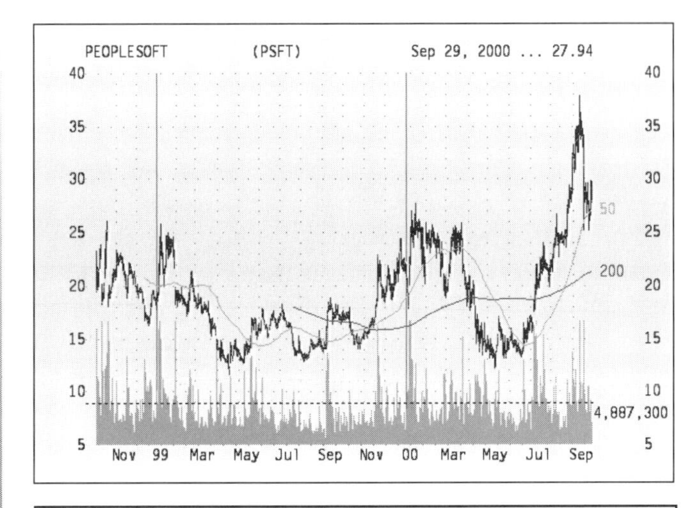

Earnings Growth Chart

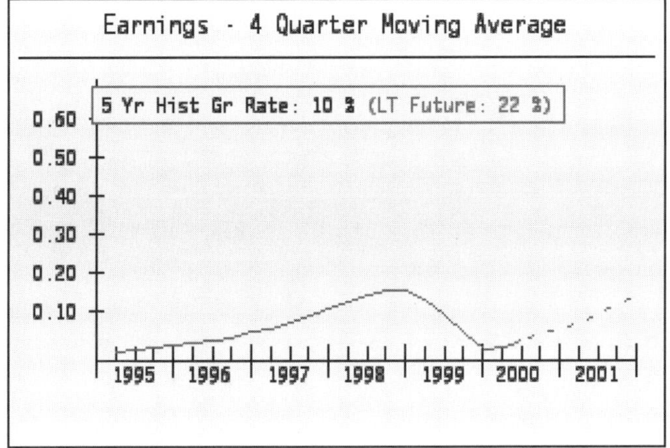

Revenue Growth Chart

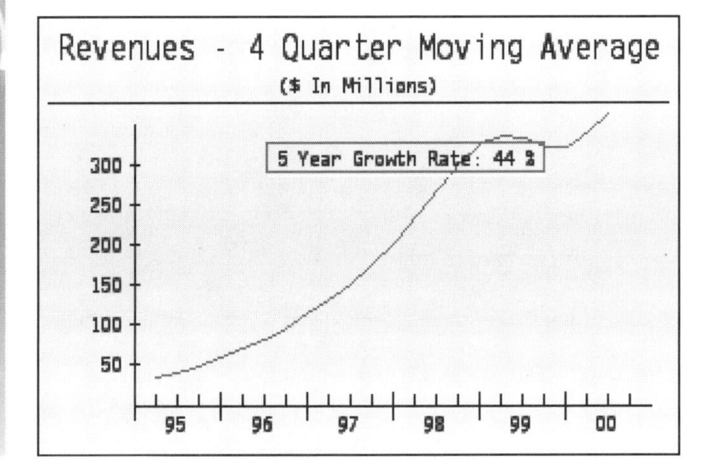

Charts provided by Baseline Financial Services.

83. QLOGIC

Symbol: QLGC
Sector: Technology (Semiconductors)

COMPANY PROFILE

QLogic designs and supplies semiconductor and board-level input–output products. These serve as interfaces between computer systems and their data-storage environments, such as hard-disk and tape drives, removable disk drives, CD-ROM drives, and RAID subsystems. In addition, the company designs and markets baseboard and enclosure management products that monitor and communicate management information related to components that are critical to computer system and storage subsystem reliability and availability. QLogic markets its products through a direct sales organization supported by field application engineers. Some of the company's customers include Sun Microsystems, Dell Computer, IBM, Fujitsu Limited, and Compaq. In 2000, QLogic acquired Ancor Communications, a leading provider of fibre channel switches.

EARNINGS

During the past 12 months, QLogic earned $0.89 per share, up 100 percent from the previous year.

REVENUES

Revenues during the past 12 months totaled $228 million, up 68 percent from a year earlier.

KEY RATIOS & MEASURES	5-YEAR RANGE	CURRENT
P/E	11–319	131.1
Price-to-Book	1.7–62.2	32.8
Price-to-Cash Flow	11.7–216.5	123.5
Price-to-Sales	0.5–79.2	45.19
Return on Equity	18.8–36.2%	36.2%
Beta		1.46

CONTACT INFORMATION

QLogic Corp., 26650 Laguna Hills Drive, Aliso Viejo, CA 92656
(949) 389-6000
www.qlogic.com

QLogic (QLGC)

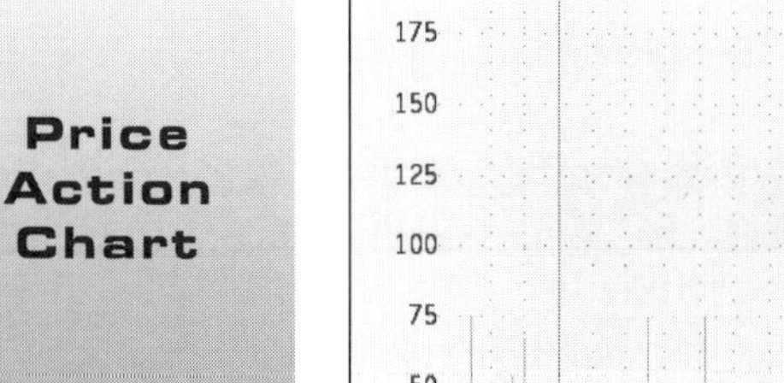

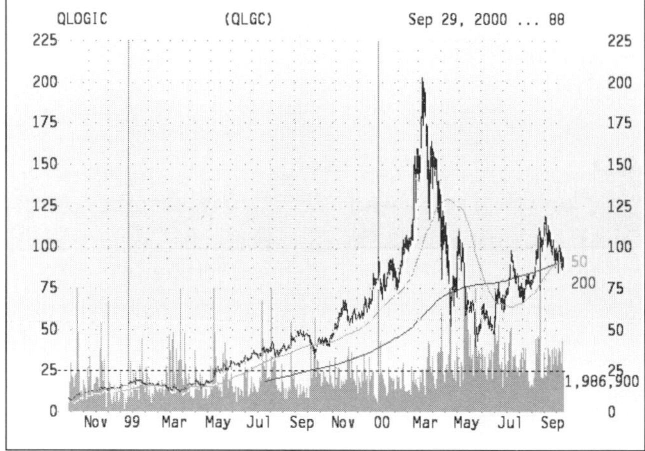

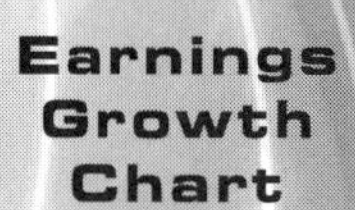

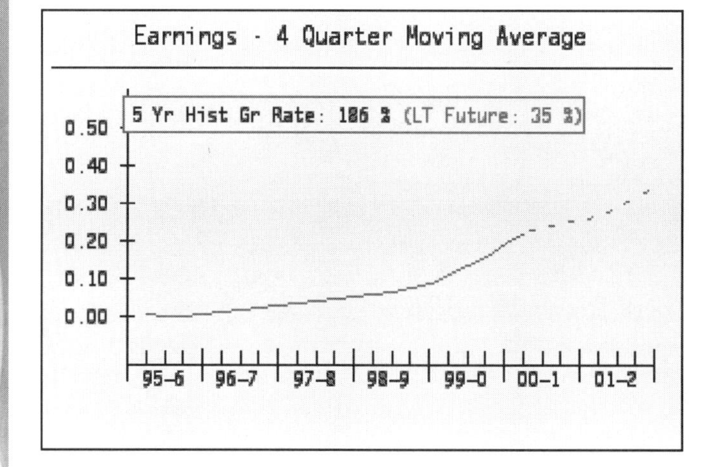

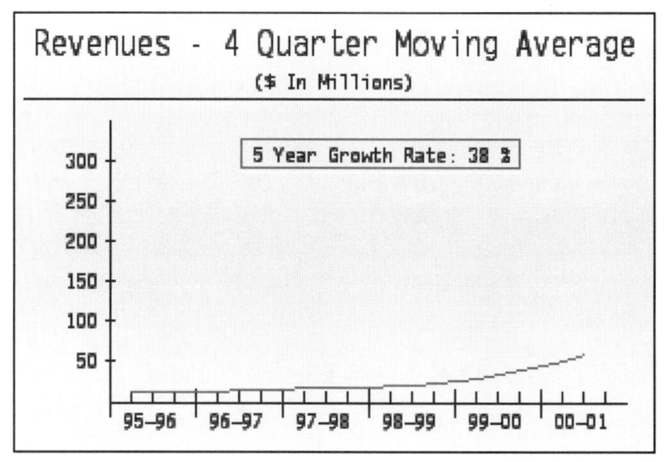

Charts provided by Baseline Financial Services.

84. QUALCOMM

Symbol: QCOM
Sector: Technology (Communications Equipment)

COMPANY PROFILE

QUALCOMM provides an array of digital wireless communications products, technologies, and services. The company designs and manufactures wireless communications, infrastructure, and subscriber products. It also creates and develops application-specific integrated circuits based on its Code Division Multiple Access (CDMA) technology. In addition, the company designs and makes products and services for the OmniTRACS two-way satellite-based data messaging and position-reporting system. What's more, QUALCOMM designs and manufactures subscriber products and ground communications systems for Globalstar L.P. In 1998 the company and Microsoft formed a 50-percent joint venture, Wireless Knowledge, to enable mobile users to enjoy secure and airlink-independent Internet access.

EARNINGS

During the past 12 months, QUALCOMM earned $1.01 per share, up 130 percent from the previous year.

REVENUES

Revenues during the past 12 months totaled $3.6 billion, down 5 percent from a year earlier.

KEY RATIOS & MEASURES	5-YEAR RANGE	CURRENT
P/E	22–310	58.8
Price-to-Book	1.4–41.7	11.3
Price-to-Cash Flow	7.7–220.6	48.5
Price-to-Sales	0.7–41	12.13
Return on Equity	2.6–20.8%	20.8%
Beta		1.62

CONTACT INFORMATION

QUALCOMM, Inc., 5775 Morehouse Drive, San Diego, CA 92121-1714
(858) 587-1121
www.qualcomm.com

QUALCOMM (QCOM)

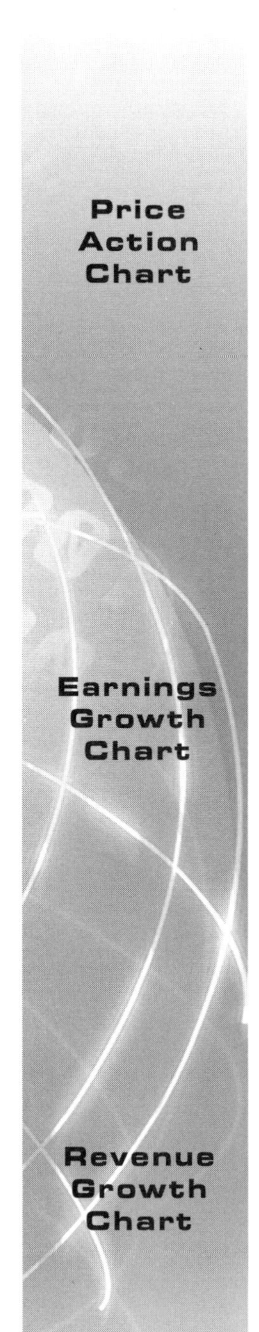

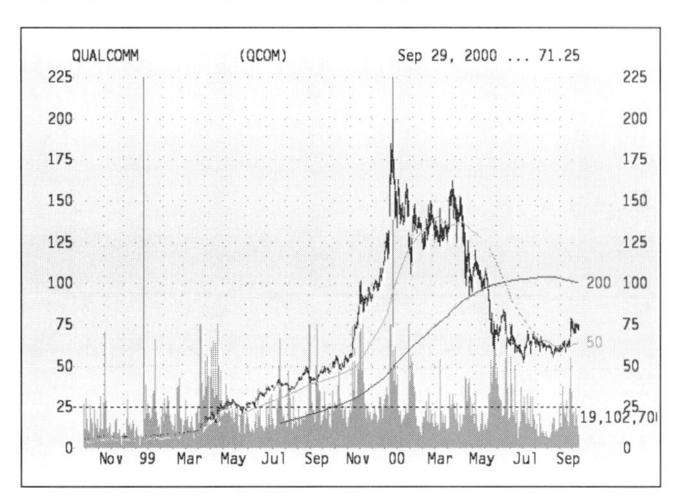

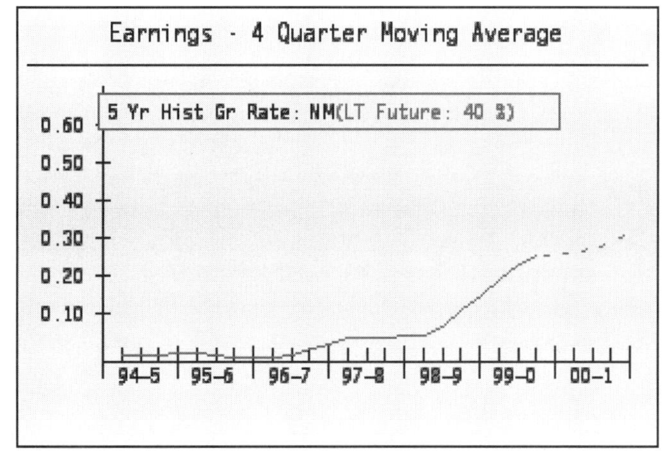

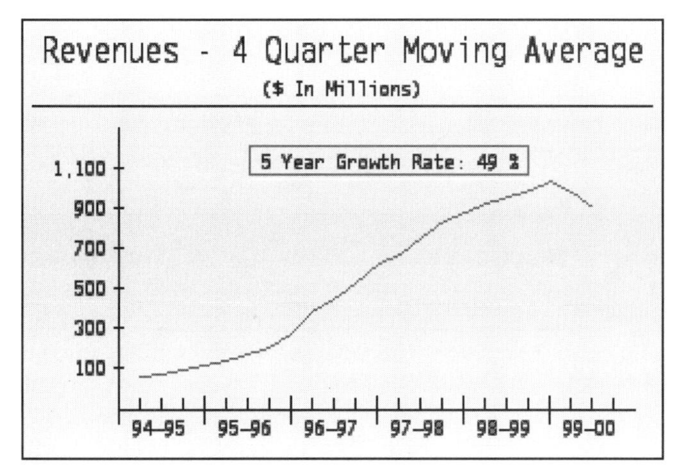

Charts provided by Baseline Financial Services.

85. Rational Software

Symbol: RATL
Sector: Technology (Software and Programming)

Company Profile

Rational Software provides integrated solutions that automate the software development process. The company serves customers in e-business, e-infrastructure, and e-devices. Rational's e-development solutions include software development tools, software engineering best practices, and services that unify cross-functional software teams. The company's products include requirements management software (RequisitePro); visual modeling software (Rational Rose); automated testing software (Rational Robot, TestFactor, Purify, PureCoverage, Quantify, and Visual Test); configuration and change management software (Rational ClearCase and ClearQuest); integrated development environment software (Rational Apex); and an integrated suite (Rational Suite).

Earnings

During the past 12 months, Rational Software earned $0.55 per share, up 53 percent from the previous year.

Revenues

Revenues during the past 12 months totaled $625 million, up 40 percent from a year earlier.

Key Ratios & Measures	5-Year Range	Current
P/E	10–129	126.1
Price-to-Book	1.4–29.3	26.1
Price-to-Cash Flow	7.2–102.2	100.3
Price-to-Sales	1.1–21.1	20.71
Return on Equity	20.4–25.2%	25.2%
Beta		1.5

CONTACT INFORMATION

Rational Software Corp., 18880 Homestead Road, Cupertino, CA 95014-0721
(408) 893-9900
www.rational.com

Rational Software (RATL)

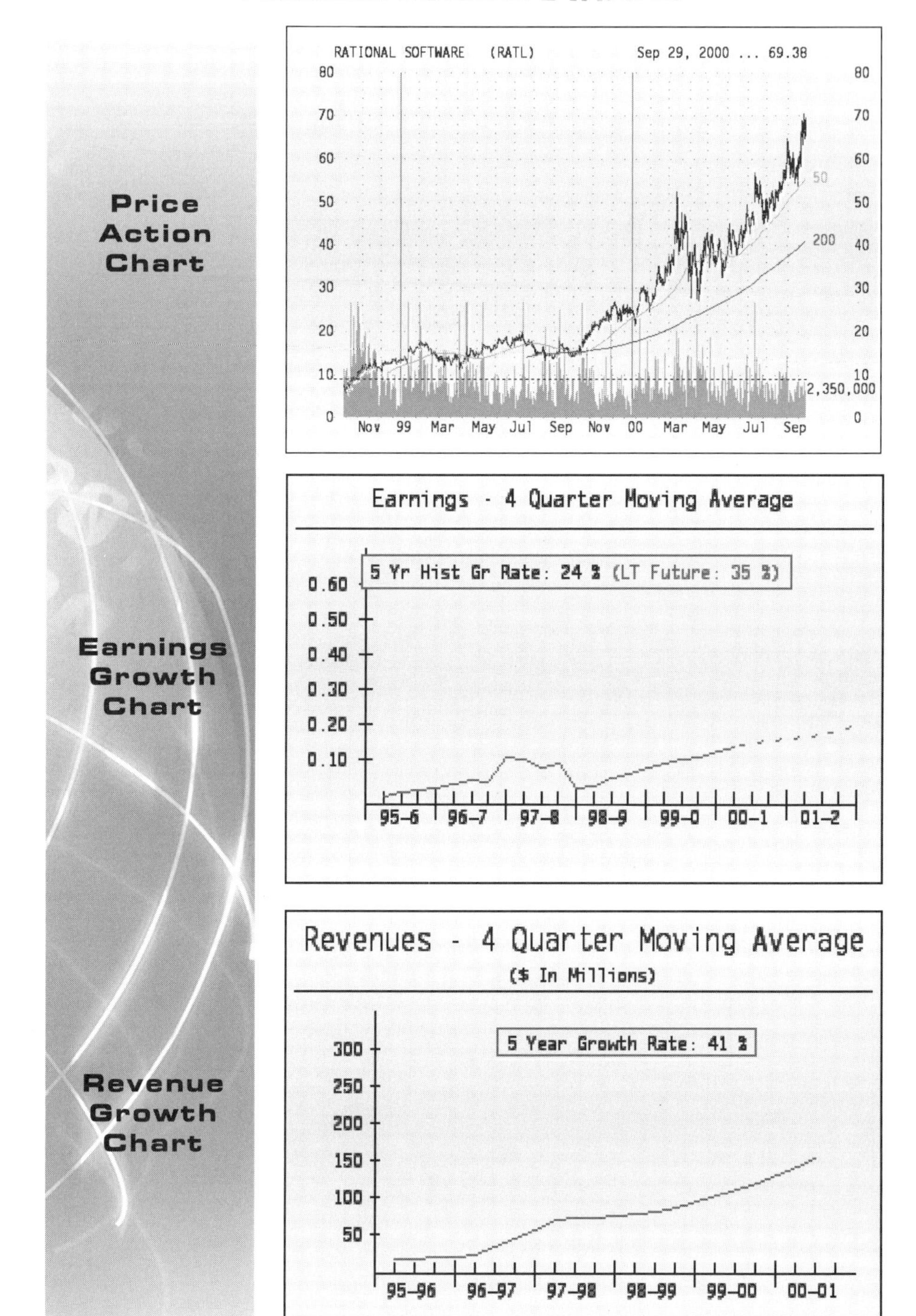

Charts provided by Baseline Financial Services.

86. REALNETWORKS

Symbol: RNWK
Sector: Technology (Software and Programming)

COMPANY PROFILE

RealNetworks provides media "streaming" software, enabling the creation and real-time delivery and playback of media content online. The company's products and services allow for the transmission of audio, video, text, animation, and other media content over the Internet on a live and on-demand basis. RealSystem G2 is a streaming media solution that includes RealAudio and RealVideo technology. The company also has an electronic commerce Web site to promote the proliferation of streaming media products, and a network of advertising-supported sites like Real.com, Film.com, and LiveConcerts.com. The RealPlayer product enables users to listen to or view content from Web sites that use the company's server products, providing basic functions like play, stop, rewind, and fast forward.

EARNINGS

During the past 12 months, RealNetworks earned $0.18 per share, up 997 percent from the previous year.

REVENUES

Revenues during the past 12 months totaled $195 million, up 119 percent from a year earlier.

KEY RATIOS & MEASURES	5-YEAR RANGE	CURRENT
P/E	NM	285.4
Price-to-Book	4–42.2	21.5
Price-to-Cash Flow	79.7–823.7	222.1
Price-to-Sales	6.9–106.6	40.21
Return on Equity	3.3–7%	7%
Beta		2.51

NM, Not Meaningful

CONTACT INFORMATION

RealNetworks, Inc., 2601 Elliott Avenue, #1000, Seattle, WA 98121
(360) 674-2700
www.realnetworks.com

RealNetworks (RNWK)

Price Action Chart

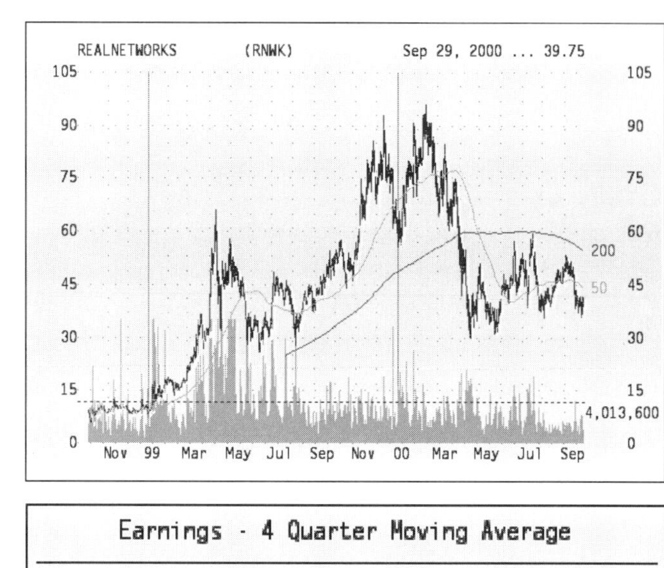

Earnings Growth Chart

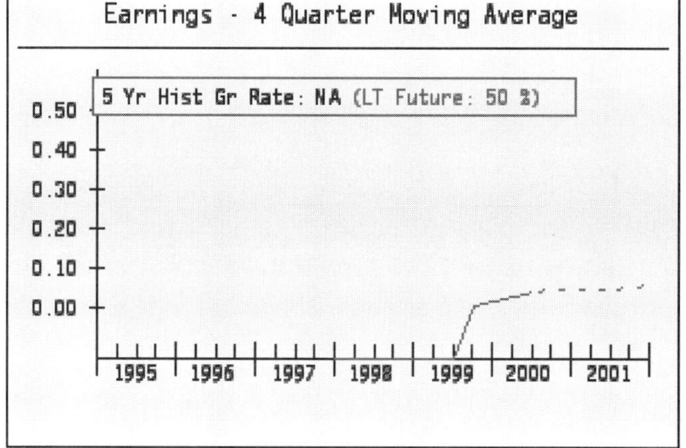

Revenue Growth Chart

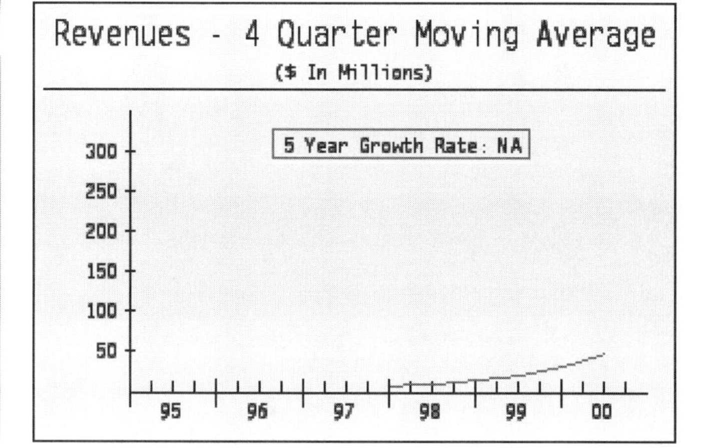

Charts provided by Baseline Financial Services.

87. RF MICRO DEVICES

Symbol: RFMD
Sector: Technology (Semiconductors)

COMPANY PROFILE

RF Micro Devices designs, develops, manufactures, and markets proprietary radio-frequency integrated circuits (RFICs) for wireless communications applications. Such applications include cellular and personal communication services, cordless telephony, wireless local area networks (LAN), wireless local loops, industrial radios, wireless security, and remote meter reading. The company offers a broad array of products, including amplifiers, mixers, modulators/demodulators, and single-chip transceivers, which represent a substantial majority of the RFICs required in wireless subscriber equipment. Customers include Nokia Mobile Phones, LG Information and Communications, Ericsson Mobile Communications, Samsung Electronics, QUALCOMM, and Motorola.

EARNINGS

During the past 12 months, RF Micro Devices earned $0.33 per share, up 82 percent from the previous year.

REVENUES

Revenues during the past 12 months totaled $325 million, up 70 percent from a year earlier.

KEY RATIOS & MEASURES	5-YEAR RANGE	CURRENT
P/E	72–336	131.4
Price-to-Book	2.3–48.8	21.8
Price-to-Cash Flow	34.2–973.2	101.5
Price-to-Sales	1.4–45.7	21.47
Return on Equity	9–18.8%	18.8%
Beta		2.1

CONTACT INFORMATION

RF Micro Devices, Inc., 7628 Thorndike Road, Greensboro, NC 27409-9421
(336) 664-1233
www.rfmd.com

RF Micro Devices (RFMD)

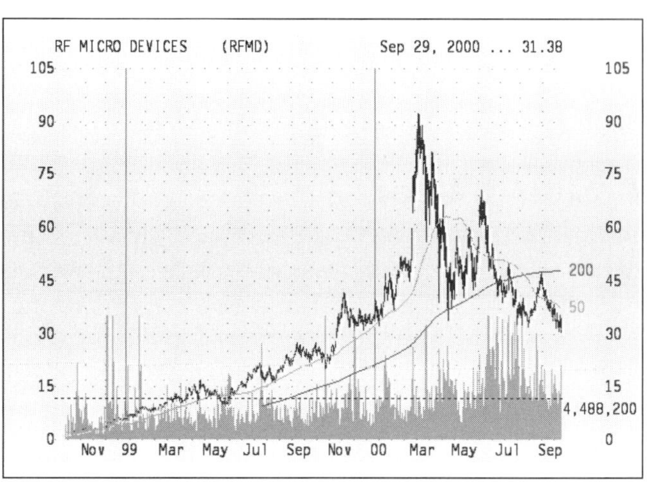

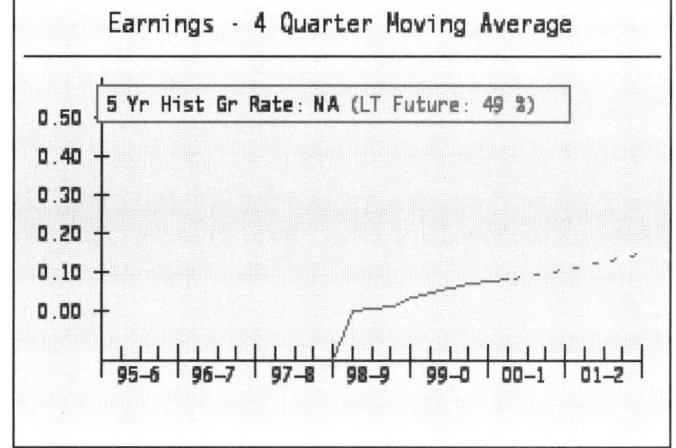

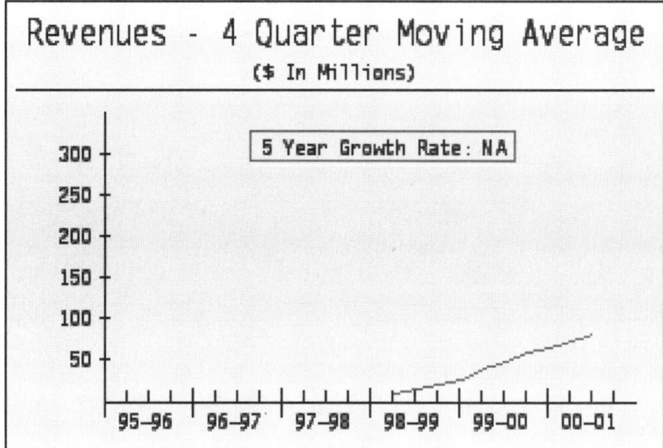

Charts provided by Baseline Financial Services.

88. SDL

Symbol: SDLI
Sector: Technology (Semiconductors)

COMPANY PROFILE

SDL designs and manufactures semiconductor lasers, fiber-optic-related products, and optoelectronic systems. Its semiconductor lasers are used in a wide variety of applications, including fiber-optic and satellite communications, cable television, materials processing, printing, data storage, medical treatment, computer displays, military equipment, and scientific instrumentation. SDL's optical communications products, led by its flagship 980-nanometer semiconductor laser pump module, power the transmission of data, voice, and Internet information over fiber-optic networks to meet the needs of telecommunications, dense wavelength division multiplexing, cable TV, and satellite communications applications. During 2000, SDL acquired Veritech Microwave and Photonic Integration Research. It also agreed to merge with JDS Uniphase.

EARNINGS

During the past 12 months, SDL earned $0.82 per share, up 178 percent from the previous year.

REVENUES

Revenues during the past 12 months totaled $289 million, up 116 percent from a year earlier.

KEY RATIOS & MEASURES	5-YEAR RANGE	CURRENT
P/E	10–562	489.2
Price-to-Book	1.2–71.7	62.4
Price-to-Cash Flow	5.7–473.4	412.3
Price-to-Sales	1–122.1	106.29
Return on Equity	3.5–15.1%	3.5%
Beta		1.56

CONTACT INFORMATION

SDL, Inc., 80 Rose Orchard Way, San Jose, CA 95134-1365
(408) 943-9411
www.sdli.com

SDL (SDLI)

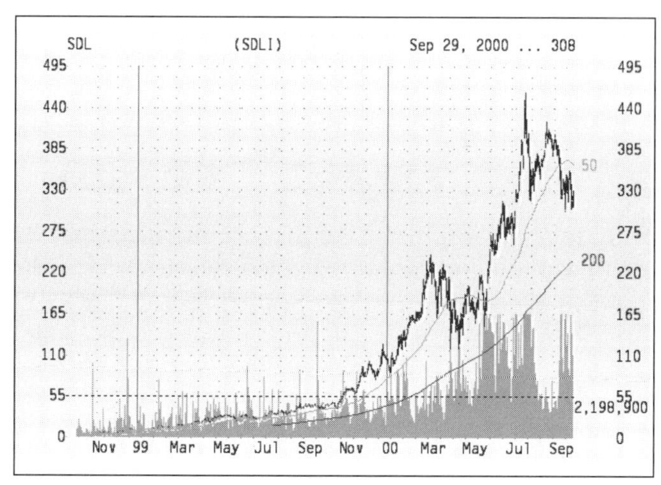

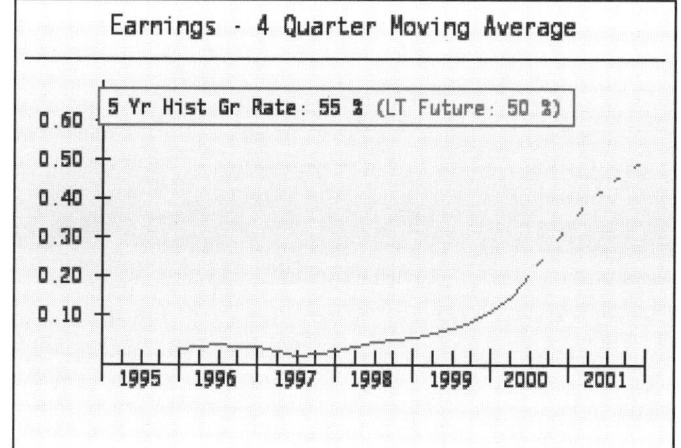

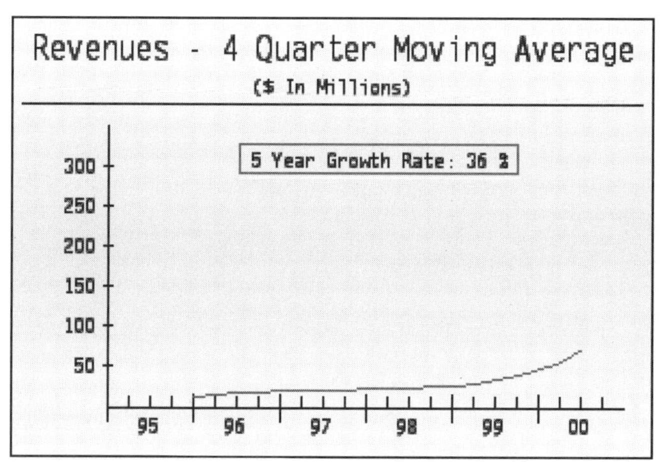

Charts provided by Baseline Financial Services.

89. SIEBEL SYSTEMS

Symbol: SEBL
Sector: Technology (Software and Programming)

COMPANY PROFILE

Siebel Systems provides customer relationship management software. The company's suite of Web-based e-Business application software provides organizations with one view of the customer across multiple distribution channels, including the Web, call centers, field sales and service units, resellers, partners, and dealers. The software is designed to provide support for sales, marketing, and customer service organizations, and to unite the company with its partners, resellers, and customers in one global information system. The software is available in versions intended for the pharmaceutical, healthcare, consumer goods, telecommunications, insurance, energy, automotive, apparel, and finance industries. During 2000, Siebel acquired both OpenSite Technologies and OnLink Technologies, both of which provide sales support software.

EARNINGS

During the past 12 months, Siebel Systems earned $0.69 per share, up 77 percent from the previous year.

REVENUES

Revenues during the past 12 months totaled $1.2 billion, up 111 percent from a year earlier.

KEY RATIOS & MEASURES	5-YEAR RANGE	CURRENT
P/E	28–337	283.6
Price-to-Book	4.1–52.8	50.7
Price-to-Cash Flow	20.2–253.9	244.1
Price-to-Sales	2.2–34.7	33.35
Return on Equity	11–25.3%	21%
Beta		1.71

CONTACT INFORMATION

Siebel Systems, Inc., 1855 South Grant Street, San Mateo, CA 94402-2647
(650) 295-5000
www.siebel.com

Siebel Systems (SEBL)

Price Action Chart

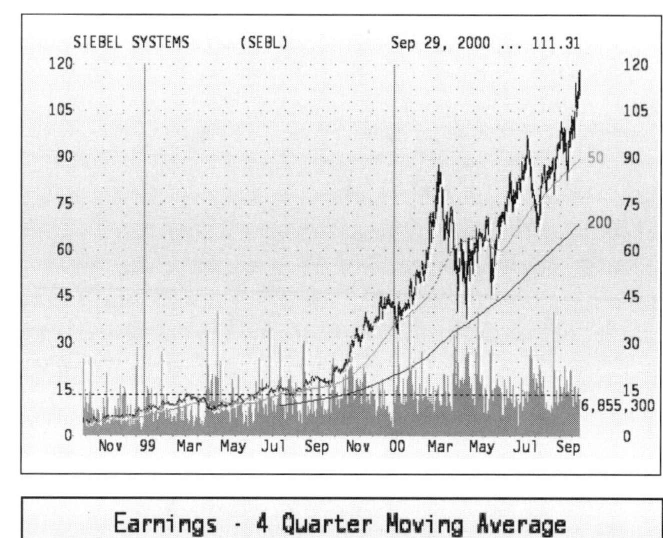

Earnings Growth Chart

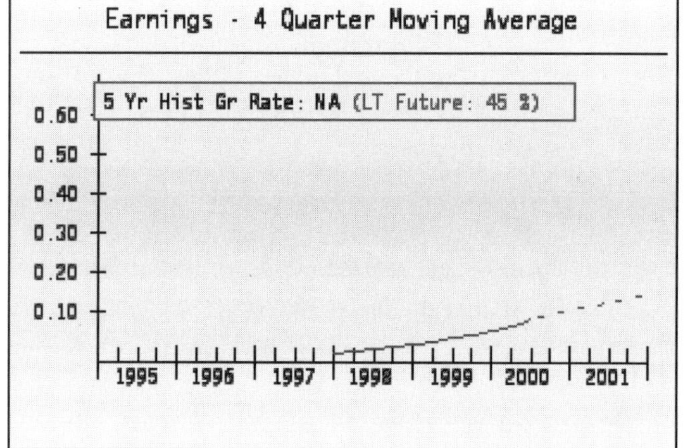

Revenue Growth Chart

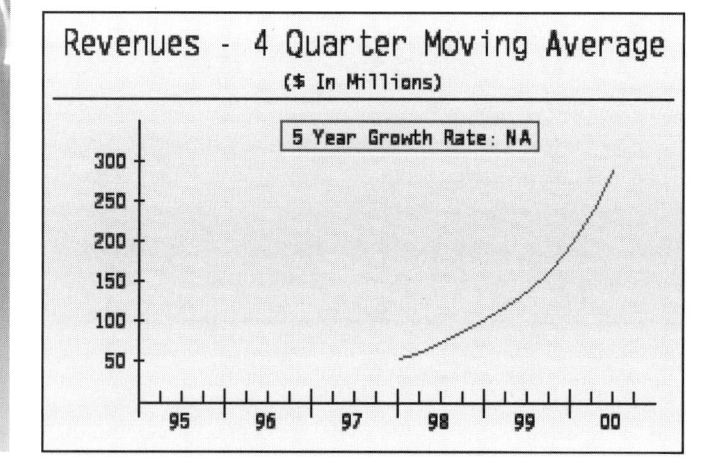

Charts provided by Baseline Financial Services.

90. SMURFIT-STONE CONTAINER

Symbol: SSCC
Sector: Basic Materials (Paper and Paper Products)

COMPANY PROFILE

Smurfit-Stone Container Corporation (SSCC) produces paper-based packaging and other products. SSCC's containerboard and corrugated containers segment makes corrugated containers, containerboard, kraft paper, solid bleached sulfate, and pulp; its boxboard and folding cartons segment produces coated recycled boxboard and folding cartons. SSCC also manufactures multi-wall bags, consumer bags, intermediate bulk containers, uncoated recycled boxboard, paper tubes and cores, solid fiber partitions, consumer packaging, and Cladwood, a wood composite panel used by the housing industry. The company, which owns some 132,000 acres of timberland in Canada, operates 285 production plants around the world. In 2000, Smurfit-Stone also acquired St. Laurent Paperboard.

EARNINGS

During the past 12 months, Smurfit-Stone Container earned $0.59 per share, up 186 percent from the previous year.

REVENUES

Revenues during the past 12 months totaled $7.6 billion, up 41 percent from a year earlier.

KEY RATIOS & MEASURES	5-YEAR RANGE	CURRENT
P/E	4–170	22.8
Price-to-Book	1.2–3.1	1.5
Price-to-Cash Flow	3.8–30.2	5.1
Price-to-Sales	0.3–1.4	0.39
Return on Equity	6.6–9.4%	6.6%
Beta		0.87

CONTACT INFORMATION

Smurfit-Stone Container Corporation, 150 North Michigan Avenue, Chicago, IL 60601
(312) 346-6600
www.smurfit-stone.net

Smurfit-Stone Container (SSCC)

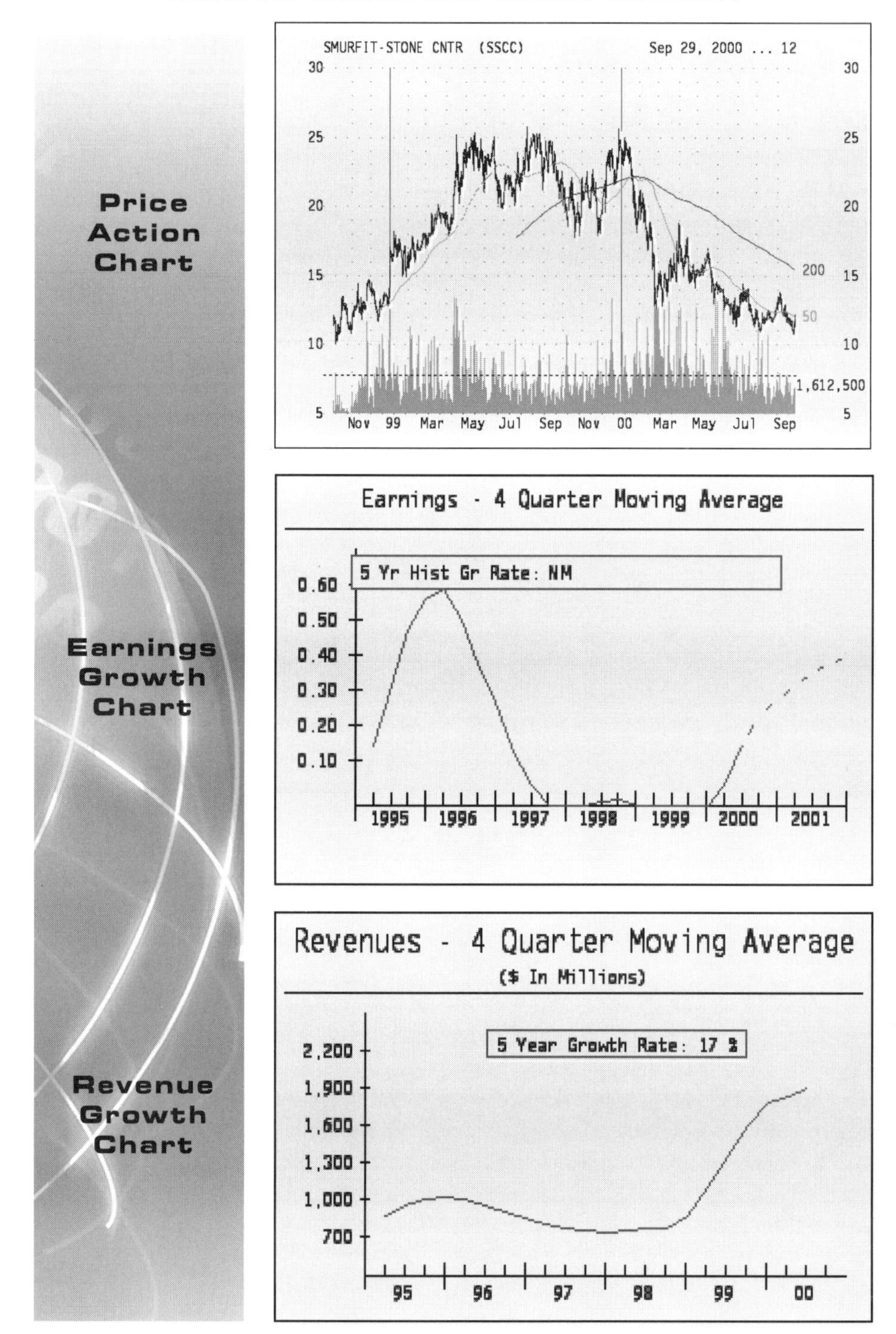

Charts provided by Baseline Financial Services.

91. STAPLES

Symbol: SPLS
Sector: Consumer/Noncyclical (Office Supplies)

COMPANY PROFILE

Staples sells office products, supplies, business machines, business services, furniture, and computers through nearly 1,130 stores in the United States, Canada, the United Kingdom, Germany, the Netherlands, and Portugal. The stores operate in the U.S. and Canada under the Staples and Staples Express names, and elsewhere under the Staples name. Usually located in the suburbs and averaging some 24,000 square feet, the Staples superstores generate most of the company's sales and profits. In selected urban markets, the company operates Staples Express stores, which range in size from 6,000 to 10,000 square feet. Staples also operates a mail-order catalog business under the Staples Direct name, and a Web-based superstore at Staples.com.

EARNINGS

During the past 12 months, Staples earned $0.72 per share, up 21 percent from the previous year.

REVENUES

Revenues during the past 12 months totaled $9.7 billion, up 22 percent from a year earlier.

KEY RATIOS & MEASURES	5-YEAR RANGE	CURRENT
P/E	18–66	22
Price-to-Book	2.7–8.9	3.7
Price-to-Cash Flow	12.2–41.4	14.6
Price-to-Sales	0.5–2.1	0.79
Return on Equity	14.1–19.5%	19.5%
Beta		1.08

CONTACT INFORMATION

Staples, Inc., 500 Staples Drive, Framingham, MA 01702
(508) 253-5000
www.staples.com

Staples (SPLS)

Price Action Chart

Earnings Growth Chart

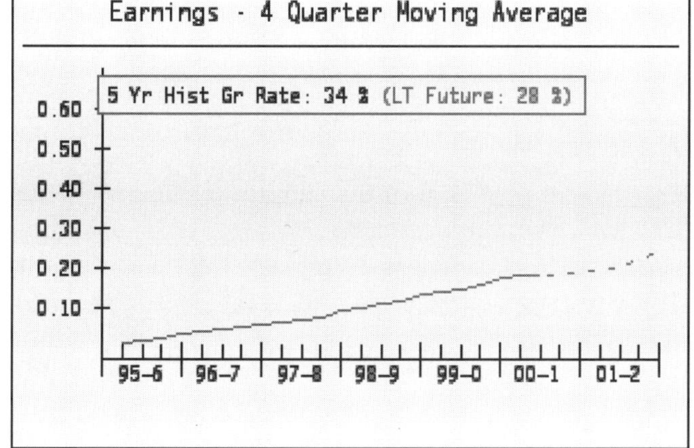

Revenue Growth Chart

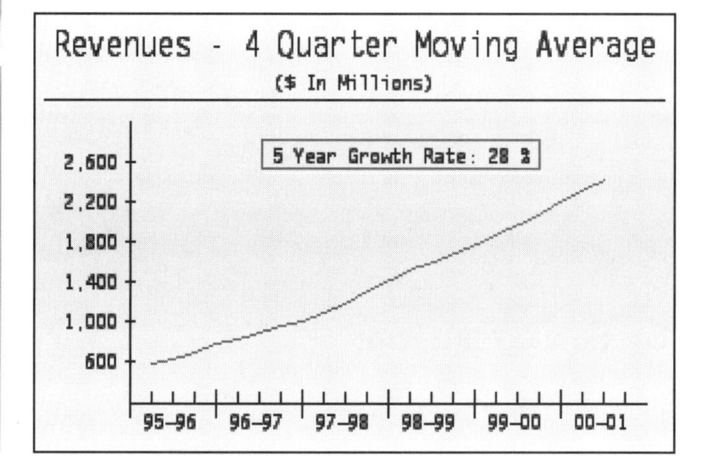

Charts provided by Baseline Financial Services.

92. STARBUCKS

Symbol: SBUX
Sector: Consumer/Noncyclical (Food Processing)

COMPANY PROFILE

Starbucks purchases and roasts high-quality whole-bean coffees and sells them (along with fresh-brewed coffees, Italian-style espresso beverages, teas, pastries and confections, and coffee-related accessories and equipment) through company-operated retail stores. The company has more than 2,100 Starbucks stores in 34 U.S. states, the District of Columbia, five Canadian provinces, and the United Kingdom. Starbucks also sells whole-bean coffees through specialty sales operations, and produces and sells bottled Frappuccino coffee drinks and a line of premium ice creams through joint venture partnerships. The company recently acquired Pasqua, a roaster and retailer of specialty coffee, and Tazo, a producer of premium teas.

EARNINGS

During the past 12 months, Starbucks earned $0.65 per share, up 26 percent from the previous year.

REVENUES

Revenues during the past 12 months totaled $2.1 billion, up 32 percent from a year earlier.

KEY RATIOS & MEASURES	5-YEAR RANGE	CURRENT
P/E	35–95	58
Price-to-Book	2.4–8	6.6
Price-to-Cash Flow	14.8–41.2	30.5
Price-to-Sales	1.4–4.2	3.35
Return on Equity	10.3–11.7%	11.7%
Beta		1

CONTACT INFORMATION

Starbucks Corporation, 2401 Utah Avenue South, Seattle, WA 98134-2028
(206) 447-1575
www.starbucks.com

Starbucks (SBUX)

Price Action Chart

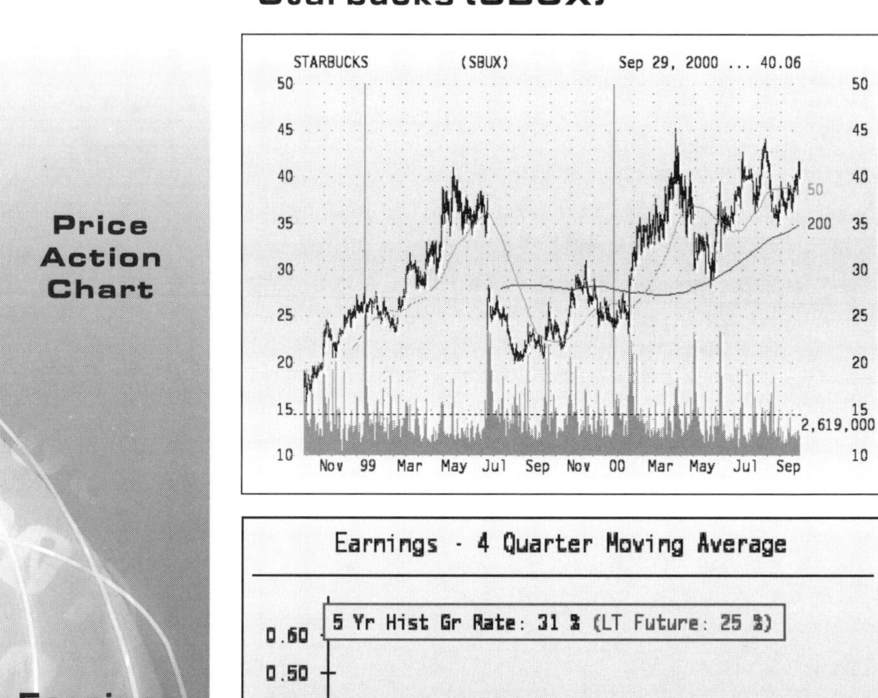

Earnings Growth Chart

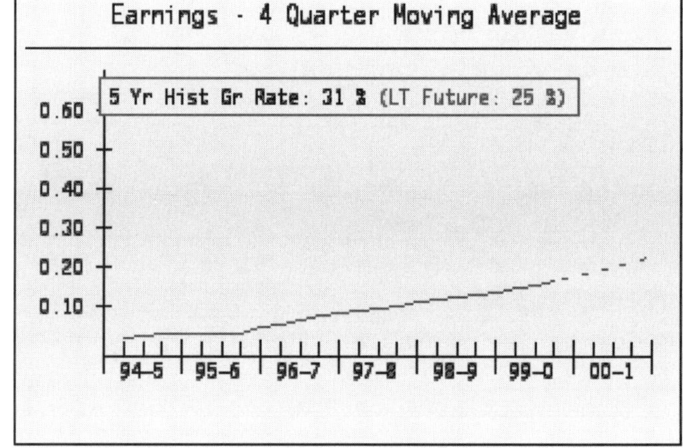

Revenue Growth Chart

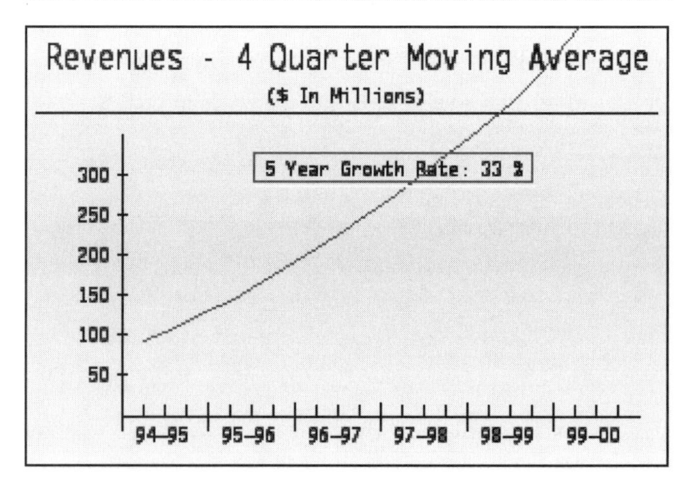

Charts provided by Baseline Financial Services.

93. TELLABS

Symbol: TLAB
Sector: Technology (Communications Equipment)

COMPANY PROFILE

Tellabs designs and manufactures digital cross-connect systems, managed digital networks, network access products, and fiber-optic systems used by a variety of customers worldwide. The company's cross-connect systems include the Titan 5500/5500S and 5300 series of digital systems. Tellabs's managed digital networks include the MartisDXX integrated access and transport system, statistical multiplexers, packet and T1 multiplexers, and network management systems. Network access products include echo cancellers, voice frequency units, and local access products. Customers include public telephone companies, long-distance carriers, alternate service providers, wireless service providers, cable operators, system integrators, government agencies, utilities, and business end-users.

EARNINGS

During the past 12 months, Tellabs earned $1.40 per share, up 23 percent from the previous year.

REVENUES

Revenues during the past 12 months totaled $2.7 billion, up 41 percent from a year earlier.

KEY RATIOS & MEASURES	5-YEAR RANGE	CURRENT
P/E	18–68	41.4
Price-to-Book	4.4–15.3	10.1
Price-to-Cash Flow	13.6–50.2	36.1
Price-to-Sales	3.1–13.4	8.63
Return on Equity	23–34.6%	29.2%
Beta		1.76

CONTACT INFORMATION
Tellabs, Inc., 4951 Indiana Avenue, Lisle, IL 60532-3818
(630) 378-8800
www.tellabs.com

Tellabs (TLAB)

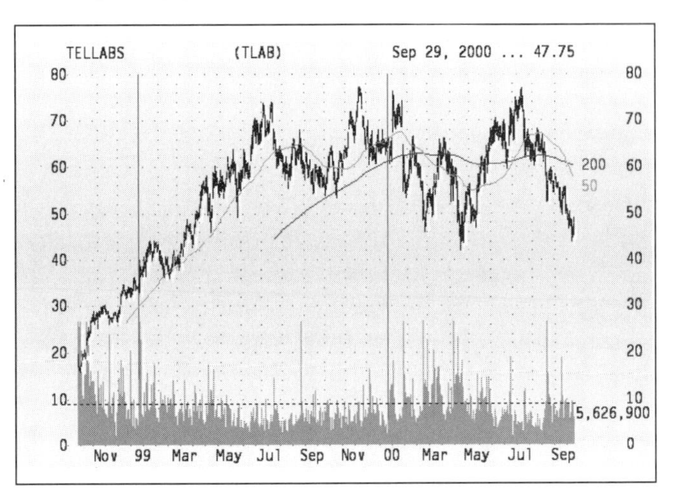

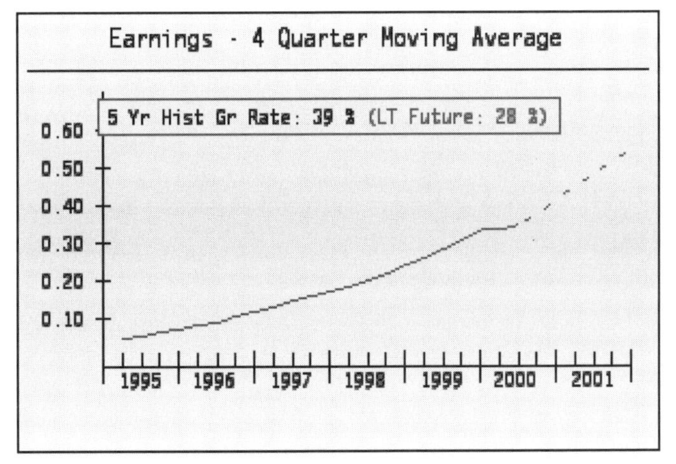

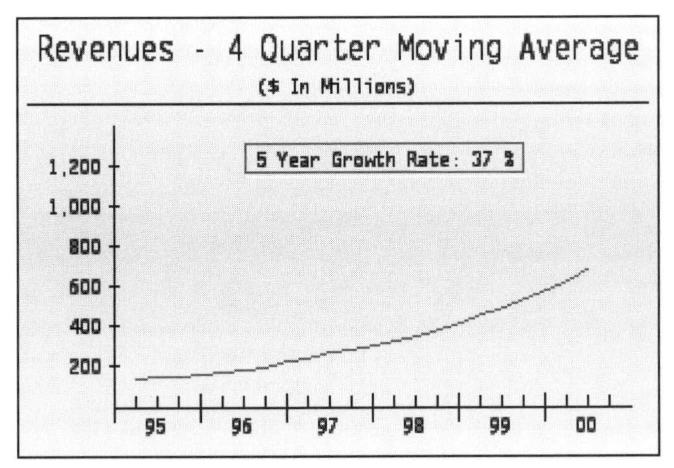

Charts provided by Baseline Financial Services.

94. 3COM

Symbol: COMS
Sector: Technology (Computer Networks)

COMPANY PROFILE

3Com specializes in products and services that provide solutions to complex networking challenges in the areas of broadband connections, wireless network access, and Internet protocol telephony. The company serves three primary customer markets: commercial enterprises with small- to mid-sized locations, general consumers, and carriers and network service providers. 3Com's commercial products include traditional access products (10/100 Network Interface Cards [NICs]), advanced access products (Gigabit NICs and mobile NICs), local area network (LAN)/wide area network (WAN) infrastructure products (switches and hubs), and LAN telephony products. Consumer products include broadband connections and home-networking products. During 2000, the company acquired Call Tech and Kerbango. It also owns a significant interest in handheld-devicemaker Palm.

EARNINGS

During the past 12 months, 3Com earned $0.07 per share, down 93 percent from the previous year.

REVENUES

Revenues during the past 12 months totaled $4.1 billion, down 21 percent from a year earlier.

KEY RATIOS & MEASURES	5-YEAR RANGE	CURRENT
P/E	2–38	33.9
Price-to-Book	0.4–2.6	1.5
Price-to-Cash Flow	2–16	12.4
Price-to-Sales	0.1–1.8	1.37
Return on Equity	1.4–30%	4.8%
Beta		1.48

CONTACT INFORMATION

3Com Corp., 5400 Bayfront Plaza, Santa Clara, CA 95052-8145
(408) 326-5000
www.3com.com

3Com (COMS)

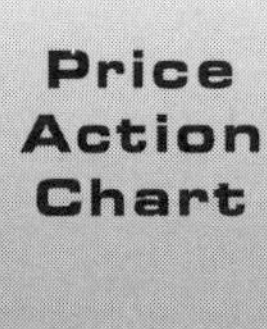

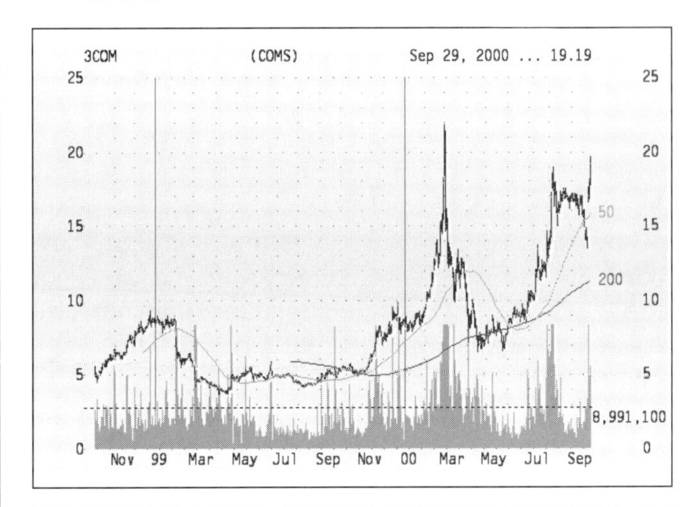

Earnings
Growth
Chart

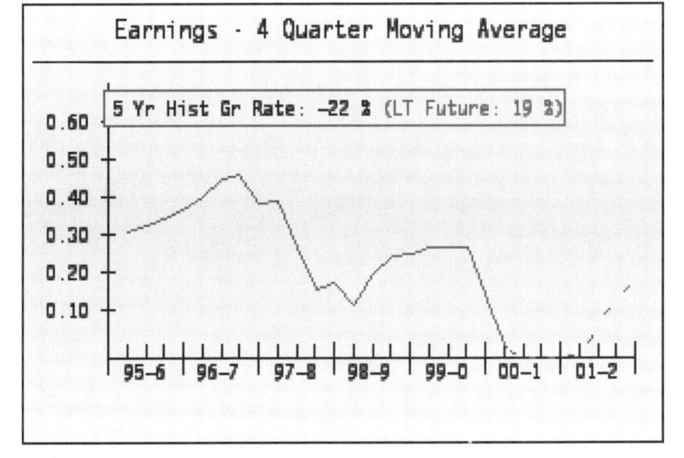

Revenue
Growth
Chart

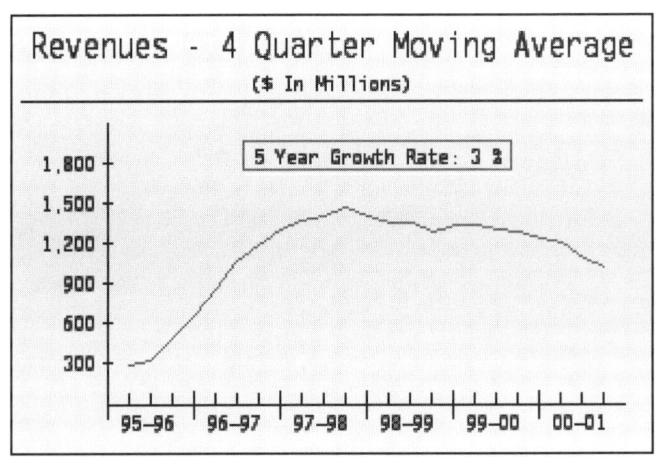

Charts provided by Baseline Financial Services.

95. TMP WORLDWIDE

Symbol: TMPW
Sector: Services (Advertising)

COMPANY PROFILE

TMP Worldwide provides recruitment advertising, yellow pages advertising, and executive search and selection services for more than 31,000 clients. TMP prospects for talent for its clients through recruiting programs that sell, market, and brand employers to job seekers looking for entry-level to $100,000-plus positions. The company also offers a range of search and selection services aimed at identifying and assessing mid-level and senior executives for its clients. In addition, TMP places advertisements in local yellow page directories for clients that sell products and services in multiple markets. The company also operates Monster.com, an Internet career destination and portal.

EARNINGS

During the past 12 months, TMP Worldwide earned $0.70 per share, up 59 percent from the previous year.

REVENUES

Revenues during the past 12 months totaled $946 million, up 39 percent from a year earlier.

KEY RATIOS & MEASURES	5-YEAR RANGE	CURRENT
P/E	25–200	115
Price-to-Book	3.4–25	21.2
Price-to-Cash Flow	9.9–83	70.6
Price-to-Sales	0.7–9.7	8.19
Return on Equity	3.9–14.7%	12%
Beta		1.57

CONTACT INFORMATION

TMP Worldwide, Inc., 1633 Broadway, 33rd Floor, New York, NY 10019
(212) 977-4200
www.tmp.com

TMP Worldwide (TMPW)

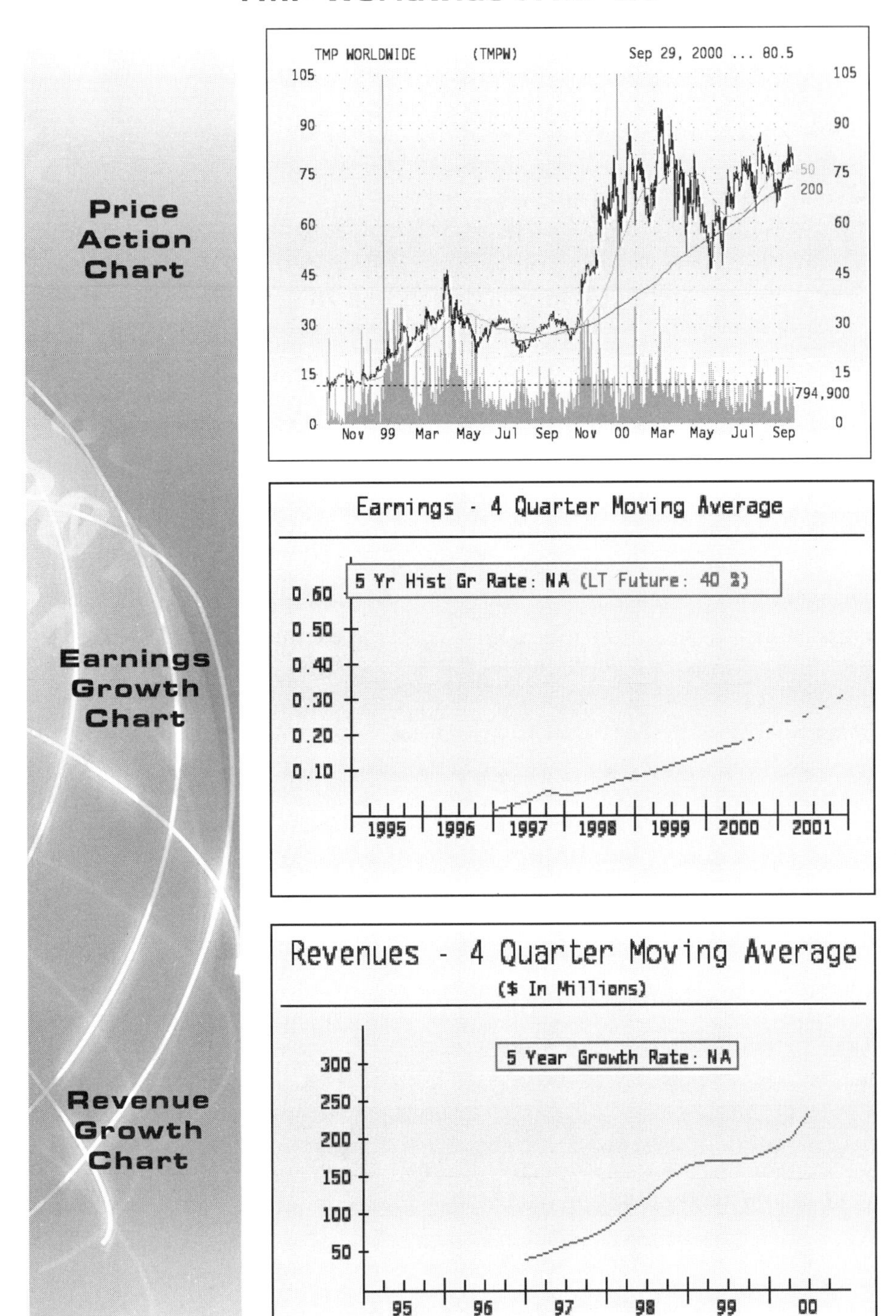

Charts provided by Baseline Financial Services.

96. VERISIGN

Symbol: VRSN
Sector: Technology (Software and Programming)

COMPANY PROFILE

VeriSign provides digital certificate services designed to enable Web sites, enterprises, and individuals to securely conduct electronic commerce and communicate over Internet-protocol networks. The company's Website Digital Certificate services are used by more than 400 of the Fortune 500 companies, and by all of the top 25 e-commerce Web sites listed by Jupiter Communications. It also offers the VeriSign OnSite service, which enables enterprises to develop and deploy customized digital certificate services for use by the company's employees, customers, and business partners. More than 300 enterprises have subscribed to the OnSite service since its introduction, including Bank of America, Hewlett-Packard, the Internal Revenue Service, Kodak, and Texas Instruments. In 2000, VeriSign acquired Internet domain-name registrar Network Solutions.

EARNINGS

During the past 12 months, VeriSign earned $0.15 per share, up 258 percent from the previous year.

REVENUES

Revenues during the past 12 months totaled $155 million, up 167 percent from a year earlier.

KEY RATIOS & MEASURES	5-YEAR RANGE	CURRENT
P/E	NM	NM
Price-to-Book	4.6–87	62.5
Price-to-Cash Flow	153.5–2411.8	1075.1
Price-to-Sales	11.4–322.8	232.12
Return on Equity	0.3–2.4%	0.3%
Beta		2.69

NM, Not Meaningful

CONTACT INFORMATION

VeriSign, Inc., 1350 Charleston Road, Mountain View, CA 94043-1331
(650) 961-7500
www.verisign.com

VeriSign (VRSN)

Price Action Chart

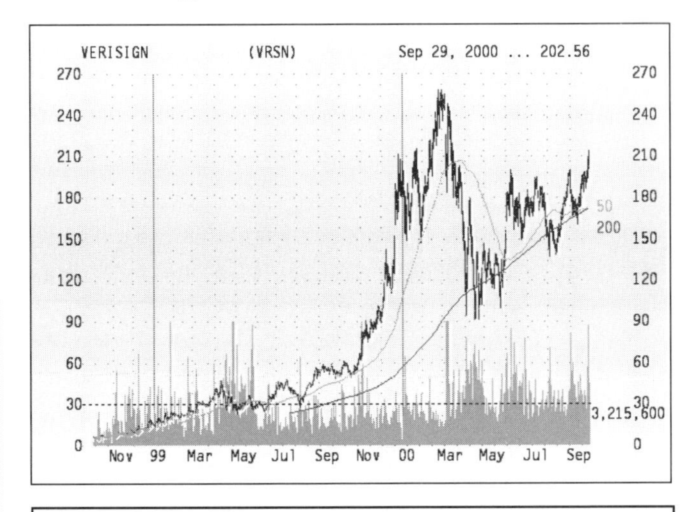

Earnings Growth Chart

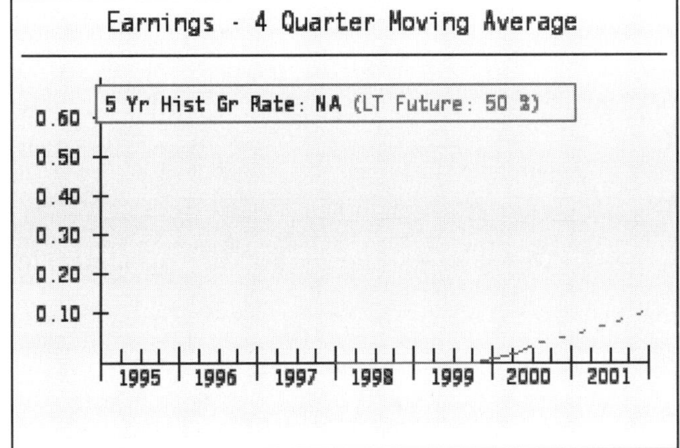

Revenue Growth Chart

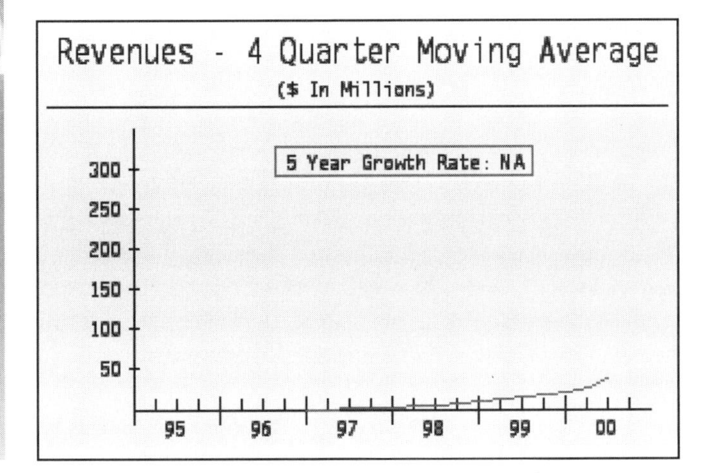

Charts provided by Baseline Financial Services.

97. VERITAS SOFTWARE

Symbol: VRTS
Sector: Technology (Software and Programming)

Company Profile

VERITAS Software develops and markets data-storage management software. The company's highly scalable products offer protection against data loss and file corruption; allow rapid recovery after disk or computer system failures; enable information technology managers to work efficiently with large numbers of files; and make it possible to manage data distributed across large networks of computer systems without harming productivity or interrupting users. VERITAS develops and sells products for most of the popular operating systems, including versions of UNIX and Windows NT. Its customers include original equipment manufacturers, value-added resellers, hardware distributors, application software vendors, and systems integrators. During 2000, VERITAS agreed to acquire Seagate Technology, which designs and manufactures a broad line of rigid magnetic disk drives.

Earnings

During the past 12 months, VERITAS earned $0.46 per share, up 93 percent from the previous year.

Revenues

Revenues during the past 12 months totaled $930 million, up 78 percent from a year earlier.

Key Ratios & Measures	5-Year Range	Current
P/E	23–493	262.8
Price-to-Book	1.4–19.5	13.6
Price-to-Cash Flow	7–89.9	62.9
Price-to-Sales	2.7–73.2	51.2
Return on Equity	5.3–37.7%	5.3%
Beta		1.89

CONTACT INFORMATION

VERITAS Software Corporation, 1600 Plymouth Street, Mountain View, CA 94043
(650) 335-8000
www.veritas.com

VERITAS Software (VRTS)

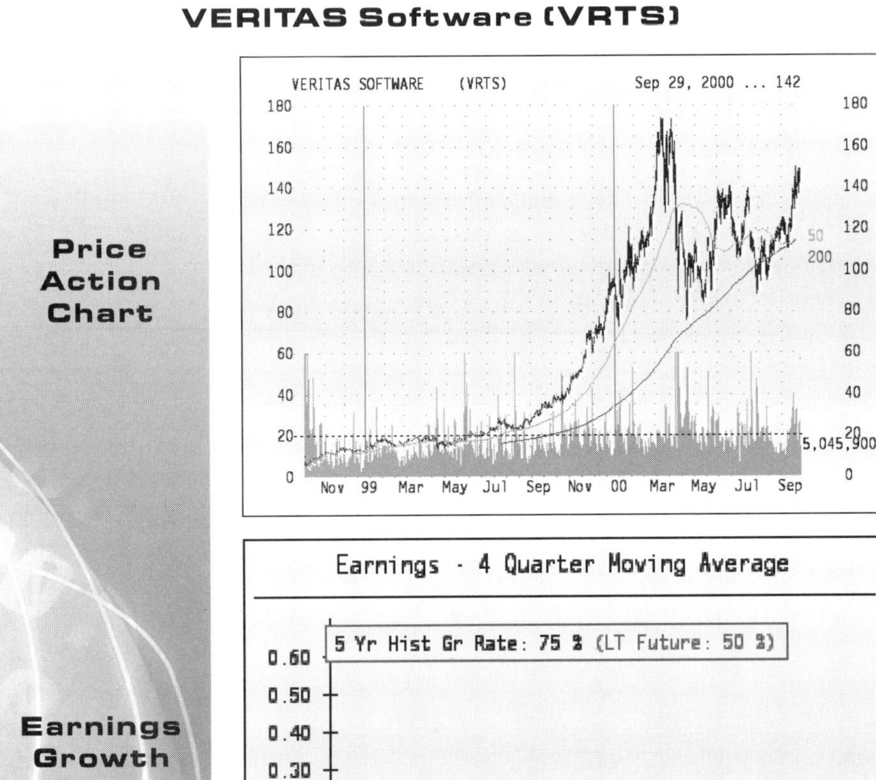

Revenue Growth Chart

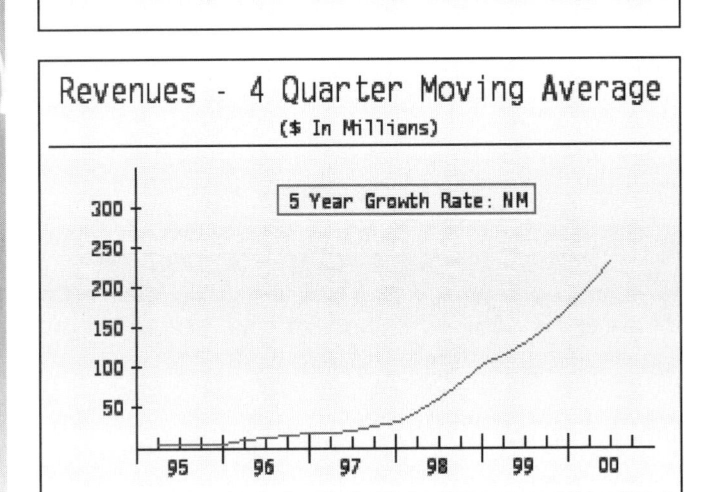

Charts provided by Baseline Financial Services.

98. VITESSE SEMICONDUCTOR

Symbol: VTSS
Sector: Technology (Semiconductors)

COMPANY PROFILE

Vitesse Semiconductor makes high-performance integrated circuits (ICs) for manufacturers of communications systems and automatic test equipment (ATE). Its communications products, which account for more than 80 percent of total revenues, include multiplexers, demultiplexers, switch cores, clock generation and recovery circuits, laser drivers, optoelectronic receivers and amplifiers, POS/ATM framers, Ethernet media access controllers, packet processors, switch fabrics, Fibre Channel Ics, and other devices. Vitesse also makes gate arrays and custom-designed products for the ATE industry. Major customers include Cisco Systems, Fujitsu, IBM, LTX, Lucent Technologies, Schlumberger, Seagate, and others. During 2000, Vitesse acquired Orologic and Sitera.

EARNINGS

During the past 12 months, Vitesse Semiconductor earned $0.60 per share, up 40 percent from the previous year.

REVENUES

Revenues during the past 12 months totaled $384 million, up 51 percent from a year earlier.

KEY RATIOS & MEASURES	5-YEAR RANGE	CURRENT
P/E	25–232	145.4
Price-to-Book	2.1–32.3	24.3
Price-to-Cash Flow	10.9–159.5	120.3
Price-to-Sales	2.5–56.2	42.37
Return on Equity	14.7–22.2%	14.7%
Beta		1.92

CONTACT INFORMATION
Vitesse Semiconductor Corp., 741 Calle Plano, Camarillo, CA 93012-8543
(805) 388-3700
www.vitesse.com

Vitesse Semiconductor (VTSS)

Price Action Chart

VITESSE SEMICONDUCTR(VTSS) Sep 29, 2000 ... 88.94

120 105 90 75 60 45 30 15 0

50 200 3,429,100

Nov 99 Mar May Jul Sep Nov 00 Mar May Jul Sep

Earnings Growth Chart

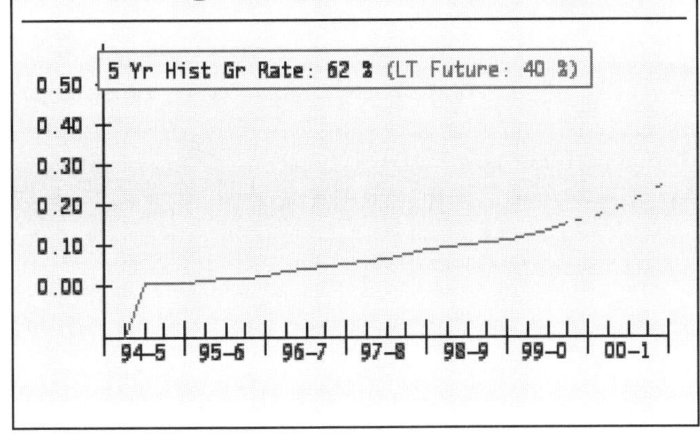

Revenue Growth Chart

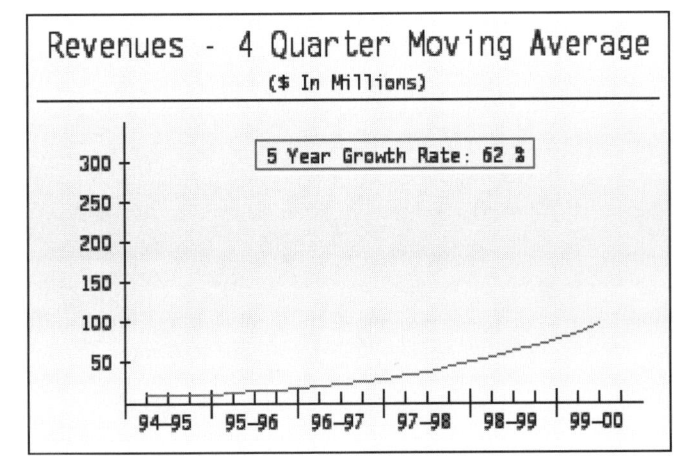

Charts provided by Baseline Financial Services.

99. VOICESTREAM WIRELESS

Symbol: VSTR
Sector: Services (Communications Services)

COMPANY PROFILE

VoiceStream Wireless provides personal communications services under the VoiceStream brand name. Its offerings include all of the services typically provided by cellular systems, as well as paging, caller identification, text messaging, smart cards, voice mail, over-the-air subscriber profile management, and over-the-air activation. VoiceStream serves 11 urban markets across the United States, including Denver, Seattle/Tacoma, Phoenix/Tucson, Portland, Salt Lake City, Des Moines, Oklahoma City, Honolulu, El Paso, Albuquerque, and Boise. The company holds 107 broadband PCS licenses covering about 62.6 million people, and serves 322,400 PCS subscribers. In 2000, VoiceStream acquired Omnipoint and Aerial Communications, and agreed to buy Powertel.

EARNINGS

During the past 12 months, VoiceStream Wireless lost $6.25 per share.

REVENUES

Revenues during the past 12 months totaled $1 billion.

KEY RATIOS & MEASURES	5-YEAR RANGE	CURRENT
P/E	NM	NM
Price-to-Book	21.6–1848.3	NM
Price-to-Cash Flow	NA	NM
Price-to-Sales	3.3–34.5	25.48
Return on Equity	NA	NM
Beta		1.95

NM, Not Meaningful; NA, Not Applicable

CONTACT INFORMATION

VoiceStream Wireless Corp., 3650 131st Avenue SE, Bellevue, WA 98006
(425) 653-4600
www.voicestream.com

VoiceStream Wireless (VSTR)

Price Action Chart

VOICESTREAM WIRELESS(VSTR) Sep 29, 2000 ... 116.06

180 160 140 120 100 80 60 40 20 0

200 50 1,945,200

Jul Sep Nov 00 Mar May Jul Sep

Earnings Growth Chart

Earnings - 4 Quarter Moving Average

5 Yr Hist Gr Rate: NA (LT Future: 20 %)

0.50 0.40 0.30 0.20 0.10 0.00

1995 1996 1997 1998 1999 2000 2001

Revenue Growth Chart

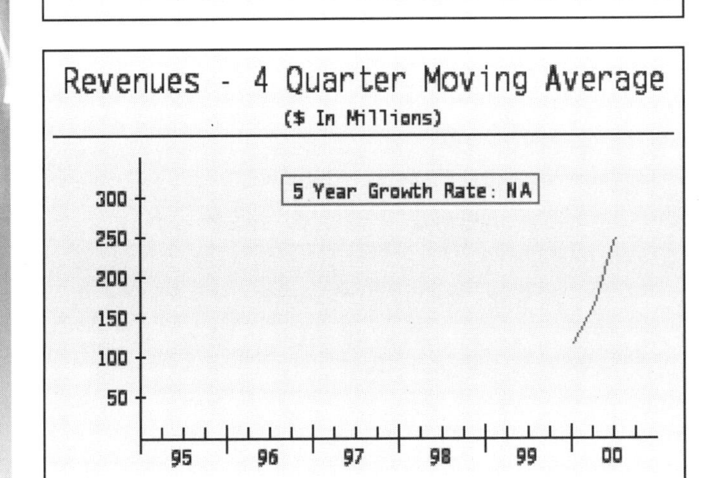

Charts provided by Baseline Financial Services.

100. WORLDCOM

Symbol: WCOM
Sector: Services (Communications Services)

COMPANY PROFILE

WorldCom is a global telecommunications company. Its products and services include: dedicated and dial-up Internet access; calling and debit cards; dedicated and switched long-distance and local products; local access to long-distance companies and asynchronous transfer mode-based backbone service; advanced billing systems; facilities management; enhanced fax and data connections; high-speed data communications; and wireless, dial-up networking, broadband data, Web-server hosting and integration, 800, conference calling, messaging, private line, and mobility services. WorldCom also provides international telecommunications services to some 65 foreign countries. Its planned merger with Sprint fell through in 2000, although the company continues to make select strategic acquisitions.

EARNINGS

During the past 12 months, WorldCom earned $1.69 per share, up 107 percent from the previous year.

REVENUES

Revenues during the past 12 months totaled $39.1 billion, up 15 percent from a year earlier.

KEY RATIOS & MEASURES	5-YEAR RANGE	CURRENT
P/E	19–196	21.9
Price-to-Book	1.1–3.6	2
Price-to-Cash Flow	10.1–40.3	11.5
Price-to-Sales	0.7–5.7	2.7
Return on Equity	8.3–9.5%	9.4%
Beta		1.11

CONTACT INFORMATION
WorldCom, Inc., 500 Clinton Center Drive, Clinton, MS 39056
(601) 460-5600
www.worldcom.com

WorldCom (WCOM)

Price Action Chart

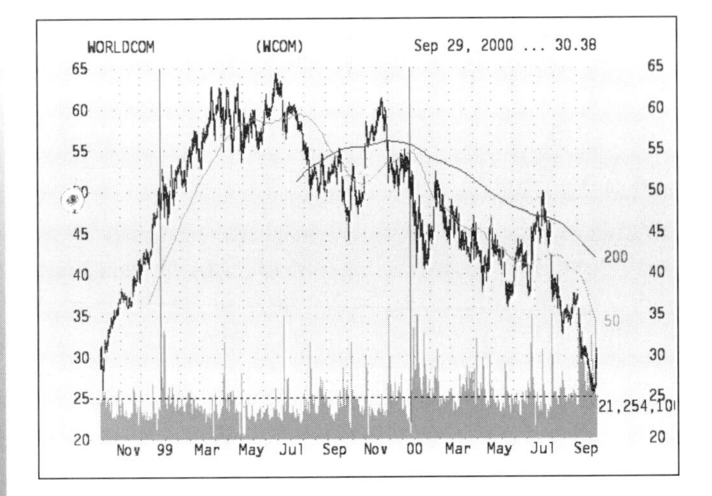

Earnings Growth Chart

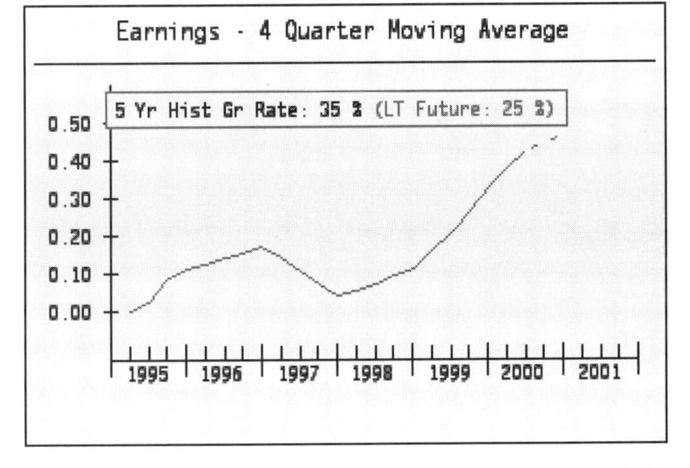

Revenue Growth Chart

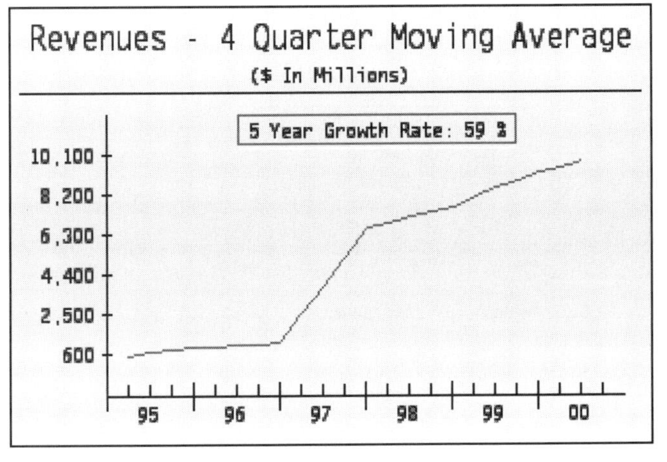

Charts provided by Baseline Financial Services.

APPENDICES

NASDAQ-100 COMPANIES BY WEIGHTINGS IN THE INDEX

	Company	% of Index
1.	Cisco Systems	6.57
2.	Microsoft	5.23
3.	Intel	4.67
4.	QUALCOMM	4.59
5.	Oracle	4.45
6.	JDS Uniphase	3.30
7.	Sun Microsystems	2.41
8.	Siebel Systems	2.35
9.	VERITAS	2.23
10.	Immunex	2.04
11.	CIENA	1.95
12.	Amgen	1.83
13.	Nextel Communications	1.65
14.	VoiceStream Wireless	1.63
15.	Juniper Networks	1.60
16.	BEA Systems	1.53
17.	Palm	1.47

	Company	% of Indcx
18.	Check Point Software Technologies	1.34
19.	Applied Micro Circuits	1.33
20.	Network Appliance	1.29
21.	i2 Technologies	1.28
22.	Linear Technology	1.21
23.	Maxim Integrated Products	1.21
24.	SDL	1.14
25.	Xilinx	1.13
26.	Dcll Computer	1.11
27.	ADC Telecommunications	1.10
28.	Comverse Technology	1.09
29.	PMC-Sierra	1.01
30.	PeopleSoft	1.01
31.	WorldCom	1.01
32.	Gemstar-TV Guide International	1.00
33.	Applied Materials	0.99
34.	Comcast	0.97
35.	VeriSign	0.95
36.	Tellabs	0.90
37.	Adobe Systems	0.89
38.	Millennium Pharmaceuticals	0.88
39.	Broadcom*	0.87
40.	Altera	0.86
41.	Ariba*	0.85
42.	Paychex	0.85
43.	Exodus Communications	0.83
44.	Flextronics International	0.78
45.	LM Ericsson Telephone	0.73
46.	Chiron	0.71
47.	Intuit	0.71
48.	IDEC Pharmaceuticals	0.70
49.	Sanmina	0.69

*Lycos and NTL were replaced by Broadcom and Ariba as this book went to press.

	Company	% of Index
50.	Starbucks	0.67
51.	MedImmune	0.65
52.	Vitesse Semiconductor	0.64
53.	Concord EFS	0.63
54.	Genzyme General	0.62
55.	Human Genome Sciences	0.59
56.	Biogen	0.57
57.	Cintas	0.57
58.	Level 3 Communications	0.54
59.	Biomet	0.53
60.	Costco Wholesale	0.51
61.	Yahoo!	0.51
62.	Bed, Bath & Beyond	0.49
63.	Mercury Interactive	0.48
64.	QLogic	0.48
65.	Rational Software	0.46
66.	PanAmSat	0.46
67.	eBay	0.45
68.	Fiserv	0.45
69.	McLeodUSA	0.43
70.	Metromedia Fiber Network	0.42
71.	KLA-Tencor	0.41
72.	TMP Worldwide	0.40
73.	Apple Computer	0.38
74.	USA Networks	0.38
75.	EchoStar Communications	0.36
76.	Adelphia Communications	0.35
77.	Conexant Systems	0.34
78.	Citrix Systems	0.32
79.	Electronic Arts	0.31
80.	XO Communications	0.31
81.	RF Micro Devices	0.30

	Company	% of Index
82.	BroadVision	0.29
83.	Parametric Technology	0.29
84.	Amazon.com	0.28
85.	Abgenix	0.27
86.	Atmel	0.27
87.	Molex	0.23
88.	PACCAR	0.22
89.	Staples	0.22
90.	Inktomi	0.21
91.	BMC Software	0.18
92.	Smurfit-Stone Container	0.18
93.	CMGI	0.15
94.	CNET Networks	0.14
95.	Novell	0.14
96.	Microchip Technology	0.12
97.	RealNetworks	0.10
98.	3Com	0.09
99.	Compuware	0.09
100.	Excite@Home	0.08

NASDAQ-100 COMPANIES BY ONE-YEAR EARNINGS GROWTH

	Company	% Earnings Growth
1.	RealNetworks	997
2.	Immunex	734
3.	Lycos	611
4.	Atmel	289
5.	Yahoo!	271
6.	KLA-Tencor	261
7.	VeriSign	258
8.	Applied Materials	246
9.	MedImmune	213
10.	BroadVision	200
11.	Smurfit-Stone Container	186
12.	SDL	178
13.	BEA Systems	158
14.	Applied Micro Circuits	155
15.	JDS Uniphase	132
16.	QUALCOMM	130
17.	WorldCom	107
18.	Network Appliance	102
19.	Palm	100
20.	QLogic	100
21.	Inktomi	93
22.	VERITAS Software	93
23.	PMC-Sierra	91
24.	Flextronics	82
25.	RF Micro Devices	82
26.	Siebel Systems	77
27.	Xilinx	77
28.	eBay	73
29.	i2 Technologies	71
30.	Abgenix	65

	Company	% Earnings Growth
31.	ADC Telecommunications	63
32.	Check Point Software Technologies	60
33.	TMP Worldwide	59
34.	Oracle	57
35.	Altera Corporation	54
36.	Mercury Interactive	54
37.	Rational Software	53
38.	Microchip Technology	52
39.	Adobe Systems	50
40.	Comcast Corporation	47
41.	PanAmSat	47
42.	Biogen	45
43.	Cisco Systems	45
44.	Gemstar-TV Guide Intl.	45
45.	Sun Microsystems	45
46.	Concord EFS	44
47.	Linear Technology	44
48.	Sanmina	42
49.	Intuit	41
50.	Vitesse Semiconductor	40
51.	Intel	39
52.	Nextel Communications	38
53.	Comverse Technology	37
54.	LM Ericsson Telephone	37
55.	Maxim Integrated Products	36
56.	Paychex	36
57.	Bed, Bath & Beyond	34
58.	Genzyme General	31
59.	PACCAR	27
60.	Starbucks	26
61.	Chiron	25
62.	Fiserv	25

	Company	% Earnings Growth
63.	Microsoft	24
64.	Citrix Systems	23
65.	Molex	23
66.	Tellabs	23
67.	Staples	21
68.	Apple Computer	20
69.	Cintas	19
70.	Biomet	18
71.	Costco Wholesale	18
72.	Dell Computer	15
73.	Amgen	14
74.	Adelphia Communications	8
75.	IDEC Pharmaceuticals	5
76.	Excite@Home	–4
77.	BMC Software	–8
78.	Compuware	–11
79.	NTL	–13
80.	Novell	–22
81.	Electronic Arts	–29
82.	EchoStar Communications	–44
83.	3Com	–49
84.	XO Communications	–51
85.	McLeodUSA	–57
86.	PeopleSoft	–57
87.	Exodus Communications	–63
88.	Parametric Technology	–71
89.	Level 3 Communications	–166
90.	Amazon.com	–186
91.	Human Genome Sciences	–228
92.	Millennium Pharmaceuticals	–291
93.	CMGI	–422
94.	CNET Networks	–494

	Company	% Earnings Growth
95.	USA Networks	–557
96.	CIENA	NA
97.	Conexant Systems	NA
98.	Juniper Networks	NA
99.	Metromedia Fiber Network	NA
100.	VoiceStream Wireless	NA

NA, Not Applicable

NASDAQ–100 COMPANIES BY ONE-YEAR REVENUE GROWTH

	Company	% Revenue Growth
1.	Abgenix	416
2.	JDS Uniphase	406
3.	Exodus Communications	346
4.	CMGI	276
5.	Excite@Home	239
6.	BroadVision	223
7.	Inktomi	222
8.	Flextronics International	218
9.	VeriSign	167
10.	Adelphia Communications	127
11.	Lycos	120
12.	RealNetworks	119
13.	Yahoo!	119
14.	eBay	118
15.	XO Communications	116
16.	SDL	116
17.	Amazon.com	115
18.	Sanmina	112
19.	Network Appliance	111
20.	Siebel Systems	111
21.	Applied Materials	106
22.	CNET Networks	106
23.	Palm	105
24.	PMC-Sierra	98
25.	Immunex	94
26.	Applied Micro Circuits	92
27.	NTL	85
28.	EchoStar Communications	82
29.	KLA-Tencoor	78

	Company	% Revenue Growth
30.	VERITAS Software	78
31.	BEA Systems	75
32.	Level 3 Communications	75
33.	Check Point Software Technologies	74
34.	Metromedia Fiber Network	70
35.	RF Micro Devices	70
36.	ADC Telecommunications	68
37.	QLogic	68
38.	CIENA	65
39.	i2 Technologies	65
40.	Nextel Communications	65
41.	Xilinx	62
42.	MedImmune	61
43.	McLeodUSA	57
44.	Mercury Interactive	57
45.	Cisco Systems	55
46.	Vitesse Semiconductor	51
47.	Altera	48
48.	Gemstar-TV Guide Intl.	46
49.	Concord EFS	43
50.	Citrix Systems	42
51.	Maxim Integrated Products	42
52.	Atmel	41
53.	Smurfit-Stone Container	41
54.	Tellabs	41
55.	Rational Software	40
56.	Linear Technology	39
57.	TMP Worldwide	39
58.	PanAmSat	34
59.	Sun Microsystems	34
60.	Bed, Bath & Beyond	33
61.	Compuware	32

	Company	% Revenue Growth
62.	Dell Computer	32
63.	Microchip Technology	32
64.	Starbucks	32
65.	Biogen	31
66.	Comverse Technology	31
67.	USA Networks	31
68.	Molex	30
69.	Comcast	29
70.	Intuit	27
71.	IDEC Pharmaceuticals	24
72.	Paychex	24
73.	LM Ericsson Telephone	22
74.	Staples	22
75.	Adobe Systems	19
76.	BMC Software	19
77.	Apple Computer	17
78.	Amgen	16
79.	Fiserv	16
80.	Microsoft	16
81.	Costco Wholesale	15
82.	Oracle	15
83.	WorldCom	15
84.	Electronic Arts	13
85.	Intel	13
86.	Biomet	11
87.	PeopleSoft	10
88.	Cintas	9
89.	Millennium Pharmaceuticals	9
90.	Chiron	6
91.	PACCAR	5
92.	Genzyme General	1
93.	Novell	1

94.	Parametric Technology	–5
95.	QUALCOMM	–5
96.	3Com	–17
97.	Human Genome Sciences	–28
98.	Conexant Systems	NM
99.	Juniper Networks	NM
100.	VoiceStream Wireless	NM

NM, Not Meaningful

NASDAQ—100 COMPANIES BY PRICE-EARNINGS RATIO

	Company	PE Ratio
1.	CIENA	575.3
2.	eBay	571.6
3.	i2 Technologies	551.5
4.	BEA Systems	502.4
5.	SDL	489.2
6.	Palm	441.1
7.	Network Appliance	440.0
8.	Applied Micro Circuits	367.9
9.	Lycos	324.5
10.	BroadVision	308.4
11.	JDS Uniphase	300.2
12.	Mercury Interactive	295.8
13.	Yahoo!	292.1
14.	RealNetworks	285.4
15.	Siebel Systems	283.6
16.	VERITAS Software	262.8
17.	IDEC Pharmaceuticals	254.1
18.	Immunex	235.7
19.	Check Point Software Technologies	203.2
20.	PeopleSoft	201.2
21.	MedImmune	177.1
22.	Gemstar-TV Guide Intl.	169.3
23.	Vitesse Semiconductor	145.4
24.	Oracle	134.2
25.	RF Micro Devices	131.4
26.	QLogic	131.1
27.	Rational Software	126.1
28.	Cisco Systems	125.8
29.	Sun Microsystems	125.5
30.	TMP Worldwide	115.0

	Company	PE Ratio
31.	Xilinx	106.2
32.	Maxim Integrated Products	99.5
33.	LM Ericsson Telephone	94.4
34.	Intuit	92.1
35.	Electronic Arts	89.3
36.	Sanmina	89.3
37.	Altera	86.5
38.	Paychex	86.3
39.	Linear Technology	82.9
40.	ADC Telecommunications	76.9
41.	Parametric Technology	76.7
42.	Comverse Technology	74.1
43.	Adobe Systems	73.5
44.	Amgen	73.5
45.	Flextronics International	68.7
46.	Chiron	66.9
47.	Atmel	59.5
48.	QUALCOMM	58.8
49.	Starbucks	58.0
50.	Dell Computer	57.4
51.	KLA-Tencor	51.4
52.	Intel	50.1
53.	Microchip Technology	50.0
54.	Molex	46.9
55.	Conexant Systems	44.9
56.	Fiserv	43.2
57.	Applied Materials	42.6
58.	Concord EFS	41.5
59.	Tellabs	41.4
60.	Biogen	41.0
61.	Microsoft	40.8
62.	Apple Computer	38.6

	Company	PE Ratio
63.	Bed, Bath & Beyond	37.6
64.	Cintas	36.9
65.	PMC-Sierra	36.3
66.	Genzyme General	35.4
67.	Novell	34.8
68.	3Com	33.9
69.	Citrix Systems	33.3
70.	Biomet	32.9
71.	PanAmSat	29.2
72.	Costco Wholesale	26.7
73.	Smurfit-Stone Container	22.8
74.	Staples	22.0
75.	WorldCom	21.9
76.	BMC Software	18.5
77.	Compuware	12.0
78.	PACCAR	5.5
79.	Adelphia Communications	NM
80.	Abgenix	NM
81.	Amazon.com	NM
82.	CMGI	NM
83.	CNET Networks	NM
84.	Comcast	NM
85.	EchoStar Communications	NM
86.	Excite@Home	NM
87.	Exodus Communications	NM
88.	Human Genome Scenarios	NM
89.	Inktomi	NM
90.	Juniper Networks	NM
91.	Level 3 Communications	NM
92.	McLeodUSA	NM
93.	Metromedia Fiber Network	NM
94.	Millennium Pharmaceuticals	NM

	Company	PE Ratio
95.	Nextel Communications	NM
96.	XO Communications	NM
97.	NTL	NM
98.	USA Networks	NM
99.	VeriSign	NM
100.	VoiceStream Wireless	NM

NM, Not Meaningful

INDEX